D1548259

Gender
& Power
in Rural
Greece

Gender & Power in Rural Greece

EDITED BY
JILL DUBISCH

PRINCETON UNIVERSITY PRESS
PRINCETON, NEW JERSEY

Copyright © 1986 by Princeton University Press

Published by Princeton University Press, 41 William Street,
Princeton, New Jersey 08540
In the United Kingdom: Princeton University Press, Guildford, Surrey

All Rights Reserved

Library of Congress Cataloging in Publication Data will be
found on the last printed page of this book

ISBN 0-691-09423-3
ISBN 0-691-02833-8 (pbk.)

This book has been composed in Linotron Sabon

Clothbound editions of Princeton University Press books
are printed on acid-free paper, and binding materials are
chosen for strength and durability. Paperbacks, although satisfactory
for personal collections, are not usually suitable for library rebinding

Printed in the United States of America by Princeton University Press
Princeton, New Jersey

DESIGNED BY LAURY A. EGAN

To Ernestine Friedl

with gratitude and affection

CONTENTS

PREFACE

W_{HEN} I arrived in Greece in the summer of 1969 to do fieldwork for my doctoral dissertation,[1] I carried in my mind a definite image of Greek culture generally and of Greek women in particular. This image had been shaped by the available literature on Greece, both scientific and popular, which I had read in preparation for my research. That literature had left me with the sense that the lives of Greek women were as much Middle Eastern as European in character. Although neither secluded nor veiled, Greek women were, I had gathered, subject to a restrictive code that circumscribed their behavior and routinely segregated them from the world of men. The emphasis in the literature on the existence and persistence of certain institutions such as "dowry" and "honor" crimes reinforced my image of oppressed and socially inferior beings.

Among the important works contributing to my pre-fieldwork knowledge of Greece was *Honour, Family and Patronage*, John Campbell's excellent monograph on the Sarakatsani shepherds of Epiros. The book is illustrated with a number of black and white photographs, and one in particular epitomized for me the restricted lives of rural Greek women. The photograph shows a group of Sarakatsani women, swathed in their traditional dark, shapeless, wool garments. They stand huddled together, their backs to the camera, their faces hidden—formless, effaced, and self-effacing. Although I knew that not all Greek women looked and dressed like these women, the photograph seemed to symbolize their generally subordinate status.

Yet even before I arrived in Greece, I had begun to be a little skeptical about my preconceived image of Greek women. Were they really that inferior, that submissive? I wondered. Much that I had read seemed to be presented from a male perspective. Did Greek women concur completely in this view or did they have their own view of things?[2] Ernestine Friedl's article (reprinted in this volume) on the appearance versus the reality of power sharpened my skepticism. Thus, when my husband and I arrived in the small village of Falatados,[3] where we were to live for thirteen months, I was not entirely surprised to find that the Greek women I encountered did not always fit my preformed picture of them.

Once I had settled in the village, it was not difficult to meet these women. In fact, most of my initial encounters in Falatados were with women. During the day, many of the men were away, working either in the fields or at jobs on other parts of the island. The women, on the other hand, were busy with chores in or around the house. Often, a woman sweeping her porch, hanging up laundry, or on her way to the store would stop to chat with us as we wandered the streets and then invite us into her home. Politely but determinedly she would seek to draw us out—who were we? why were we there? who were our families—as we chatted in halting Greek over coffee, *raki*, and spoons of sweet jam, the requisite trappings of Greek hospitality.

As time went by, as my Greek improved and my friendships with villagers developed, as I gradually began to learn the ins and outs of village life, certain aspects of my earlier image of Greek women began to be altered and modified and, occasionally, completely overturned. I observed my landlady managing the affairs of her household, including its relations with the world outside. I heard women scolding their husbands, accusing them of ineptitude around the house, and men and women engaging in arguments about the relative virtues of each sex or exchanging bawdy banter. Women joked with me, and sometimes even with my husband, about sexual matters, and one teen-age girl took advantage of our presence to maneuver a clandestine meeting with a young man.

At the same time, however, it was undeniable that in many ways these village women's lives were more restricted than those of the men. Only recently have women been permitted to enter the coffeehouses (*kafenia*), and then only on special occasions and in the company of male relatives. While young men roamed freely around the island, young women were supposed to be chaperoned on expeditions outside the village, and they never went on "dates" or attended festivals on their own. Women, young and old, maintained certain standards of modesty in dress, and tourists who failed to observe such standards were severely criticized by men and women alike. (Since it was the era of miniskirts, opportunities for such criticism were frequent.) In addition, a number of ritual observances and taboos placed burdens upon women that were not placed on men. For example, they were not allowed to enter church during their menstrual periods, and they wore black for long periods of mourning following the death of close relatives. Even though I was free of most of the specific taboos and obligations, I felt something of their restrictiveness. The specific sources of such a feeling were difficult to pinpoint or define, demonstrating both the subjective effects of cultural patterns and their often subtle coercive power.

By the time I left the field, it had become obvious to me that while my earlier image of Greek women had not been entirely false, neither had it been completely accurate. Constructing a more realistic picture, one which took into account all the apparent contradictions and anomalies in the status of rural Greek women, was one of the tasks which faced me on my return to the United States, and it led me not only to reevaluate the earlier stereotype of Greek women, but also to question the ethnographic presentation of women in other societies as well.

My pre-fieldwork questions regarding women had seemed a little unusual at the time, certainly far removed from the interests of my professors and fellow students in graduate school. However, they turned out to be not as extraordinary as I had thought, for by the time I returned from fieldwork, I found that the sort of observations I had made were also being made by others. Impelled by the women's movement, scholars in anthropology and other disciplines were beginning to question many previous assumptions about gender roles in both our own and other societies. Such questioning has now evolved into a major area of academic research spanning a number of disciplines, and the literature is vast and constantly growing. Within anthropology, the study of women and gender has become an established sub-field, one which has challenged us to examine our previous thinking about, and presentation of, women in other societies, and which has sought to provide us with the questions, concepts, and methodologies upon which to build a more complex and less biased comprehension of gender than has been possible in the past.

This movement in anthropology is one of the roots from which the present volume has grown and by which it has been nourished. A second root is Greek ethnography itself, a field which has grown significantly in the last fifteen years, and which has become increasingly sophisticated in its approach to understanding contemporary Greek culture. Since I began my fieldwork, the anthropological literature on Greece has been steadily increasing, and because each piece of research has been built on previous studies, each can, on the one hand, be increasingly refined in its theoretical focus and, on the other, be placed in the broader comparative context of Greek ethnography. No longer is our picture of Greek life based on a few ethnographies of rural communities. Instead, we can work with a range of studies that not only cover different geographical regions, but also include towns and cities.[4] While this proliferation of material increases the complexity of our analysis, it also makes research in Greece more exciting and rewarding than ever before and allows us the opportunity to raise—and to answer—more sophisticated and interesting questions than was previously possible.

Gender roles and the relationships between men and women seem to draw the attention of most fieldworkers in Greece, even when gender is not the central topic of research. In fact, most of the contributors to this volume did their initial field investigations in other areas. Yet all of them had data on women and theories about gender roles that they felt the need to explore. The topic is one which cannot be ignored. Not only do sexual segregation and gender roles play a large part as organizing principles in Greek society, both on the ideological plane and in the ongoing activities of daily life, but, in addition, the researcher today, influenced by the questions regarding the "problem of women"[5] that are current in her or his own society, carries into the field a heightened consciousness of the topic. Moreover, explorations of gender have stimulated some of the most interesting and fruitful anthropological research undertaken in Greece in recent years. The present volume, inspired by such explorations, is designed to draw together recent work on the subject. These studies do not necessarily lead to agreement regarding the nature and significance of gender roles in Greece, but they should at least point the way to fuller and more complex understanding of such patterns. Yet achieving this understanding, while exciting in itself, is actually the means to a greater end: a better and more general knowledge not only of gender roles in all societies, but also of society itself. The study of gender roles and ideology can sharpen our conceptual tools and aid us in our attempt to understand social structure, cultural systems, and social change. It is no longer possible to take for granted a male-oriented view of society or to see culture as a male-created, male-dominated phenomenon. To my mind, the focus on women in anthropological research has been not only a useful one, but also probably the most stimulating recent trend within the discipline. We have begun to fill in the gaps that, until recently, we did not even perceive were there, and we have also begun to look afresh at our field and to reevaluate many previously practiced approaches and previously held assumptions. The interest in women and gender has helped to make anthropology more self-conscious with respect to both our discipline and the culture from which it springs. It also has led to new insights in many areas of study, from social structure to politics to kinship to symbolism, and it has caused us to reevaluate the very conception of "culture" itself. In this sense, then, no study including the ones in this volume, is ever "just" about women.

NOTES

1. Research in Greece was carried out from 1969 to 1970 under a grant and fellowship from the National Institute of Mental Health.
2. My original doctoral dissertation proposal in the Department of Anthropology at the University of Chicago focused on this problem of the "separate

culture" of women, but the actual dissertation, as it evolved during my field-work, dealt with the consequences of rural-urban migration (see Dubisch 1972).

3. The village in which I did fieldwork was on the island of Tinos, one of the Cycladic Islands, about five hours from Piraeus by boat. I returned there for visits in 1972, 1973, 1975, and 1979.

4. The amount of ethnographic research on and number of publications about Greece are constantly increasing, and some material is too recent even to have been taken account of in this volume (see, for example, Handman 1983; Herzfeld 1985).

5. The phrase is borrowed from Edwin Ardener (1975).

ACKNOWLEDGMENTS

THERE are always numerous people who are responsible for the publication of a book, especially when the book is a collection of the work of many authors. Thus, I would first like to thank all the contributors, without whose hard work, faith, and patience this volume would never have been possible. Many thanks are also due to Ray Michalowski, friend and colleague, who, along every step of the way, from inception to completion, has given me invaluable criticism and encouragement. Michael Herzfeld, Muriel Dimen, and Anna Caraveli made many helpful comments on earlier drafts of the Introduction, and Harold S. Shapiro was a source of both moral and practical support during fieldwork. Gail Ullman of Princeton University Press has been patient and encouraging throughout various stages of the book, and thanks go also to Doris Carter for her excellent job of typing various sections of the manuscript. Most of all, the contributors and I would like to express our appreciation to the men and women in villages throughout rural Greece who have inspired us to record our observations in this collection.

NOTE ON TRANSLITERATION

SEVERAL systems of transliteration from modern Greek to English are currently in use. Since there is no universal agreement as to which one is most accurate and/or effective, and since the decision to employ one system rather than another can be a matter of controversy, the choice of transliteration has been left up to individual authors. While this has resulted in a certain amount of inconsistency from one article to another and in some variable renditions (for example, *filotimo* and *philotimo* both appear), such minor problems seem preferable to the imposition of a single system.

Gender
& Power
in Rural
Greece

Introduction

JILL DUBISCH

WOMEN have a peculiar place in the study of society, for they are not regarded as part of society in the same way that men are. Since women are not the subjects of society, but rather its objects, to study women is, as Simone de Beauvoir has written, to study "the Other" (de Beauvoir 1952). In each of the social sciences, the implicit assumption is that those who make society (or culture or politics or history) are men.[1] Although this view is changing, both in anthropology and in other academic disciplines, the basic observation, that women are objects, remains unchanged; the topic "women" is still a separate category, a special area of study, in a way that the topic "men" is not. Thus, women studying women find themselves simultaneously subject and object. This focus on women carries the danger of "ghettoizing" them, for women and their activities may be presented as "something of a subculture" and the study of women as "something akin to a subdiscipline" (Strathern 1981:683). If to be separate is, inherently, to be unequal, then it is only by integrating the study of women into the study of society that "women's studies," by ceasing to exist, will, paradoxically, have had the impact on academic fields that it deserves. This volume is intended as one more step toward this integration. As such, it is part of a larger process within anthropology, which, through a focus on women and gender, is beginning to broaden our concepts of human society, both of the past and in the present.[2]

Following the recognition that women's lives and their role in the social system have been overlooked and/or misrepresented, the first step has been to fill in the gaps, that is, to "straighten out the record" and document more fully the role of women. This seemingly straightforward task, however, has opened up (appropriately enough) a Pandora's box of further questions. It has become clear that to include women in the study of society is more than a matter of filling in the ethnographic record; it also requires changing the very concepts, theories, and methodology with which we work and, ultimately, the field of anthropology itself. A seemingly simple question such as, for example, "What factors lead to the exercise of power by women in society?" leads to other im-

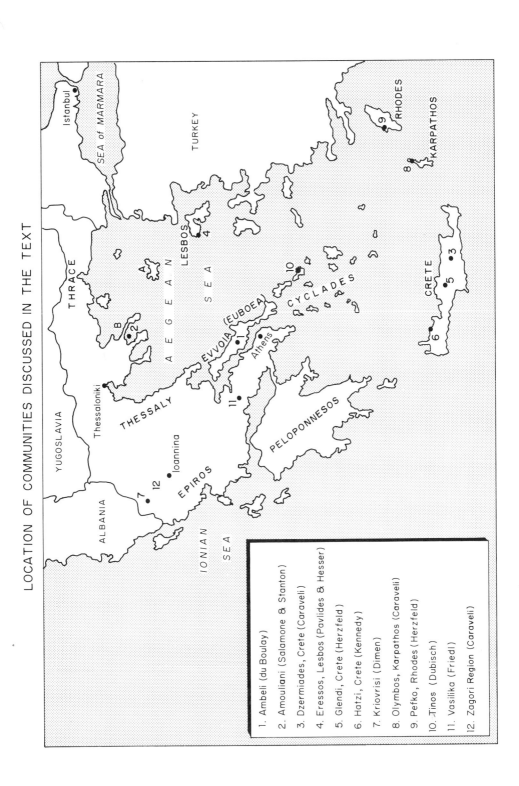

LOCATION OF COMMUNITIES DISCUSSED IN THE TEXT

1. Ambeli (du Boulay)
2. Amouliani (Salamone & Stanton)
3. Dzermiades, Crete (Caraveli)
4. Eressos, Lesbos (Pavlides & Hesser)
5. Glendi, Crete (Herzfeld)
6. Hatzi, Crete (Kennedy)
7. Kriovrisi (Dimen)
8. Olymbos, Karpathos (Caraveli)
9. Pefko, Rhodes (Herzfeld)
10. Tinos (Dubisch)
11. Vasilika (Friedl)
12. Zagori Region (Caraveli)

portant questions regarding the definition of power and its operation in society. Exploration of how women acquiesce in the "dominant" values of society and to what degree they have their own "muted" culture (E. Ardener 1975) raises questions about the very definition of culture itself and about the role of the anthropologist as participant and observer.

Looking at society from the point of view of women thus leads us not simply to a different view of women but to a different view of society itself; it also points us toward our ultimate goal, which is not to understand "women" as a separate and isolated category, as object and "other," but rather to understand gender in its broadest terms. To achieve this understanding requires that we reshape our study of society. To some extent, at least, this is a goal toward which anthropologists and those in other academic fields have been working in recent years, and the questions we have been asking have become increasingly sophisticated and have produced increasingly more exciting and challenging answers.

Greek society is a particularly appropriate context in which to explore gender-related questions and to analyze their social and cultural significance, for not only does gender play an important role in Greek social and conceptual life, but also the history of the anthropological study of gender in Greece parallels, and has influenced, the interest in women within the field of anthropology as a whole. The first published ethnography of a Greek community, *Vasilika: A Village in Modern Greece*, which appeared in 1962, was written by a female anthropologist, Ernestine Friedl. Friedl also explored some of the problems of sex roles in fieldwork in her contribution to Peggy Golde's volume *Women in the Field*. But it was her seminal article, "The Position of Women: Appearance and Reality," originally published in 1967 and reprinted in this volume, that provided considerable impetus for further research into gender-related issues in Greece and elsewhere. Friedl went on to expend her interest in gender roles into a full-length volume, *Men and Women: An Anthropologist's View* (1975), which takes an ecological and structural-functional approach to understanding gender roles. Since Friedl did her ground-breaking fieldwork, a number of anthropologists, both male and female, have worked in Greece, and many of them, regardless of their own gender,[3] have responded to the "raised consciousness" regarding women.[4] Their work has expanded our understanding of gender not only in Greece, but also cross-culturally. As the title indicates, this volume focuses both on women and on the larger issues that are raised by the study of women and gender.

Universals in Gender Roles:
Biology versus Culture

An important issue in the study of gender has been the extent to which women's roles (and, to a somewhat lesser extent, men's) are determined, or at least highly conditioned, by their reproductive roles. While the essays in this volume do not speak to the issue of biology per se, there are certain aspects of the debate which do bear directly upon our discussions of gender in Greece, and which are worth covering briefly here. Particularly pertinent is the question of whether universal features of female and male roles exist, as well as the relationship of such features to women's power and status.

Anthropologists are by no means in agreement regarding the issue of universality and variation in gender roles. While the existence of some cross-cultural variation in roles is generally acknowledged, there is wide disagreement about the significance of this variation, as well as about its degree, nature, and cause. To some analysts, variations in gender roles are mere decoration on underlying basic and universal themes, themes which are based in the genetics of the species (see, for example, Tiger and Fox 1971). Thus, both physical differences between the sexes and certain behavioral traits (for example, aggression, propensity for group cooperation, and polygamous mating strategies) are seen as consequences of natural selection, and they, in turn, serve as the underpinnings of human social arrangements, both past and present. To these anthropologists, then, gender roles are a product of our evolutionary history, which limits to some extent our options for change (see, for example, Tiger and Fox 1971; van den Berghe and Barash 1977). For others, however, the differences observed in these roles from one society to another challenge such notions of biological determinism (for example, Mead 1935), as well as many of our assumptions about the human past (for example, Dahlberg 1981). In addition, there is a political aspect to the debate. It has been suggested that the arguments of biological determinism tend to support male dominance and social arrangements advantageous to men, as well as reflecting features and values such as hierarchy, competition, and the male role as "bread winner" which are characteristic of western, particularly American, society but are not necessarily universal.[5]

Challengers of biological determinism have suggested that biological concepts themselves are culturally created, and that our bias toward such determinism may be due to the "assumption that male and female are predominantly natural objects rather than predominantly cultural constructions" (Ortner and Whitehead 1981:1). For this reason, it is now common in anthropology to make a distinction between *sex*, which refers to biologically determined phenotypical features, and *gender*, which refers to the socially assigned attributes of sex (see, for example, Martin and Voorhies 1975:3). This distinction seems to be gaining acceptance in a number of disciplines. Biology, rather than being viewed as automatically producing certain significant features of gender roles, is seen instead as a cultural construct which must itself be explained. This means that part of our task as anthropologists should be to explore the emic dimensions of gender, that is, to determine what constitutes a culture's own concepts of the biological nature of male and female (see Ortner and Whitehead 1981), since "[w]hat it means to be a woman in this or that situation must rest to some extent on the cultural logic on which gender is constructed" (Strathern 1981:683). Such an exploration is undertaken by du Boulay as part of her essay for this volume.

To accept the culturally created nature of gender, however, is not necessarily to argue against the existence of universal features of gender roles. But while both biological and cultural determinists might identify similarities in such features, their explanations for these similarities differ significantly. Those emphasizing the cultural malleability of gender seek explanations for universality not in the biological givens of sex but in the constant features of human social arrangements which are, in turn, responses to certain necessities of human existence. These constant features, it is argued, center around women's roles as the bearers and caretakers of children. While at first this view sounds much like biological determinism, in fact cultural determinists emphasize the significant though sometimes roundabout roles played by the biological facts of pregnancy, childbirth, and nursing, as organized and interpreted by culture, in shaping women's tasks and position in all societies. In terms of cultural adaptation, then, women are associated with those tasks that are compatible to the fundamental and essential job of bearing and raising children. This association places certain universal constraints on women, resulting in the role similarity that is seen from one society to another. For example, the explanation for why women generally do not hunt in foraging societies lies not in some "hunting instinct" that has evolved in men and not in women, but rather in the fact that pregnancy and the care of small children limit a woman's mobility, making it more practical for her to forage close to camp while men engage in the time-consuming task of chasing game at great distances. The nature and extent of women's participation in different social activities in turn determine women's general position in society (see Friedl

1975; Martin and Voorhies 1975) and also create a "women's world," making women's experience of society different from that of men.[6]

At another level, Sherry Ortner has proposed a set of features which she feels are universally part of gender. She notes that "we find women subordinated to men in every known society" (Ortner 1974:70), a phenomenon, she suggests, that is culturally rather than biologically determined. There is no evidence, she argues, that women are "naturally" submissive and men "naturally" dominant, so we must seek our explanation for such characteristics in social rather than biological facts. These social facts, however, derive from cultural interpretations of biology. Taking a structuralist approach, and drawing upon Claude Lévi-Strauss's ideas regarding the opposition between nature and culture, Ortner suggests that women, because of their bodily processes and social roles, and because of the psychic structures which develop as a result of those social roles, are universally perceived as being closer to nature than are men. Men, on the other hand, because they are cultural (rather than "mere" biological) creators, are perceived as being closer to or representing culture. Since culture is valued over nature in all societies, and since it is the role of culture to control or regulate nature, women's status is subordinate to that of men.[7]

Although proponents of cultural determinism may stress different arguments, they all make two important points. The first is that women's social roles do not arise directly from reproductive roles per se, but rather from the ways in which such roles are culturally defined, interpreted, and evaluated. Thus, explanations for universal features of gender roles are to be found in *cultural* invariants rather than in biological ones. From this argument follows the second important point: since culture is changeable (or at least more changeable than genes), present social arrangements are not inevitable; neither can we establish the limits of gender role possibilities simply by considering the range of roles that now exist. As one author has put it, we cannot necessarily predict *variability* by studying *variation* (Callan 1978:205). Thus, it follows that if cultural interpretations and arrangements were to be altered, what is now "universal" would not necessarily any longer be so.

The notion of universal gender constructs has itself been challenged, however, including the relationship male:female :: culture:nature :: public:domestic (see, for example, MacCormack and Strathern 1980; Ortner and Whitehead 1981; Reiter 1975; Strathern 1981). Such a challenge not only raises important issues regarding gender roles, but it also leads to questions about power and subordination, as well as about ethnocentric bias in the way these concepts are defined and analyzed. (This issue will be discussed more fully later.)

While the question of change and changeability is significant from a political or practical point of view, it also has broader implications for the interpretation of gender roles. Cultural explanations take us deeper into culture itself, prompting us to seek there both the causes and the significance of gender and deepening our understanding of cultural systems.

This book is such a step into culture. By exploring certain gender issues, particularly the relationship of gender to public and private, to power and lack of power, and to the "outside" and the "inside" within the context of a single yet diverse cultural setting, we can test the validity of certain hypotheses regarding gender constructs. The articles in this volume speak implicitly and explicitly to many of the issues surrounding gender role universals: Are there universals? To what extent are women's roles limited or determined by their reproductive roles? How do cultures define these roles? What are the causes and consequences of culturally varying definitions of gender? What does gender "mean" in a larger cultural context? By exploring such questions in specific ethnographic settings, the authors challenge a number of previously held ideas regarding gender roles and expand our understanding of gender in society.

GENDER AND DOMESTIC LIFE

Despite disagreements about the existence and nature of universal features of gender roles, anthropologists generally have found women's association with the domestic sphere to be strong in all cultures. While some observers have challenged the universal validity and/or utility of the domestic/public distinction, most discussions of women, either in general or within the context of particular societies, begin with or at least include a description and analysis of the domestic realm, regardless of how domesticity is defined or what women's extra-domestic roles may be. This realm, and its conceptual opposition to the public realm of social life, is a promising place to begin both analyzing gender in Greece and exploring some of the important issues related to gender, power, and the status of women. The title of Michael Herzfeld's paper, "Within and Without," suggests the importance of the division between inside and outside, between private and public, for understanding such issues and, as we shall see, also points the way to some of the complexities inherent in what at first seems to be a relatively simple social and conceptual division.

Domestic life is an area about which many people feel they have an intuitive understanding. We are born into domestic units of one form or another, and it is the context in which we have our first and some of our most intimate experiences of life. We also tend to recognize domestic life readily in other societies. However, such intuitive understanding can obscure the profound variations that occur in domestic life from society to society. For example, in some societies men sleep and eat in men's houses, separate from women and children. Husbands and wives may have intercourse in the bush, not in their homes. Men may contribute economic support to, or father children in, a household in which they do not live or be only transient visitors in the houses of their wives and children.[8] There may also be variations by class. At certain periods in history, the "private" activities of kings and queens—eating, sleeping, dressing—have been matters of public observation. In addition, there are other, less immediately observable variations in the domestic life of different societies—variations in roles, emotions, and rules, for example. Nevertheless, there are certain activities that we generally associate with this sphere of social life. These activities usually (though by no means always) include preparation and consumption of food, cleaning, grooming, disciplining of the young, sleeping, and adult sexual intercourse (Harris 1975:310). Moreover, we often determine domestic life and its boundaries by examining spatial arrangements. Domestic life and the social units with which it is associated are most often delimited by physical markers of some sort, whether they be the high, windowless, mud walls which surround the households in a Middle Eastern village, the lawns and fences of a middle-class suburb in the United States, the individual cooking hearths separating one family from another in the communal dwellings of a Yugoslav *zadruga*, or the simple and quickly constructed grass huts in a camp of the foraging !Kung San. Variations in such markers often can tell us something about social life and about gender roles (see, for example, S. Ardener 1975). Beyond such markers, there is a psychic dimension to interiority, a dimension which appears to be more developed in some societies than in others.

Domesticity, then, and its degree of separateness from other realms of social life, needs to be explored in the context of specific social settings. In addition, the boundaries between domestic life and the public realm, the nature of their interrelationships, and the symbols that express these boundaries and interrelationships may vary considerably from one society to another.[9]

Investigation of the domestic (or private)/public dichotomy[10] and its relationship to gender roles is especially important in Greece where, as in other Mediterranean societies, the dichotomy is highly developed and strongly gender-linked. Within any Greek village (and, to a great extent, in towns and cities also), there is a sharp physical demarcation between the private sphere, bounded by the walls of the house, and the public areas—the street, the *platia* ("square"), and the shops (see in this volume Dubisch; Friedl; Pavlides and Hesser; on the city, see Hirschon 1978, 1981). In some areas of Greece, the house is likely to be occupied by an extended family; in others, the conjugal family is the more common residential unit. But whatever the social composition of the unit, its privacy is guarded both symbolically and physically by the house in which it dwells. Although the houses in most Greek villages are clustered closely together, forming a nucleated structure, they are arranged so that maximum privacy is assured, and it is difficult to see into one house from another or from the street (Dubisch 1976; Friedl 1962; on the urban house, see Hirschon and Gold 1982).

The division between private and public is behaviorally demarcated as well, particularly with respect to gender roles, for as many anthropologists working in Greece have noted, the roles of women and men are strongly linked to the division between domestic and public realms. The house, the center of domestic life, is both physically and morally associated with the woman (see du Boulay 1974 and this volume; Dubisch, this volume; Hirschon 1978). Women are, ideally, restricted to the house, the location of many of their basic tasks, although in agricultural communities women also have important duties outside the house, such as caring for animals and working in the fields. Women's association with, and restriction to, the house may actually be stronger in urban areas, where such duties are nonexistent, although even in cities there may be public activities for women (see Hirschon 1981 and 1983).[11] In some areas of Greece, women may own their own houses, having received them as dowry (see, for example, Casselberry and Valvanes 1976; Dubisch 1976; Hoffman 1976; Kenna 1976), and, as Eleftherios Pavlides and Jana Hesser show in this volume, women, through their dowry and their handicraft activities, have played an important role in shaping the physical setting in which domestic life is lived.

Conversely, the public sphere is open freely to men, and, ostensibly, it is men who shape events in this sphere. Women do not loiter in public space as men do, but rather enter it only to perform specific tasks or on particular occasions, such as *paniyiria* or saint's day celebrations (see Friedl, this volume; Hoffman 1974 and 1976). But it could be argued that exclusion works both ways, and that generally in rural Greece it is considered better for a man not to spend too much time at home but instead to pass his leisure hours with other men in some public space like the *kafenio*, "coffeehouse," a place traditionally forbidden to women (see Loizos 1981; Kennedy, this volume).[12] We must be careful, however (and several of the papers in this volume, particularly that of Salamone and Stanton, emphasize this point) not to view gender roles and the division between private and public as coterminous. The private and public realms also represent two sets of values in Greek life, values which are significant to both men and women. (Both du Boulay's and Herzfeld's articles in this volume explore this topic; see also Herzfeld 1982b.) Moreover, as we shall see, women are concerned with the public realm and even have important roles in it, and men have significant associations with the house. The intimacy provided by domestic life is important to both sexes (a point emphasized by Herzfeld; see also Campbell 1964), even if more of the men's lives is lived in public. In Greek life, private and public are complementary and connected. It is precisely because of this interrelationship that the division between the private realm of domestic life and the public world has such important implications for Greek society, implications that go beyond gender roles. Before exploring some of these, however, we need to examine the relationship between the private/public dimension and power.

GENDER, POWER, AND SUBORDINATION

Given what may be a universal tendency of women to be associated, if not exclusively, at least significantly, with the private or domestic realm, and given the assertion made by some authors that women's position is universally subordinate to that of men, discussions of the relationship of power, prestige, and subordination to gender inevitably lead us into an examination of the private/public dimension of social life. Michelle Rosaldo, for example, notes that "the extra-domestic or 'public' ties . . . are primarily available to men" (Rosaldo 1974:17-18), and she suggests that the private/public distinction is the key to understanding the source and nature of women's power. Where women are barred from the public realm of activity, the power they wield will be of a different kind than the public power of men.

Two different arguments are offered about the relationship between power and the private/public distinction. One is that where the distinction is highly developed, women, because they are associated with the private realm, have a lower status and more circumscribed power. Peggy Reeves Sanday, for example, suggests that while segregation does not necessarily imply inequality, it is a necessary precondition. "Men and women must be physically as well as conceptually separated in order for men to dominate women" (Sanday 1981:7; see also Martin and Voorhies 1975). Where the private/public distinction is weak or non-existent, however, "where neither sex claims much authority and the focus of social life itself is the home," the relationships will be more egalitarian (Rosaldo 1974:36). Implicit in this argument is the assumption that the public or extra-domestic realm is the source of greatest power and prestige, and that certain universal features of their roles cause women to be exclusively or primarily associated with the domestic realm and to wield less power than men (compare this position with Ortner's arguments, discussed above).

The second argument pertaining to the relationship between power and domestic roles suggests that when the private/public distinction is highly developed, such roles give women a separate sphere of power and authority, one in which they may actually be dominant. If we neglect the domestic realm as a source of power, it is argued (and it seems to be ignored or downplayed in many cultural ideologies, including our own), we overlook an important source of power and status for women and therefore obtain a distorted view of their position in society generally. This issue is discussed from varying perspectives in several of the articles in this volume.

It appears, then, that there are two quite contradictory views of the relationship between the private/public division and women's status and power. One argues that women's domesticity, their association with the "inside," leads inevitably to their being "without," that is, without the ability to exercise control over their own lives and the lives of others. The opposite view suggests that such domesticity may itself provide the basis for power, although not necessarily "legitimate" power (see Lamphere 1974). Thus, depending upon one's viewpoint, women's roles in the private realm either contribute to their subordination or are an important means by which they can seek to overcome or compensate for such subordination.

Underlying these conflicting viewpoints are certain ethnocentric and androcentric assumptions that have become part of the definition and analysis of power. Until we confront these assumptions, our discussion of the relationship between gender and power will remain limited and culture-bound. Such assumptions first become apparent when we attempt to define sexual subordination and to determine its distribution. Are women, in fact, "universally devalued" and universally subordinated, and are these the same thing? Is inequality or sexual asymmetry a fact of life in all societies? If not, what constitutes equality?[13]

Jane Collier and Michelle Rosaldo define sexual asymmetry as "a basic imbalance in the nature and organization of obligations and the availability of public reward" (Collier and Rosaldo 1981:281). Susan Bourque and Kay Warren stress that sexual subordination "is not simply a status or a state" but is related to other aspects of social life, including other inequalities, and is "the product of social processes and structural relations between men and women. Thus . . . sexual subordination involves broad structural limitations that stress the quality of femaleness over more variable individual qualities and other social identities (such as age, occupation, ethnicity and family)" (Bourque and Warren 1981:48). Sexual parity, on the other hand, involves "relationships of equivalence, though not necessarily sameness or identity (in the mathematical sense) between the sexes" (Bourque and Warren 1981:48). But can "sexual parity" exist, or must difference always mean inequality? Ortner and Whitehead argue that the very existence of gender differentiation in and of itself implies hierarchy and therefore the differential evaluation of male and female. "[A] gender system is first and foremost a prestige structure" in which the category of "men" is valued more highly than the category of "women" (Ortner and Whitehead 1981:16). In other words, wherever the categories of male and female are contrasted, however those categories might be defined within a particular culture, one category is necessarily regarded as superior to the other. Similarly, Collier and Rosaldo claim that "cultural conceptions of the sexes are intimately linked to the organization of social inequality" (Collier and Rosaldo 1981:275). Given that some gender differentiation is found in all societies, we would have to conclude, then, that female subordination is, in fact, universal.

Other anthropologists have challenged these assumptions, however. Karen Sacks, for example, claims that to view subordination as an inevitable concomitant of gender differentiation is culture-bound, an example of what she calls "state-specific thinking" which insists on perceiving hierarchy, even when it may not be present in the minds and lives of the natives (Sacks 1976). (The private/public distinction also may be more characteristic of state societies—see Reiter 1975.) L. L. Jordanova criticizes the concept of universal subordination on similar grounds, claiming that it "assumes a model of society where there are unambiguous, rigid hierarchies, and so clear criteria for assigning their rank to any individual" (Jordanova 1980:65). Nancy Scheper-Hughes, reviewing her fieldwork in rural Ireland, has also questioned the assumption that sexual segregation is a male-enforced phenomenon which necessarily implies male domination; she terms the Irish situation one of "consensual segregation" (Scheper-Hughes 1983b). Herzfeld, in this volume, argues that male authority often has been overemphasized in Greek ethnography; such authority frequently turns into a measure of male subordination in the home. Thus, while the male/female distinction could be said to be a necessary condition for female subordination, it is not a sufficient one.

Sanday suggests that the power relationship between the sexes in a particular society exists in one of three forms: "mythical" male dominance, a situation in which men and women have equal power but men deny women's power and assert their own superiority; actual male dominance; and sexual equality which is both actual and acknowledged (Sanday 1981:8). (The issue of "mythical" versus "actual" male dominance will be discussed below.) Sanday further suggests that it is not differentiation per se, but rather the *degree* of differentiation, that is linked to female subordination. When maleness and femaleness are sharply distinguished, male dominance is more likely to occur, although why it is men who dominate rather than women still remains to be explained. When gender is a less significant aspect of identity, women's subordination qua women is reduced. As Sanday has noted, in societies in which the relationship between men and women approaches sexual equality, sexual differentiation is less pronounced, although not entirely absent. This argument parallels that discussed above relating a strong private/public distinction to women's status.

This discussion suggests that an important consideration in our study of gender, power and subordination is the question of *context*. For example, Bourque and Warren's observation that sexual subordination emphasizes the identity of femaleness over other qualities suggests that it is not just the degree of differentiation of the categories of male and female, but the extent of their "penetration" into a variety of contexts, that accounts for variation in sexual subordination from one society to another. In some societies, gender identity is contextual, that is, it is significant only in certain aspects of a person's life rather than being a determinant of identity in all contexts. Seen in this light, the cross-cultural study of women's equality or inequality becomes more complex than simply determining a particular society's position on a continuum ranging from equality at one end to extreme female subordination at the other. Subordination or devaluation may exist in one context and not in another. Attention to this dimension of "penetration" also may help to explain certain apparent anomalies in gender roles, such as societies in which women seem subordinate within the domestic context, as wives, daughters, and daughters-in-law, and yet appear to be relatively undiscriminated against as women when they enter the extra-domestic world of work.[14]

We cannot adequately analyze the problem of gender differentiation and gender power, however, without exploring some fundamental questions regarding the definition and sources of power, particularly its material roots versus its ideological roots. Let us first examine the question of definitions.

POWER: PROBLEMS AND DEFINITIONS

Power is commonly distinguished from authority, influence, and prestige, to which it is related but with which it is not necessarily coincident. Bourque and Warren, for example, view power as being structured and based on the socially approved control of resources, whereas they define personal influence as the ability to redirect or affect the power of others (Bourque and Warren 1981:52, 55). Influence is more often wielded by women, while power is usually the property of men (Lamphere 1974:99). Rosaldo, on the other hand, differentiates power, "the ability to gain compliance," from culturally legitimated authority, the recognition that such ability is right. Since women often wield power but lack authority, this distinction is "crucial to our understanding of women" (Rosaldo 1974:21). Denied authority in the public sphere, women may seek to exercise power in illegitimate ways.

While at first these two definitions of power might appear to be inconsistent, both make a distinction between acts that are politically sanctioned or culturally approved and those which, however effective they might be, are not. To these distinctions can be added another—the distinction between power and prestige or status. This distinction is the essence of Friedl's article, which begins this volume; she contrasts the "appearances of prestige" with the "realities" of power in Greek village life, suggesting that the ideology of male dominance and the public manifestations of masculine prestige can lead us to overlook the very real and important power exercised by women in the domestic sphere.

In general, distinctions such as these are useful for analyzing women's roles in Greece and other societies. Yet they can be difficult to apply in specific situations and may obscure, rather than illuminate, our understanding of women's position and the options open to them. In Greece, for example, the legitimate/illegitimate distinction becomes evident when we analyze the role dowry plays in women's domestic power. As Friedl points out, the possession of a dowry gives women a culturally recognized right to a say-so in household affairs, a right acknowledged by husband, wife, and the community at large. Women may also engage in activity that is socially disapproved, such as nagging, to prompt their husbands to carry out their wishes. However, while the distinction between the two methods of exercising power—

one socially acceptable, the other not—may be important in certain respects, they are similar in that both are means by which women "get their way." Women who nag or deliberately burn their husbands' evening meal or withhold sex are behaving in ways that are viewed with disfavor, but which nonetheless may be acknowledged as effective. The *poniria*, "cunning, deviousness," attributed to Greek women by Greek men (see Herzfeld, this volume) is a cultural acknowledgment of women's ability to get their way and, in a larger sense, of the ability of anyone who is weak to resort to deviousness. Indeed, in appropriate circumstances, men, whose position in the public world is similar to that of women in the house, may, Herzfeld points out, imitate this poniria themselves (Herzfeld, this volume). In addition, women's ability to disrupt or subvert normal social relationships, to "cause trouble" through disapproved actions, may give them a measure of control over their own lives and the lives of others, especially in rural Greek communities where the reputation of a family depends so much on the appropriate behavior of its women. Friedl suggests that this dependence of Greek men upon their women for the maintenance of their reputation gives women a sort of "latent power" in the relations between the sexes.[15] Perhaps the widespread belief that women are polluting stems in part from fear of their "negative" (illegitimate and disruptive) power. Rosaldo suggests that the commonness of such a belief may be due to the fact that "societies that define women as lacking legitimate authority have no way of acknowledging the reality of female power" (Rosaldo 1974:34).[16]

Some have argued that discussions of power and the way it is exercised suffer from a "state bias"; that is, our characterization of power as being politically sanctioned and our tendency to distinguish power from personal influence are rooted in our experience of the hierarchical power system of state societies. Such a definition, it is argued, is not necessarily useful when we examine non-state societies or the exercise of power in communal or nonpublic settings within state societies. In Greece, for example, while it is necessary to take into account the hierarchical public power system and the impact of legally defined structures on gender roles, concepts of power derived only from such sources may prove inadequate when we attempt to understand power at other levels.

Thus, while it may be somewhat useful to distinguish between illegitimate and legitimate exercises of power, between power and authority, this distinction should not blind us to the fact that not only may both be effective (and illegitimate power may be even more effective than legitimate power, since the way it is used is less circumscribed by social rules), but also they may both be culturally recognized. Such recognition can be explicit, as in the case of the Greek *poniria*, or more indirect, as in beliefs about pollution and the evil eye.[17] Moreover, when we are discussing the illegitimate exercise of power, we must also determine in whose eyes it is illegitimate. Men and women may not have the same opinion about what is legitimate and what is not (an issue explored more fully in the section on muted models).

The distinction between power and personal influence is an even more difficult one to apply in specific situations. Rather than exercising power directly, women in many societies often have to work through others to get their way, and this process may be analyzed more productively in terms of different *spheres* of power, rather than in terms of power versus "influence."

Renée Hirschon has suggested that "the domestic/household sphere has been greatly devalued in the western view," and that "our own preconceptions regarding power and its proper locus in the public domain hinder us from appreciating its different expressions in other societies" (Hirschon 1984:19). Given the importance of the domestic sphere in Greece, several authors in this volume argue that women's roles within this sphere are highly significant for the society as a whole, and that the power they wield in the domestic realm has effects that extend beyond the household itself. Friedl suggests in Chapter 2 that if Greek women do exercise real power in domestic life (as she feels they do), and if "the life of the family is the most significant structural and cultural element of the Greek village, then there is unmistakable need for a reassessment of the role of the Greek woman in village life." In Chapter 3, Muriel Dimen points out the vital role of Greek women in social reproduction, that is, in "the reproduction of social relations through the creation of the new generation and the daily biological and psychological renewal of the present," a process essential to the maintenance of the state itself. S. D. Salamone and J. B. Stanton argue in Chapter 5 that the institution of the *nikokyrio*, "household economy," spans both the private and public realms of Greek life and dictates a "balance of power" between men and women. For both husbands and wives, social prestige depends upon public recognition of the family's success (cf. Dubisch 1974).

Others have suggested that, ironically women's power may stem from submission to the system that seeks to deny it to them. In her article in Chapter 7 of this volume Juliet du Boulay argues that it is through their acquiescence to the cultural value system that women find not only satisfaction, but also the route to power: "a women increasingly exercises power as she succeeds in embodying the maternal ideal which is open to her." Elsewhere, Loring Danforth has suggested

that women who join the ritual of the Anastenaria gain "an opportunity to act with an authority that is normally possessed only by men"
(Danforth 1983:221). Yet at the same time, he points out, such authority is gained through submission to males, including their husbands
(whose permission they must obtain); the male leader of the ritual; and
St. Constantine, a male saint. In this sense, power is available to
women, but it is power that is "inside" in the sense of being constrained
within a larger, male-dominated system. While they see the relationship
between husbands and wives as more egalitarian, Salamone and Stanton likewise stress fulfilling the expectations of the ideal female role (in
this case as *nikokyra*, "female householder") as the means by which
women enjoy the prerogatives inherent in that role.

All these observations suggest that the important question is not so
much whether women have power (or if they have something else instead—influence, for example), but rather in what ways is power exercised. Examining power in terms of the private/public distinction allows us a clearer view of the nature and dimensions of women's power.
Power is always social. The domestic arena is no less a power arena
than any other. Within the domestic context, women often can exercise
their power in a direct manner, whereas in many societies they must
work through others, or through their impact on others, to affect matters in the public sphere. Viewing power contextually, then, may be
more worthwhile in terms of arriving at an understanding of women's
power and the nature of female subordination in Greece (and in other
societies as well) than trying to distinguish power from influence. For
du Boulay, for example, context is the key to understanding the apparent anomalies in the position of Greek women, a point made also by
Herzfeld, who in Chapter 10 contrasts the behavior of women toward
their husbands in the home with their more submissive stance outside.[18] By focusing on the private/public dimension of Greek life, we
can better appreciate the need to distinguish arenas or spheres for the
exercise of power, and we can also begin to pinpoint the different
sources of power and status. Power is always relative and is always exercised in certain spheres and over certain matters, and not over
others.[19]

However, as useful as the private/public distinction might be in help-
ing us to untangle the issues surrounding the exercise of power in Greek
village life, we must be careful not to assume a simple isomorphism between gender roles and the domestic and public spheres. Even women's
domestic roles, including their economic and religious roles, may have
a public dimension (see, for example, Salamone and Stanton, this volume; Dubisch 1983; Hirschon 1983). Conversely, men can be seen as

intrinsically connected to the house. Detailing how both men and
women are engaged in a partnership that supports the house, du Boulay
speaks of the "often tyrannous service to the house" to which men must
submit in their constant struggles to support it. It is also important not
to overlook the vital connections between the domestic and private arenas. We need to consider the ways that each supports and articulates
with the other (for example, see Dimen, this volume), as well as the
ways that power in one sphere is translated into power in the other
sphere. Pavlides and Hesser point out in Chapter 4 that both the exterior façade and the interior furnishings of the village house serve to display a family's wealth and its women's industry. On occasions such as
name day celebrations, there is a public "penetration" of the domestic
sphere, in which the husband of the house presides as host over a table
set in the *saloni*, "parlor"; both the room (the location of the family's
best possessions) and the table laden with refreshments serve as public
displays that uphold a family's communal reputation (see Danforth
1979b). In addition, as I have argued elsewhere (Dubisch 1974), the
prestige of each partner, earned through appropriate behavior in his or
her respective arenas, can translate into power in the other arena. A
man granted respect by his wife at home gains prestige and influence in
the public world; someone nagged by his wife, on the other hand, is
pitied and looked down on. A women with a good reputation (reputation being by nature a public matter, based on community judgment)
enjoys power and respect in her relations with her spouse.[20]

But are "prestige" and "respect" the same as power? If not, how are
they related? The distinction between power and prestige is best discussed within the larger context of the basis of power, specifically
whether its roots are material or ideological. It is to this topic that I will
turn next.

THE ROOTS OF POWER: MATERIAL OR IDEOLOGICAL?

Sexual subordination has both material and ideological components.
By stressing one or the other, and sometimes by confusing the two, researchers may arrive at very different conclusions about gender equality, even when examining the same society. Material and ideological
factors may reenforce each other, as, for example, when ideological justification is offered for material inequality, but they may also diverge,
as Friedl points out in her article in this volume. Where they do diverge,
we are faced with questions regarding the "real" status of women in the
society in question. In her book *Men and Women: An Anthropologist's*

[handwritten margin note: private becomes public.]

View, Friedl suggests that the following are indicators of overt power: (1) control over production and distribution of economic resources, (2) rights of participation and leadership in political and religious activities, and (3) autonomy in decision making in matters affecting one's personal and familial life (Friedl 1975:6-7). Friedl's approach is frankly etic. Examining the issue of female power and subordination from an emic point of view, however, points up discrepancies between the two types of analyses. An ideology that embraces female subordination or the devaluation of women can exist in societies in which women actually exercise considerable control over resources and possess the power of self-determination, an example of what Sanday has termed "mythical" male dominance (Sanday 1981; see also Hirschon 1984 for further examples). The reverse situation also exists, that is, societies in which women are "valued" but are denied the right to exercise power or run their own lives. There are also societies which exhibit a conflicting mixture of gender ideologies, and in which women are granted simultaneously an equal (or valued) and a subordinate status. Anna Meigs (1984) has suggested that this situation exists in the highland New Guinea society she studied, and Herzfeld (this volume) suggests that it exists in Greece. How, then, are we to determine, from one society to another, what constitutes a "better" position for women? In which situation are they more subordinate? Can power result from being "valued," even if the material bases for power do not exist for women? And even if the material bases for power do exist, does the "devaluation" of women reduce their power or is it irrelevant? When ideology and material conditions do not completely reflect each other, which one is the "true" indicator of women's position?

These questions are especially important to our study of Greece, which, like other countries of the European Mediterranean and like those of Latin America, places a strong emphasis on motherhood and female purity, qualities that women use to bolster their own sense of worth (see, for example, Rosaldo 1974:38-39 on Spain; Giovannini 1981 on Italy) or, as Evelyn Stevens argues in her discussion of the Latin American concept of *marianismo* (the feminine counterpart of *machismo*), to attain a privileged position for themselves (Stevens 1973).

Some anthropologists regard material factors as the key to understanding variations in women's status and power. Where women have access to their own productive resources, it is argued, or where they play vital roles in the productive process, their personal power and their status are higher. However, it is not only women's role in production that is significant. As Friedl has argued, even more important may be women's culturally acknowledged right to dispose of the products of their own labor (Friedl 1975). For example, a Greek woman's right to a say-so in the disposal of her dower property grants her power within the domestic sphere, a power that may not coincide with the image of women reflected in the dominant ideology of gender, but which is nonetheless real and significant. To ignore the "reality" of this power and to focus only on "appearance" and on the ideology of gender distorts our understanding of women's position in rural Greek society.[21]

To what degree can the ideology of gender in and of itself confer or deny power? While some claim that there is no real evidence that being a moral symbol endows women with any real power or influence (see, for example, Bourque and Warren 1981:60-61), others disagree, claiming that realization of the feminine ideals of their culture can provide women with a measure of control over their lives, even when the material conditions for such control are lacking. Furthermore, to overlook this component of women's position is ethnocentric and materialist (see, for example, Sanday 1981). Hirschon, defining property as a "socially valued resource," suggests that it may take a nonmaterial form—for example, ritual knowledge, special skills, or even honor and reputation (Hirschon 1984:9). Such arguments are particularly germane to the studies in this volume. While Friedl regards the possession of dowry as the major (though not the only) factor in women's domestic power, du Boulay and Dimen take somewhat different views. Du Boulay suggests that we should not consider the impact of women simply in terms of power and authority, but rather in terms of their spiritual importance. The major *structural* factor that gives women power is, in her view, the fulfillment of the maternal ideal; other factors, such as possession of dowry, are idiosyncratic and may or may not have an impact on a woman's position in the household. In fact, du Boulay presents us with instances in which a wife's possession of material resources has called forth even greater abuse and/or authoritarianism from her husband, who is determined to maintain his position in the household. Dimen suggests that while "economics and politics are conventionally thought of as sources of power . . . control of the individual psyche and of ideology is vital." She points out that Greek women both symbolize and recreate important features of society, including the social and economic isolation of the house, the value of hard work, and "the inevitability and personal necessity of social connection." Both authors seem to suggest that it is important to focus on women's ability to shape society and on their important roles in symbolizing and maintaining central values.

Another aspect of the ideology of gender and its relationship to power is religion. Gender roles and the values attached to them often have a religious justification. Sanday regards religious codes as an important part of the "sex role plans" of a culture. These plans affect both the behavior of and the value placed on each sex, and they play a significant part in determining the symmetry or asymmetry of male and female powers within a society (Sanday 1981). In Greece, the behavior expected of and the values associated with men and women are inextricably linked to the Orthodox religion. As du Boulay points out, women are associated with Eve and with all the evil and wickedness she represents, thereby justifying male superiority and men's control over women. Yet at the same time, women also are associated with the Mother of God (the *Panayia*). We can understand neither the apparent anomalies of women's status in rural Greek society, nor the value and necessity of their role, unless we consider these dual aspects of femaleness in the context of the religious value system. Outside of their proper roles as wives and mothers, women are Eves and the root of all evil; yet in their fulfillment of these roles, they become reflections of a divine archetype. Women's subordination, then, is part of an overall symbolic order. If they were to rebel against their association with Eve, writes du Boulay, "they would also . . . be forced to overthrow their association with the myth of the birth of Christ and the honour given to women through the figure of the Mother of God." Anna Caraveli, on the other hand, sees women as constructing an alternative religious system, one that is outside and even to some extent opposed to the dominant religion. That women wield power through their performance of religious laments is, according to Caraveli in Chapter 8, evidenced by the history of attempts by (male) authorities to suppress them.

Overemphasis on material factors as the root of power, then, may lead to neglect of other possible sources of power. Moreover, attributing the possession of power to control over material resources might be putting the cart before the horse. While there may be a relationship between the two in many societies, it is not necessarily clear whether material control is a cause of power or whether it is instead its consequence, with power itself a result of ideology. Sanday has suggested as much. Abandoning her earlier materialist position regarding gender and power, she has concluded that symbolism plays "a key role in channeling secular power roles" (Sanday 1981:xv) and suggests that "secular power roles are derived from ancient concepts of sacred power" (p. xvi). It could be argued that the belief that certain individuals have power, or that the possession of certain kinds of things grants people power, leads, in fact, to their having it. When we cast arguments pertaining to women's power in different societies in a mold of material determinism, we may simply be exchanging one bias for another.[22]

But the argument goes deeper than the issue of possible materialist bias in our examination of the roots of power and status. We must also free ourselves from the androcentrism that continues to permeate the very definitions of what we study. Male activities and male views still influence much of our research, despite attempts to correct for this bias. We tend to see power in what men control, in the events and activities associated with men, and our questions about women and power are couched in terms of the extent to which women control similar things or engage in similar activities. This proclivity is particularly evident in the study of both politics, which tends to focus on the public (male) world, and history, which focuses on public events, that is on male activities (Sherman and Beck 1979). The political activities of women, which in many societies are carried out outside (or alongside) the formal political structures that delineate the male political world, or inside, in a domestic context, are treated as peripheral, intrusive, and often illegitimate, instead of as an integral part of the political process.

Our very definitions of "political" are based on an androcentric model. Women's activities often are not viewed as political precisely because they *are* women's activities and women are not defined as political actors (see, for example, Bourque and Grossholtz 1974 on sexual sterotyping in political analysis; see also Morgan 1983). Women's strategies and their attempts to get their way are viewed as idiosyncratic and personal rather than as political acts shaped by structural factors. Moreover, the private/public distinction suggests that the sphere in which women are more likely to exercise power is subordinate to, or outside of, the world of "real" (public) power. Women's exercise of power is thus viewed as an unpredictable intrusion into the body politic rather than as an integral part of its anatomy. Women's roles "behind the throne," for instance, are considered to be illegitimate interferences in the formally constituted, public political system rather than an integral part of the functioning of power—expected, patterned, and predictable, even if undefined and unacknowledged. From the anthropologist's standpoint, however, such roles should be viewed as being as institutionalized as any others; most (male) rulers have had wives, mothers, sisters, and mistresses whose exercise of a degree of power over the "legitimate" rulers has been generally accepted.

Rayna Reiter has reported that in the southern French village she studied, women explicitly reject the notion that power resides in the public (male) world alone; they view the private domain as no less important than the public one (Reiter 1975:258). Often, however, informants, like some anthropologists, deny a political role to women. Collier suggests that while conflicts between men may be explained "in terms of culturally recognized rules, women's quarrels are often attributed to personal idiosyncrasies or to particularistic circumstances" (Collier 1974:89-90; cf. du Boulay, this volume). Yet this exercise of "negative power," the power to make trouble, is also a generally unacknowledged political act, aimed at achieving control over others. We may overlook this activity because of the "trivial" nature of the means employed (nagging, delaying supper, and withholding sex, for example), but as Collier points out, "Women . . . may ostensibly fight over trivialities, but the real stakes are political—the capacity to determine the actions of others" (Collier 1974:94).

During the course of my fieldwork, I collected information about several such quarrels between women living in the community. Villagers were quick to point out to me that these quarrels were almost always among "foreign" women (*ksenes*), that is, women who had not been born in the village but had married into it.[23] The implicit or explicit assumption behind such statements was that these women were of weaker or more questionable character (otherwise they would have been able to find spouses in their natal villages), hence the higher incidence of quarreling, both among themselves and with others in the village. I came to realize, however, that such quarrels were less an indication of character flaws than of the weak structural position of the ksenes who, without relatives in the village, often formed friendships and alliances with each other. Because of these women's more isolated position, such alliances were subject to strain and breakage. Without the backing of kinsmen in the community, these ksenes were more likely to resort to nagging and quarreling in their efforts to achieve their ends. This behavior was socially disapproved of and was interpreted by the villagers not as political strategy but as defective character.[24]

Such examples demonstrate that, in analyzing power, we may have to overcome not only our own biases, but also those of our informants. "Our own culture (and probably all others) is characterized by an ideology dictating that women's lives are relatively uninteresting" (Rosaldo and Lamphere 1974:15). Yet, while du Boulay reports that in the Greek village where she lived both men and women view women's activities as trivial, Dimen points out that these very trivia of domestic life are essential parts of the process of social reproduction upon which the entire society rests. In the community studied by Salamone and Stanton, men regard the *rouha*, the trousseau and household goods that form part of the dowry, simply as part of the "burden" of having daughters, but in fact such goods (produced by the women) can be an important part of the household's wealth.

In the activities that structure part of women's daily lives, we find clues not only to the puzzles of gender roles and status, but also to many of the other patterns and processes that form an essential part of Greek society. In the quarrels of "foreign" women, we see the operation of political strategies within the village social system, as well as the opposition between "inside" and "outside" that is so fundamental to Greek social concepts; in gossip, we see the operation of important mechanisms of social control and the expression and maintenance of village values (du Boulay 1976); in women's cooking and cleaning and the observation of rules about pollution, we discern statements about social order, nature, and culture (Dubisch, this volume); in the perpetual sewing, embroidery, and other "handicraft" activities (the very term suggests relative unimportance), we find economic significance and the base of a family's prestige (Pavlides and Hesser, this volume; Salamone and Stanton, this volume). We must not let the division between private and public spheres blind us to the interrelationships between the inside and the outside. By ridding ourselves of the preconception that women's activities are "only" domestic, we begin to realize the relationship of such activities to the "larger" system.

At the same time, we must recognize that sometimes the women's world is more obscure precisely because so much of it centers on the "inside." This inner world of domestic life may be difficult for any outsider to penetrate, particularly for a male outsider in a society with a high degree of segregation of the sexes.[25] As Herzfeld suggests, we need to be aware of our own role as observers and the extent to which this role influences the information we receive. We also need to be aware of the biases resulting from participation in a male-dominated and male-defined profession, biases incorporated even by female anthropologists (see, for example, Friedl 1975; Scheper-Hughes 1983a). Although such cultural biases can never be completely surmounted, we can strive to become conscious of them and, in this reflexive fashion, make ourselves an integral part of our own fieldwork.[26]

WOMEN AS ACTORS

How can we overcome some of the biases and pitfalls which seem to be inherent in our study of gender? One approach that may help uncover the "hidden" world of women and avoid some of the androcentric bias that pervades our studies of gender is to view women as actors, that is, to see them as individuals who seek, in culturally structured ways, to achieve desired ends (Rosaldo and Lamphere 1974:9). In this view, women are no longer portrayed simply as interchangeable parts within social systems in which men are the prime movers and decision-makers. Instead, they are considered to have their own goals and strategies that they seek to realize within socially defined contexts (although, as suggested above, not necessarily through socially approved means). Implicit in such an approach is the idea that culture does not consist of a fixed set of roles and rules for behavior, but rather is "negotiable"; that is, within any set of prescriptions, there is room for ambiguity and flexibility, and there is a willingness to acknowledge the necessity for variation. T. P. Beidelman regards "ambiguity, contradiction and conflict" as the "essence of social life" (Beidelman 1980:30). This point is particularly important when we are dealing with gender roles. Mari Clark has proposed "that we analyze the concept of gender as a generally ambiguous cultural construct that is elaborated in response to constraining factors and individual goals in particular situations" (Clark 1983:129). This concept is demonstrated in du Boulay's article, in which she recounts instances of how seemingly rigid rules about female deportment are in fact contextually interpreted and applied. Once we see women as actors, both shaped by and shaping the social system, their significance in the operation of that system becomes clearer, and they are no longer its passive objects but reveal themselves instead as active subjects.

Viewing women as actors pursuing strategies does not necessarily mean that we need view them as always seeking power. Overemphasis on this aspect of negotiation of the world reflects the individualistic bias of Western, particularly American, culture, which sees power largely in terms of personal goals. As Dimen suggests in this volume, Greek village women do not work "as persons in and for themselves only, but as merged parts of social units as well." In Greece, the goals of both men and women may be social rather than personal in nature, concerned with the protection and advancement of family rather than self (a point emphasized by Salamone and Stanton). We also need to consider the extent to which power comes from having an impact in a culturally determined manner, through conformity to cultural role expectations for example. Such conformity can be as much a strategy as is circumvention of cultural pressures and requirements. (This point is discussed by du Boulay.) Such strategies need not be conscious. For example, in his study of a northern Greek village, Danforth describes how women who join the religious cult of the Anastenaria find in their membership in the cult a means of resolving certain conflicts with their mothers-in-law. These women are not consciously motivated to join by their domestic difficulties, however. The immediate cause is usually some persistent illness for which other sources of cure have failed (Danforth 1983). Caraveli suggests in this volume that through their performance of ritual laments for the dead, women may give voice to a sense of "communal victimization." By such means, women turn institutions of oppression into sources of fulfillment, endeavoring to create for themselves, perhaps, a positive personal and gender identity. Such an endeavor is, according to Robinette Kennedy, what lies at the root of the psychologically satisfying personal friendships that Cretan women create with each other. Although "friends" for these women are by definition people who have power over each other (to the extent that power is derived from the possession of secrets), Kennedy stresses that the relationship is not based on such power.

By viewing women as actors, with a variety of strategies and goals that result from both personal and structural factors, we can begin to perceive some of these patterns in the fabric of social life. In addition, an actor-oriented approach can help us to understand gender constructs and gender symbolism, not only as they are contextually interpreted and manipulated by both men and women within a particular culture, but also in terms of how they shape actors' perceptions so that such constructs come to be regarded as inevitable features of the "natural" world (Ortner and Whitehead 1981:5).

This actor-oriented approach has not been free of criticism. One objection to it is that it can take us only so far in understanding women's position in society. For example, in the Peruvian communities they studied, Bourque and Warren collected data which, they feel, "demonstrate that despite women's analysis of subordination and their efforts to devise strategies to respond to it, there are structural forces arrayed against them" (Bourque and Warren 1981:217). Likewise, Sohier Morsy, utilizing data from an Egyptian village, questions "the utility of approaching sex roles in terms of individual strategies and competition for power"; she suggests that women's "power and capacity for choice are ultimately regulated by structural principles similar to those which underlie male positions of power in their respective societies" (Morsy 1978:137, 138).

Such criticisms speak to an important point, namely, that whatever their opportunities for choice and manipulation, women often have little control over the larger structures that shape their lives (although it might be pointed out that, in many societies, neither do men). Yet in certain ways, the debate is a false one, for most actor-oriented analysis neither ignores nor denies the broad structural constraints on women (or men), but rather proposes that women's roles and their exercise of choice and power may be more flexible and variable than a simple description of these constraints suggests.

Friedl, for example, in her article on dowry, is not claiming that women's use within the domestic context of the advantage bestowed on them by possession of a dowry is the sole key to understanding their position in Greek society, or that it necessarily compensates for inequality in other spheres. Rather, she is saying that it is an aspect of women's position which, if ignored, leads us to believe that women have far less influence in society than in fact they have. Dimen has characterized Greek village women as both "servants and sentries," for while in some ways they serve the power of the state, they also stand guard at the boundaries of the domestic domain, striving to protect the private realm of life from intrusions. Thus any actor-oriented analysis, if it is to be convincing and not simplistic, must take into account the complex interaction between actor and system rather than viewing either as the sole determinant of the other.

The problem is not limited to the study of women and gender roles. No individual, male or female, is simply either the passive pawn of social forces or the sole determiner of his or her own fate. This point is emphasized by Nicos Mouzelis, who, in his analysis of classes in Greece, emphasizes that an approach that views collective actors as "mere products of the social system" (Mouzelis 1978:51) is as unsatisfactory as one that reduces social structures to individual acts and motivations. He suggests that change and development can be analyzed successfully only by "seriously taking into account the truism that men are both the products and producers of their social world, by stressing both the system-actor and the actor-system relationship" (p. 53), and by examining both "how institutional structures impose constraints on specific actors, and how these actors either accept or try to overcome such constraints" (p. 53). Although Mouzelis is discussing development and class analysis, his statements apply equally well to women in society. What the study of women and the study of social change have in common is that both often challenge existing theories of society and culture. Just as certain classes are more constrained in their ability to act, so women usually are more constrained than men (although we must not overlook the ways in which men are constrained also). Within the limits of these constraints, however, women seek to realize their goals and sometimes strive to change the system itself. Despite their criticism of actor-oriented approaches, Bourque and Warren conclude that "the lives of Andean women demonstrate . . . inequality is not mechanically perpetuated. Instead, it is negotiated, disputed, and ultimately changes through the conscious actions of individuals" (Bourque and Warren 1981:218). Such themes are clearly sounded in a number of the essays in this volume. Whether or not they explicitly take an actor-oriented approach, they seek to explore various dimensions of the actor-system (and system-actor) relationship and to understand both the options and limitations this relationship presents for Greek women.

The complexity of women's position in Greek society and the necessity for taking an actor-oriented approach become evident when we examine social change in Greece and its impact upon women. To the extent that gender concepts and gender roles place one sex in an inferior or disadvantaged position, change in these concepts and roles seems a desirable goal. "Modernization" and the spread of the women's movement with its concepts of sexual equality would seem to be steps in the right direction. Yet at the same time, as the preceding discussions have shown, the issue of women's status and power is not a clear-cut one, not even to the women involved.

While industrializaton and the spread of a market economy can lead to greater options for women, as well as to alterations in the legal and economic system that may work to their benefit, the forces of "modernization" can also bring about a deterioration in the position enjoyed by women in many "traditional" societies (see, for example, Boserup 1970; Reiter 1975). Sometimes women's traditional skills continue to be of use, but often such skills become marginal and unrewarding in a rapidly changing industrial world. In addition, the availability of unskilled jobs may decline, while those that require education and training are available only to men. Because their plans for development are derived from androcentric western models, agents of change may ignore women's traditional economic roles and rights. To some extent, we can view this process as a shift in the "balance of power" from the domestic world to the public world. It is no wonder, then, that women in American society feel that their route to equality lies in the public arena of work rather than in the domestic sphere (though there are women who still argue the importance and effectiveness of domestic power), and it is significant that for such women the least rewarding activities, particularly from a financial standpoint, are the ones which replicate domestic labor, such as nursing, cleaning, and child care.

In Greece, such changes have had a varying impact. The opening of factories provides opportunities for local women to perform wage labor (Lambiri 1968). Pavlides and Hesser report a decline in the importance of women's contributions to the furnishing of houses, because men earn enough money through wage labor to purchase items. Yet Salamone and Stanton found that the traditional handicrafts practiced by the women of the community they studied have continued to be valued. This is due, primarily, to both a nationalistic emphasis on local handicrafts (products of the "inside," we might suggest) and the tourist industry, which has, in various areas of Greece, provided an impetus to continue the production of traditional (and pseudo-traditional) crafts.[27] Such crafts, then, are shaped and encouraged by the act of presenting oneself to the "outside," of conforming to what tourists' images of such Greek crafts should be.[28]

The position of women is influenced by international forces other than economic ones. As Herzfeld points out, Greeks have long been sensitive to Western standards regarding women's position. Such sensitivity, however, does not necessarily mean uncritical acceptance of these standards. Greek writers of the past, Herzfeld suggests, advocated education of women not as a step toward their emancipation but as a way to enhance their domestic role. While American feminists see the entrance of women into the marketplace as a step forward in the struggle for social and economic equality,[29] women in certain segments of Greek society may regard not having to work outside the home and, in particular, being relieved of the burden of heavy agricultural labor, as an improvement in their position. Their identity and self-worth are derived from sources other than their extra-domestic labor. Indeed, as Salamone and Stanton show, contact with urbanites and foreign women does not necessarily bring dissatisfaction; villagers may actually feel pity for the American woman who has neither a firm sense of identity nor the security and peace of mind that accompany it.

These observations bring us back to one of the paradoxes discussed in the Preface: many Greek women seem to possess a strength of character and a firm sense of self in what to the outside observer seems a restrictive society. I think that one of the keys to understanding this paradox is understanding the domestic realm and its significance. With their feet firmly in this realm, fulfilling their roles as wives and mothers, many rural Greek women feel confident and certain of themselves, whatever else they do. Although many writers stress that Greek women gain their *social* identity through their ties to men (particularly to father and husband), nonetheless, most Greek women do not seem to depend upon men for their *personal* identity and sense of self-worth. If we are to see women as actors making choices in a changing world, we need to understand how their own perceptions of their situation influence the types of choices they make.

CULTURE AND THE "MUTED MODEL"

Focusing on the "women's world" and viewing women as actors with goals and strategies leads us into a broader theoretical issue: From what and from whom are we to construct our model of culture itself?

Have our descriptions of particular cultures sometimes been androcentric, either because we rely too heavily on male informants or because informants of both sexes tend to present the dominant, public, male point of view? Edwin Ardener has suggested that we ought to look for what he calls "muted models" in our investigations of particular cultures, that is, models of the social and natural worlds which are held by subordinate groups within a society and which differ from those of the dominant group. Such models are "muted" in the face of the dominant ideology and may be only vaguely articulated by the members of the subordinate group themselves (E. Ardener 1975). Women in particular may have different ideas about themselves, about their relationships with men, about the structuring of society and the nature of the world, and about the symbolism and significance of sex and gender categories than do men. But their models may be overlooked by anthropologists, even by female anthropologists, because fieldworkers may accept the ideology of the male world as *the* cultural model—it is after all, the visible, public, and culturally approved viewpoint—and because alternative models, being muted (private, hidden, and often unarticulated) are less accessible to researchers. As both Caraveli and Herzfeld document in this volume, a certain degree of acceptance is required before such alternative models are revealed to ethnographers.

Once we are alert to the possibility of alternatives, however, we often find that evidence of them is not difficult to obtain. For example, Daisy Dwyer, working in Morocco, has recorded interesting differences in men's and women's views of female sexuality (Dwyer 1978). Men and women in the Peruvian villages studied by Bourque and Warren have different views about the extent and value of women's contribution to agriculture. The men use their belief that women contribute less to justify male dominance, but the women do not necessarily agree with the men's evaluation (Bourque and Warren 1981). In Greece, women's views as to what constitutes appropriate social behavior may differ from those of men, and they may attempt to act as agents of social control to curb what they define as male excess. Men, on the other hand, do not necessarily agree with women's assessment of what is appropriate. Regarding such acts as drinking and high-spirited public behavior as an important part of being a man (*andras*), they may resent and resist women's attempts to curb or reprimand them (Bernard 1976; Campbell 1964; Dubisch 1983; Friedl 1962). Obviously, this is an area in which there is no single agreed-upon standard of behavior. Yet even if we do not want to describe this example as a "muted model" (it could be argued instead that men and women represent conflicting community standards), it does suggest the necessity for a complex view of culture, one which not only can incorporate women's views and behavior, but which also can take account of the cultural expectation that men and women have different views and that both sets of views are "legitimate" and equally a part of the culture.

A clearer case might be made for the "muted model" in Greece in the area of sex and childbirth. Despite the importance of the mother role and the status it confers upon women in Greek society, I sensed a certain ambivalence among women regarding children. While the dominant ideology stresses the importance of having children (and women will express agreement with this ideology), men seemed to be more insistent than women in urging my husband and me to start a family. Women, on the other hand, were more likely than men to comment on the greater freedom they enjoyed before they became mothers. One women even confided to me that not only had she not wanted her fourth and last child (which was certainly understandable in a village where most people recognized that "many children are poverty"), she really had not wanted any of them. If a method of preventing or aborting pregnancies had been readily available, she said, she would have resorted to it. While not all village women felt this way, it does suggest that there may be more tension between the dominant ideology regarding children and women's own perspective on the subject than one might at first think. However, since women are unlikely to express such views in any but the most intimate situations (and not in the presence of their husbands), male ideology dominates.[30] This reluctance to express their way of thinking reflects Herzfeld's ideas regarding inclusion and exclusion, inside and outside, and the position of the ethnographer. To hear such views expressed, one must be an "insider"; in this particular instance, being part of the "inside" meant being female. I found it interesting that, although during my fieldwork I had come to know well the woman who did not want children, and although I had visited her and her family on several occasions afterwards, it was not until I returned to the village one summer without my husband that we had this intimate conversation (cf. Clark 1983). Another example is Caraveli's experience with women who told her that mourning laments were worthless, but who gave a different account when she was alone with them.

But are these examples really instances of the "muted model" that Ardener suggests we seek? Or are they simply what du Boulay would consider Greek women's realistic assessment, and resentment, of their disadvantaged situation in relation to men? After all, having children is more difficult for women, who must both bear and care for them. (Not surprisingly, it was women with young children who complained the most.) Explicitly rejecting the idea that Greek women have an alternative model, or what she refers to as a subculture, du Boulay argues that structural factors (particularly virilocal marriage and the allegiance owed to the family) militate against the formation of any separate "women's world," and that, moreover, both men and women share a basically similar view of women. Women find their satisfaction not in developing an alternative model, but rather in seeking to realize the positive side of a conception of feminine nature that views women as having the potential for both evil (as Eve) and good (as the Panayia, the Mother of God). On the other hand, Kennedy, in her investigation in this volume of women's friendships, claims that such relationships provide women with the opportunity to share confidences that must be kept secret because "they consist of material which is unintegrated into the dominant culture." While she does not suggest that such material represents an alternative cosmology, she does believe that friendships allow women a context in which they can experience self-esteem with an equal, free from the pressure of other role definitions, and she warns against seeing women's friendships as a simple "microcosm of the total social structure," for "the content of women's friendships is distinctly different from the social relationships in the dominant culture of Greek society."

Of the papers in this volume, the one which comes closest to suggesting a muted model is Caraveli's analysis of ritual laments. Such laments are performed with, and judged by, other women; they often celebrate women; and they may be carried out without men's knowledge or approval. In such laments, women not only give voice to their own personal grief, but also express such ideas as the sisterhood of women and their "communal victimization." Moreover, the laments may constitute an implicit or explicit protest against official religion, for they reveal a notion of death "contrary to Christian views of a rewarding afterlife for the pious," a view of death as dark, grim, and final. Caraveli suggests, then, that laments are a form of "folk religion, outside the official church." Whether or not men share this view of religion, it is one that is articulated and expressed by women, for it is women, not men, who are the creators and performers of ritual laments.

Women are not the only people who may be "muted." Any subordinate or disenfranchised group in society may define and present itself in terms of the values articulated by the dominant group and yet at the same time possess a muted model. This point is stressed by Dimen in her discussion of the position of the villagers in relation to the state, and Herzfeld suggests that, in certain circumstances, women represent Greeks generally as a dominated people. Caraveli notes that women may take on the voice of the weak and downtrodden in their laments, speaking out against the situations that oppress them, including, for example, doctors and modern medicine. Villagers may present themselves to individuals of the dominant group (the "outside") as possessing a certain ideology, one that they themselves wish to have seen or which they feel the outsiders wish to see. Village women are thus doubly subordinate, doubly "muted," and if they do possess alternative models, it may be necessary to dig deeply to uncover them. On the other hand, the anthropologist, as Herzfeld points out, is doubly an outsider, being neither a villager nor, usually, a Greek. At the same time, however, it is important to consider the extent to which women acquiesce in and support an oppressive or restrictive system, and why, and to uncover the ways in which they strive both to "get around" the system and to find satisfaction within it. The fact that the authors in this volume, although researching a single society, are not in agreement on this matter illustrates quite pointedly the complexity of the issues, both conceptually and ethnographically.

BEYOND GENDER

These last remarks suggest that for a true understanding of gender we must move—paradoxically—beyond gender, seeking out its relationship to other aspects of social life. Gender, sexuality, private and public, inside and outside are elements of important and powerful symbolic systems. They are ways of talking about society and individuals' experience in society. But they are more than simply an expression of social order. They are the means of creating and interpreting that order and, beyond that, of ordering and talking about life itself. Ideas of male and female, inside and outside, are related to conceptions of self and to one's experiences as a member of certain social groups in their relations with other social groups. In Greece, the separation between private and public is paralleled socially by the concepts of "insider" and "outsider." Those who are "inside" are *dhiki mas*, "our own," while all the outsiders are kseni. Dhiki mas may include one's own immediate family, all one's relatives, all fellow villagers, or even all Greeks. The two terms are relative and expand or contract depending upon context. As Herzfeld points out, to move from one realm to the other, from the outside to the inside, is to change drastically the quality of one's social relationships. It also changes the images of self that are presented. Inside and outside reflect the interior self versus the exterior self, what we know we are as opposed to what others think we are or what we wish them to think we are. Groups also experience this interior versus exterior image. As Herzfeld shows, the image presented to the outsider differs from that which is seen within the physical and social boundaries of the group. Thus, private and public do more than delimit spheres of activity and domains of power. They also define realms of experience of self and society. Within the confines of the domestic realm are found safety, security, and the freedom to be "oneself," however that is defined. This inside also represents the hidden, the secret, the ability to manipulate the outside. Women, the "insiders," the "weaker," the subordinate, the "hidden," symbolize this "inside" aspect of personal and social life and the qualities associated with it. Such symbolism, as Herzfeld points out, can be carried to the national level of Greek life, where the category of "insiders" (*dhiki*) includes all Greeks, while the "outsiders" are various dominant foreign nations. One's own view of the society will be shaped largely by one's position relative to inside and outside, and this applies, of course, to the anthropologist.[31]

Thus, we have moved "beyond gender" in the sense that we are no longer concerned with gender roles; with what concrete men and women do in specific social situations; and with power, economics, and related issues. As Herzfeld rightly emphasizes, we must not confuse the symbolism of female and male and inside and outside with gender roles, for they are only partly isomorphic. While notions of inside and outside are important features of Greek life, and essential for our understanding of it, both men and women move across what Herzfeld calls boundaries of inclusion and exclusion. Moreover, men may take on qualities associated with the "inside," and women occasionally may take on qualities associated with the "outside."

Going beyond gender in this fashion can help us to understand somewhat the apparent disparity in some societies between gender ideology and gender roles. The ideology may not be "talking" about gender roles but may instead have a broader reference. Herzfeld, for example, has suggested that when the Cretan villagers told him that in the old days women were more virtuous than they are now, they were not necessarily implying an actual decline in female chastity but, instead, were positing an earlier state of more stringent adherence to moral standards to "justify what would otherwise seem an unreasonable and unrealistic morality" in the present day (Herzfeld 1983:161). Sexuality and the behavior of women were being used to make a larger statement about social ideals. And in this volume, Herzfeld proposes that gender roles can be seen as "epiphenomena of a more fundamental concern with concealment and display," which is a general feature of Greek life. In a similar vein, I suggest in my own article that beliefs regarding purity and pollution and nature and culture should not be seen simply as aspects of gender roles, but rather as representations of more general features of Greek social and symbolic life.

"Inside" and "outside" are also important components of concepts relating to the body and sexuality. The body is what Mary Douglas calls a "natural symbol" (Douglas 1970). Concern with bodily boundaries and entries and exits represents a concern with social boundaries, a concern which, as we have already seen, is an important theme in Greek culture. (This idea is elaborated upon further in my own article later in this volume.) Dimen suggests that women's solitary labor both symbolizes and attempts to preserve the isolation and autonomy of the household in the face of the increasing penetration of the state. Likewise, sexuality "naturally" lends itself to symbolism. It is not surprising that in Greece, as in other societies, women and their bodies symbolize the relationship of inside and outside and the penetrations of one by the other. Women's experiences of the problems of boundary maintenance (menstruation, sexual intercourse, pregnancy, and childbirth) represent more general experience of all members of society, both as individuals and as members of groups. Women embody, so to speak, the paradox of this dual experience. They also tend the boundaries of life itself, for they both give birth and care for the dead (see Danforth 1982).

By moving "beyond gender," we can begin to understand such representations, for concepts of gender are simply the framework upon which are hung important social values, as well as expressions and interpretations of life and society. It is through such oppositions as female/male, inside/outside private/public, intimacy/separation, self/other that people construct a language for talking about and reconciling the diverse experience of their lives, experiences that include life and death, sin and salvation, superiority and subordination, competition and communality. Thus, women represent aspects of life important to both sexes: the cunning (poniria) of the oppressed and the intimacy of self-knowledge (Herzfeld), the pain (*ponos*) of grief which seeks an outlet in laments (Caraveli), and the maintenance of boundaries necessary for social life (Dubisch).

Women play a dual role in such conceptual systems, for they serve not only as symbols but also as mediators between symbolic realms, connecting one to another and seeking to overcome the contradictions inherent in these oppositions. If we analyze concepts of gender only in relation to the social roles of male and female, we miss the significance of gender as a powerful organizer of life at the social, psychological, and symbolic levels. This is true not only for Greece, but, to some extent at least, for all societies, for although the content and pervasiveness of gender distinctions vary considerably from one society to another, there appears to be no society in which such distinctions are absent altogether.

Within these conceptual systems, however, women seem to bear a heavy symbolic load. When we discuss gender constructs, we inevitably seem to focus on women as the bearers of meaning (although see Brandes 1980). Perhaps women are a kind of "natural symbol" because they always are regarded, to some extent, as objects, not only within the framework of scholarly scrutiny but also within their own societies. And what men symbolize may be less carefully examined simply because it is taken for granted. If it is true that women as objects tend to "stand for" things, what, then, does it mean to the women themselves to labor under this "burden of symbolism," a burden that is more than symbolic, since it must affect women's perceptions of themselves as well as their activities in society? Does the dual role of social actor and symbol mean that women must always be divided against themselves?

THE ESSAYS in this volume move through a range of topics related to gender in rural Greece, from women's role and position in the domestic sphere (Friedl, Pavlides and Hesser, Salamone and Stanton) and the connections of this sphere to the larger world (Dimen) to women's role and image in the religious system (du Boulay) and their attempts as actors to create emotionally satisfying relationships and activities (Kennedy, Caraveli) to the symbolism of gender itself (Dubisch, Herzfeld). While these essays cannot supply definitive answers to all the questions I have raised, their different approaches to gender within one cultural setting provide a rich body of data and insights. In addition, they seek to convey something of the ethos of contemporary Greek life, particularly as it affects and is shaped by women. It is obvious from a number of the essays that this life is not always easy; that in rural communities everyone, male and female, must struggle to make a living; and that women, in addition, feel the burden of their oppression. And yet the essays also document the ways in which women transcend these limitations and the means by which they find satisfaction in their lives. They remind us of the complex structure of social conceptions of gender and the multifaceted nature of sexual subordination, as well as the complex ways these are experienced by both women and men. And underlying all of these essays we find a profound appreciation both of the people about whom they have been written and of the ways these people have responded to and articulated the conditions of their lives.

Notes to Chapter One

1. Examples of this view include Hart and Pilling (1960), Chagnon (1983), Evans-Pritchard (1940, 1951), and Barth (1965). For a contrasting approach when the perspective of women is included, see Goodale (1971), Gough (1971), and Weiner (1976).

2. For perspectives on human evolution that take women into account, see Gough (1975), Leibowitz (1975), McGrew (1981), Slocum (1975), Tanner (1981), and Zihlman (1981).

3. Although gender is a factor in access to information in fieldwork, men are not necessarily excluded from the world of women in societies such as Greece, nor are women totally excluded from the world of men. For a discussion of role factors affecting fieldwork in Greece, see Clark (1983).

4. In 1980, the Modern Greek Studies Association held a multidisciplinary symposium entitled "Men and Women in Greece: A Society in Transition." A number of the papers from this symposium were published in two issues of *The Journal of Modern Greek Studies* (1983 1[1] and 1[2]).

5. See, for example, Sahlins (1976). For a discussion of sociobiology as an "ethnosociology of American culture," see Gray and Wolfe (1982).

6. For an example of how different this world can be, see Kaberry (1970); cf. Hart and Pilling (1960). See also Gough's (1971) reanalysis of Evans-Pritchard's data on Nuer Kinship.

7. Ortner's article is more complex than I have been able to indicate in this brief summary, and she also emphasizes the woman's role as mediator between nature and culture. For disagreements with Ortner's conceptual scheme, see MacCormack and Strathern (1980) and also E. Ardener (1975). For critiques of its application to Greece, see my article in this volume and also Dubisch (1983).

8. See, for example, Tanner (1974) on the matrifocal household.

9. Regarding American cultural definitions of public and private, see Schneider (1968) and Gray and Wolfe (1982).

10. It should be made clear that when we speak of *private* in this context, we are not necessarily referring to "privacy" in the western sense but to a certain way of dividing social life. (For a discussion of privacy versus private in Greek culture, see Sciama [1981].) It should also be noted that while here I have used the terms "domestic" and "private" almost interchangeably, I do not mean to suggest that they are always synonymous.

11. The Greek word for *depression* (*stenahoria*) means "a narrow place." It is a condition more often complained of by women than by men and suggests the greater restriction of women and the symbolism of closed versus open (see Hirschon 1978; Danforth 1979a, 1983; Herzfeld, this volume).

12. Villagers told me that the kafenio used to be completely forbidden to women, and that any celebrations involving both sexes were always held in the home. Nowadays, I was told, it was perfectly acceptable for women to "hang out" in the kafenio, and I was encouraged to join my husband when

he did so, but in fact no village woman would join her husband on such everyday occasions. Usually, women would go to the kafenio only for special events but always in the company of their husbands or male relatives. (One woman in the village adopted my husband and me as her "chaperones" to allow her to make such excursions more frequently.) Many women never set foot in the kafenio even on business; instead, they send a child in to fetch their husbands or deliver messages, or even to make small purchases. It might be added that as a woman's "passport" into the public arena, a husband is criticized if he does not take his wife out occasionally (and a woman is criticized if she insists always on staying at home).

13. We might add here an even more fundamental question posed to me by Michael Herzfeld: Is the very idea of such universals an androcentric invention?

14. See Fallers and Fallers (1976:251-252) for an example from Turkey.

15. Danforth disagrees with Friedl on this issue of "latent power" (see Danforth 1979b). See also Kennedy's article in this volume.

16. In discussing the "powers of the weak," Janeway (1981) examines the ways in which the powerless, or at least the illegitimate, can have an impact. One of the problems in analyzing such a phenomenon is the often unstructured nature of the power exercised.

17. On the evil eye in Greece, see Dionisopoulos-Mass (1976) and Herzfeld (1981c).

18. The question of context is one which needs more careful examination. As Clark (1983) points out, context can have a temporal dimension; gender roles, for example, need to be considered in the context of the life cycle. Danforth (1983) discusses the ways that the Greek village house can, on occasion, be a public place.

19. See Jordanova (1980:65-66) for a discussion of this issue.

20. We should not lose sight of the fact that men's power is also limited, even in the public world. They themselves may be powerless in relation to the apparatus of the larger state society (see Dimen, du Boulay, and Herzfeld, this volume).

21. For a general discussion of property (including dowry) and woman's status, see the essays in Hirschon (1984). Hirschon suggests that the analytical concept of property can serve as a link between the domestic and public realms (p. 5).

22. For a discussion of bias and its implications for cross-cultural analysis, see Beidelman (1980). On bias with respect to the relationships between people and property, see Whitehead (1984).

23. Although I have chosen to gloss it as "foreigner," the term *ksenos* (masc. sing.) could be translated in a variety of ways, depending on context: "foreigner," "stranger," "outsider," and even, when used as an adjective, "someone else's." I have used the word *foreign* in the text to attempt to convey some of the flavor of the term as used in this particular context, although "outsider" might have been equally appropriate.

The village was large enough (larger in the past, before extensive emigration) for many marriages to have taken place within it. However, when inter-village marriages took place, virilocal residence was usually the rule, with the bride moving to her husband's village unless he came from a particularly poor family or village (on the in-marrying son-in-law, or *sogambros*, see Friedl 1962). Neolocal residence was the norm within the village, but in-marrying spouses might move in with in-laws, thus exacerbating the pressures on "foreign" brides.

24. It should be pointed out that not all ksenes were thought to be of questionable character. Some had integrated themselves into village life, and their status as outsiders was seldom, if ever, mentioned. It is obvious that the designation of *kseni* (sing.) was simply useful for explaining, not predicting, behavior. In addition, by blaming quarrels on "outsiders," villagers denied the existence of tensions and conflicts inherent in village life (cf. Friedl 1962:60; Giovannini 1981:18).

25. For a good discussion of this problem, see Clark (1983).

26. For a discussion of reflexivity in fieldwork, see Karp and Kendall (1982).

27. Tourism often provides new opportunities for women in rural areas and provincial towns, because it allows women to earn money through the kind of work that is compatible with home and child care, such as tending a store, renting rooms, or making objects in the home that can be sold in shops.

28. Often, such crafts are based on real or imagined ancient Greek culture—for example, "Greek" sandals not normally worn by present-day Greeks or cotton dresses with "Greek" designs. In addition, articles characteristic of one segment of the population, such as the woven bags carried by shepherds, are made into tourist items. These items frequently are purchased by Greeks themselves, so that they will be seen wearing "Greek" sandals and carrying "Greek" bags. Thus, outer image becomes the inner self.

29. On sex discrimination in the marketplace in Greece, see Psacharopoulos (1983).

30. Among the factors determining the nature of the information that can be elicited are the characteristics of the fieldworker. Age, sex, family situation, and chance features all affect how the fieldworker will be received and what information she or he will be able to collect. For discussions of this issue in Greece, see Clark (1983) and Friedl (1970).

31. One's position in this respect is not necessarily fixed but often changes over the course of fieldwork and with particular situations (see Herzfeld, this volume). We saw a shift in our own position when certain families began to receive us in the kitchen (the private domestic room) rather than in the saloni (the room for more public, formal display of the family).

TWO

The Position of Women:

Appearance and Reality

ERNESTINE FRIEDL

THE PURPOSE of this paper is to describe the ways in which the appearances of prestige can obscure the realities of power. More specifically, the substance of this discussion is an analysis of the position of
women in the social structure of a Greek village community. As the first
sentence indicates, I believe the elements of Greek culture and society
that lead most observers to consider it strongly male-centered do, indeed, exist but that they may mislead the observer into a polarized view
of the relative power of men and women in Greek society. The problem
is not unique to Greece. It is possible to argue that male activities have
more prestige than those of females in all societies, and if this is true,
the discovery of the relative social power of men and women may require more careful investigation in each case than is usually given to the
question.

One of the factors of this investigation which, so far as I know, has
been generally neglected, is the distinction between the public and the
private sector as far as the actual importance of each in the power-
structure of the community is concerned. From the standpoint of the
ceremonial mores of the community, there may be many cultures in
which male activity is accorded pre-eminence in the public sector. But
if a careful analysis of the life of the community shows that, pragmati-
cally the family is the most significant social unit, then the private, and
not the public sector, is the sphere in which the relative attribution of
power to males and females is of the greatest real importance. If, as I
hope to show, the women in a Greek village hold a position of real
power in the life of the family, and, as I have shown earlier, the life of
the family is the most significant structural and cultural element of the

This paper was read at the December 1966 conference held in Athens, Greece, by the Social Sciences Centre of Athens under the direction of Professor John Peristiany. The paper
originally appeared in *Anthropological Quarterly*, vol. 40, no. 3, July 1967, pp. 97-108,
and is reprinted here with permission of the publisher.

Greek village,[1] then there is unmistakable need for a reassessment of the role of the Greek woman in village life.

For the Greek village of Vasilika, I shall begin with those appearances which express high male prestige. Most conspicuous in this regard is the segregation of men and women in the public space of the village, and the ritual deference accorded men by women in public situations. Stress on the distinction between public and private contexts is essential for the understanding of much of Greek social life; it is a binary classification especially important for analyzing the roles of men and women.

The most conspicuous public space in the village of Vasilika is the agora; that portion of the main road where the two stores and coffee houses face each other. The area is a thoroughfare for the various kinds of traffic moving through the village as well as a convenient stopping place for visitors and vendors. In its function as a thoroughfare, it is not closed to women; they walk through it on their way to and from the fields, or on their way to church, or to the main bus stop located on the asphalt road about a quarter of a mile away. Women may even wait briefly at the agora to board the bus that stops there to pick up passengers twice a day. But no female over the age of 14, in the ordinary course of events, goes to the agora as a final destination. They do not sit in the coffeehouses; they do not even go to the store connected with the coffeehouses to make purchases. Nor will they buy from itinerant vendors when these vendors are in the agora. On ordinary days, then, the agora, as a public place, is a male place. Little girls and young boys may run errands to the stores and may be sent to fetch their fathers, but with other evidence this fact indicates the immunity of children from many types of sex role expectations.

There are a few exceptional occasions when the women do go to the agora and its establishments. The most traditional of these are the festival days at Christmas, Easter, and the village patron saint's day when the coffeehouses' owners provide musicians and dance space and sell beer to their customers. Accompanied by their male relatives, women sit at tables listening to the music, sipping beer very slowly, and watching the dancing. Sometimes the men will underwrite a dance for them and the girls and women dance alone or along with some of the men.

In the last year or two a movie truck has come to the village on some Sundays and movies are shown in one of the coffeehouse. I do not know what the pattern of attendance at the movie is; the one time I went the audience consisted largely of children, but a few older men and women were there as well. Movies apparently are being assimilated into the special occasion festival pattern rather than into the patterns of daily routine.

The village churches are, of course, also public places. Inside the church, the condition of femaleness results in social segregation on certain occasions throughout a woman's lifetime. No female may go behind the altar screen, female infants, in contrast to males, are not carried there as part of the baptismal ceremonies, and women and girls stand in the rear of the church throughout the services, while men and boys stand in the front. Like the situation in the agora, however, there are certain occasions when the spatial separation of men and women in the main part of the church is not maintained; at baptisms when all gather round the baptismal font and at weddings when the guests crowd in a semi-circle around the bride and groom.

Still another public place in Vasilika is the school and here there is no spatial segregation. Boys and girls sit together according to grade level and not according to sex, but of course these are children.

That the pattern of public adult male and female segregation I have just described constitutes an expression of higher male prestige is obvious.

Differential right of access to space is a common cultural form for expressing superiority and inferiority in social position. The daily prohibitions on adult women may be presumed through sheer frequency of occurrence to have a greater impact than the exceptions for children at all times and for women on special occasions.

Public situations in Vasilika are not limited to activities in public space. On certain occasions, the homes of the villagers take on the aspect of public places in a festival setting. The most conspicuous of these is the celebration of the Saint's Day of the head of the household, when the family is "at home" to visitors. As Gearing has indicated, all villagers are entitled to come, even enemies.

On Saint's Days more men than women actually visit the celebrants. Inside the house male guests are seated nearest the fire, if it is winter, and they are traditionally offered refreshments before the female guests even though these arrived at the same time or slightly earlier. If there are not enough chairs to go around, the women of the household, not the men, remain standing. Although daughters or wives serve the guests, it is perfectly clear that the celebrating father is the host. He prompts his women when he thinks they are too slow at serving, he and not his wife slices the bread and distributes it to the guests; he, and not his wife picks out the choice morsels for direct presentation on a fork to a male guest; and he is the one who urges his guests to eat. A man is a host on these occasions but his womenfolk are not hostesses. They serve his and his household's honor by their good cooking and by the proper presentation of enough food, but they do not create honor by being in charge of the festivities.

In this connection, I remember my surprise at a lecture on table manners given at the King's Institute to village policemen and village secretaries when the men not only showed considerable interest in the subject, but also asked many detailed questions about what the correct sequence was in serving food and drink to visitors. In the villages, they consider the solution of these questions a part of their responsibility, and a proof of their culture, and not something to be learned from the womenfolk in the family.

What is of interest to my thesis also is the discovery that festivals and therefore extraordinary public occasions are accompanied by a change in the permitted movements and activities of women. And, indeed, I should like to suggest that this change may be their most distinctive feature. Men listen to radio music and even occasionally dance in the coffeehouse: they do regularly sit around sipping coffee or soft drinks and occasionally ouzo, wine and beer. They can pay calls on each other at home during negotiations of contracts and receive some sweet and drink as a part of the hospitality of the house. On Saint's Days and holidays the food and drink are more abundant and of higher quality and the entertainment more intense and concentrated. But for men, what is most extraordinary about festivals is that women who are not relatives are around in large numbers as audience and participants. The song "Ime andras" exemplifies the spirit of this unusual circumstance. The lyrics imply that a man is defying the female audience which he sees as trying to curb his exuberance and enjoyment of the events.

A reversal of roles, particularly among role sets in which one is recognized as superior and the other inferior, as a concomitant of celebrations is common enough in human societies. The Greek village pattern I have described does not constitute a reversal of roles for both men and women, but it does involve a change of role for women, and for the period of the holiday, entitles them to privileges similar to if not entirely equal to those of men.

In Vasilika, there are two occasions on which there is an actual reversal of roles; the celebration of the carnival, and the skits performed for the national holiday on the 25th of March.

At carnival, some unmarried men and women become transvestites; they wear the clothes of the opposite sex and march around exaggerating the gestures and mien of the sex they are imitating. One of the playlets put on for the 25th of March by the unmarried young men of the village involved a boy who played the part of a woman. He wore women's clothes and much of the amusement of the audience derived from his deliberate awkwardness in the role. The license afforded by this situation did not extend to girls playing men's parts.

Too much need not be made of this transvestism. My point is that the decrease in the physical and symbolic separateness of women from men permitted on holidays underlines the significance of such separateness in the course of routine existence in the village.

To return to our main theme, the deference accorded men in public situations is paralleled by public comments about the relative merits of men and women. The birth of a son is reason for rejoicing and happy congratulations to the father in the coffeehouse, that of a daughter, reason for some teasing and behind the scenes amusement on the part of the villagers. Both men and women warn their sons about the dangers of associating with loose women who can ruin a man's life; in cases of marital discord, if there is any possible way of blaming the women, the villagers do so. They tell tales about how the wife runs around with other men, neglects her children and her household. They say these things often on the flimsiest evidence or on none at all. Clearly in her role as potential sex partner, a woman is assumed to be a danger to men. The laments about the economic burdens of raising daughters add to the chorus of verbal expressions of irritation with women.

Let us shift from symbolism and attitudinal expressions of higher male prestige to the differences in the activities available to each sex and to the prestige evaluation of these activities. The only prestige-bearing public professional activities available to women in the village are school-teaching and other civil service posts. Vasilika has no resident female school teacher, but one of the village girls is now a civil servant in Athens. At the lower end of the scale of public professions, girls who accompany the musicians and sing with them at village festivals are classed as somewhat shameless. In between are girls who sew for others, or who work as agricultural extension agents, and the like.

There are two significant types of public official statuses in the village from which women are barred. One is the higher religious offices and the other the village political posts. Women may not be priests or cantors, nor do they get elected to the village council. The latter is based on custom rather than law, but even though the women have the vote, there is no indication that any one of them will be elected to office in the near future. With respect to religious offices, women may perform service functions as sextons, but they do not get elected to the council of laymen who help the priest to run the affairs of the church. Nor are there any women doctors around Vasilika.

In sum, with the putative exception of school-teaching, the public female roles with which the villagers have experience do not include persons with public power. Higher echelon provincial or national government officials who visit the village are always men, religious officials are men, and their own village officers are men. For the moment our interest is in the fact that regardless of the reason, there are more prestigious public roles open to men than to women and by a wide margin.

When we turn to analyzing differences in prestige with respect to the standard division of labor within the household's economy, the matter is considerably more difficult. Certainly, there are household tasks carried out by men and others usually handled by women, and still others taken care indifferently by either or both. A listing is not complicated.

For the most part men do work outside the house itself, in the fields and barns and storehouses. The field jobs include pruning grape vines, deep hoeing the vineyards, plowing with horses or tractors, cultivating grain fields, planting wheat and cotton, running irrigation pumps and clearing irrigation ditches. Young men also collect the brush used for firing ovens. Within the house compound, men store cotton, press and store tobacco bales, and make and store the household's supply of wine. They take care of any horses or donkeys owned by the household, and generally look after carts and any farm machinery belonging to them. Men do not work inside the house at cooking, baking, cleaning, washing clothes, sweeping, or the like. They do, however, regularly purchase household supplies like rice, pasta, olive oil, kerosene, canned goods, and other staples, as well as meat and fresh vegetables brought by vendors. In the States when men started pushing supermarket carts and collecting groceries from a list, the fact was cited as evidence for the proposition that men were taking on more women's household tasks. In Vasilika, the purchase of supplies for cash requires leaving the home and negotiating with outsiders in a public context—activities the villagers consider improper for women.

The activities I have listed so far are carried out almost exclusively by men; but there are some in which they assist women in tasks more typically done by women. In the fields, men help the women hoe cotton, they help pick the cotton and they can join the women in transplanting and picking tobacco. Men even pick wild greens for food and collect wild plant fodder for the sheep and goats if the need arises. When a mother is ill and there are no daughters in the household, a husband and sons may even take on the cooking and washing.

Women's tasks inside the house have been mentioned. To these, caring for infants and children, sewing, mending, weaving, embroidering and similar trousseau preparations, and caring for the household religious shrine can be added. Women also supply the church with the necessary sacred breads and memorial wheat when it is the household's turn to do so. Within the house compound, women feed and care for the chickens and look after new lambs and kids. They tend to care for small vegetable gardens now planted near the house because water is piped into the house yards, and they also have responsibility for the household's decorative plants and flowers. Women also are expected to keep the house compound tidy.

The jobs connected with the agricultural cycle that can be done near the houses rather than out in the fields also tend to be female tasks. Women plant tobacco seedlings, string the tobacco, and put the poles on drying racks. They also pick cotton from the pod when, in wet weather, they have been unable to make the separation at the original picking. Their field tasks have already been mentioned as those with which, when necessary, men will assist.

The sexual division of labor in Vasilika is part of the private realm of life. It concerns the economic welfare of the household, of the family consisting of a husband and wife and their unmarried or resident married children and an occasional elderly parent or in-law. A kind of continuum of tasks may be observed under three headings. (1) Those inside the house, linked with women, (2) those in the house compound, linked with both men and women, and (3) those in the fields, linked preponderantly with men. The division of these familial tasks is complementary; there appears to be no noticeable conception among the villagers that either the men's or the women's jobs have the greater prestige. If anything, they share a common attribution of distaste.

Unlike the situation among the shepherds of Epirus, Vasilika's men are not called upon to exhibit heroic feats of endurance, strength, and skill simply to be able to maintain themselves and their families. Men's and women's tasks require similar expenditures both of energy and skill; kneading dough for ten large loaves of bread and washing clothes thoroughly clean in a wooden trough are comparable in their calls upon skill and strength with ploughing or cultivating. If there is any deficit in energy expenditure in any single woman's task, it is made up for by the longer duration of her jobs and their repetitive quality. In Vasilika, both men and women dislike physical labor and especially that which is dirty and messy. From the latter standpoint, the men have an edge on unpleasantness, because nothing women do covers them with mud the way channeling irrigation water does men. It appears to be no more disgraceful or ignominious for a man to take over a woman's job like cooking and washing up if an emergency requires it, than it is for a woman to take over the man's job of deep hoeing if there is no other way of getting it done.

These are the shared physical tasks imposed by the household economy. Its public managerial roles, however, are assumed by men when the household must be represented to the outside world. The men do the job. They talk to government officials, merchants, the school teacher, and any strangers who may come to the village. The husband in a household in which his wife takes over these public functions is ridiculed and despised by all. Of these public functions the most significant in relation to women is the set of marriage negotiations undertaken by a father in his daughter's behalf. In the discussions preliminary to the agreement in a dowry contract, the men of the bride's household speak to the go-between and represent her interests. The groom may represent himself or may have his father with him. In any case, it is the men who formally and overtly oversee the establishment of the marriage connections between households.

To summarize, the evidence that male prestige is higher than that of females in Vasilika lies in the nature of routine segregation in contrast with what is permitted at celebrations, in the esteem accorded public and extra-household occupational and political roles held by men, and in the man's representation of the household to the outside when he functions as host, entrepreneur, and marriage negotiator.

So much for appearances, that is for prestige and esteem. Let us now turn to the realities of power which may be discovered as operating behind the external patterns we have discussed. We shall begin with the social power of women within the economic structure of the households. In Vasilika, land still constitutes the most significant investment. It produces income by virtue of the subsistence and cash crops that can be raised on it. The economic power of women lies in their ability to bring land into the household as part of their dowry, and to maintain control of that land, which cannot be alienated by their husbands without their consent or, in some cases, without the consent of their fathers, brothers, or guardians. The trousseau and the household goods a woman brings with her add to the prestige of the new household but only indirectly to its ability to produce income. In the traditional structure of the village, a man is expected to find a wife who would bring in the equivalent of the land he would inherit upon the division of the patrimony of his own family. Therefore, although his wife had no more control over the household property than he did, she had at least as much. That the husband's symbolic prestige as a male did not entirely override the wife's position as a substantial contributor to the new household is proved negatively by the position of the *soghambros*, the in-marrying son-in-law. Man or no man, his prestige and the esteem accorded him is seriously impaired by the fact that it is his wife who provides the land from which he derives his and his children's livelihood. It is assumed that he makes fewer decisions in his household than a man is expected to make. No in-marrying son-in-law of the village has been elected to the village council or to the church council, although at least two of them are strong personalities interested in politics. This is an index of lack of public prestige. Within the household, since the processes of decision making are not easily observed, and because I conducted no systematic investigation of the question in the soghambros households, my evidence for the superior decision-making power of the women in this situation rests on impressions, and the clear evidence that the children of the soghambros households established connections with their mother's relatives outside the village and not with those of their fathers. Moreover, my recent studies in Athens indicate that the choice of career of the sons of one of the soghambros families was determined by the advice of the mother's sister; a particular kind of kin affiliation that is rarely influential in this regard in the village as a whole.

Within the ordinary land owning household, the power of the women over their dowry properties is reflected, I believe, in the degree of give and take in the private discussions leading to entrepreneurial decisions as to how to utilize the property. In the households, where I could observe the process, women participated vigorously in decisions concerning what and how much to plant, how many laborers to bring in, whether to sell crops or to hold them for higher prices, what credit to accept and what sums to pay back, and the like. All this is hidden behind the façade of public male dominance.

The same control over property gave the concern of women over the future of their daughters a base in something more than affection and sentiment. The dowry of the girls consisted partly of property their mothers had contributed, and their mothers felt quite free to engage in the discussions about a future son-in-law. This was partly in terms of his potential as a conserver of the mother's original property. Mothers of sons were eager to have daughters-in-law who would not squander their grandchildren's patrimony.

The suggestion that the power of women over household economic decisions and over the marriages of their children is dependent on property control should be tested by research in the contemporary village situation. If Vasilika is typical, the urban marriages of rural girls with substantial dowries have left for the rural men only girls with poor dowries. A village farmer, we're told, can no longer expect to marry a girl who will bring in land equivalent to the value of his, but may have to take girls with smaller properties because they are the only ones left who will consent to live in the rural villages and to do farm work. For a poor rural girl, marrying a man who brings to the marriage more land than she herself can contribute as a dowry is a form of hypergamy from her point of view just as is the marriage of a farm girl to an urban husband. The current gossip in the village suggests that there is less respect for the poorer new brides and an examination of decision making within their households would be instructive.

My hypothesis can also be tested in urban centers where the substantial dowries of the village girls who marry low salaried husbands would be expected to give them an excess of power in their households. I do not believe they do. The reason may be that the husband's educational qualifications and his urban sophistication (both greater than those of his rural wife) added to what is after all a steady low income combine to become the equivalent of his wife's seemingly disproportionately large dowry. For the urban family, a job and the knowledge of how to get along in the city is just as important for the continued welfare of the family as the husband's contribution of land is in the farming communities. Education and access to employment are not quite as easily and directly transmitted to a new generation as land is. Neither is an urban woman's property consisting of a house and its furnishings. If the erstwhile farm girl is to continue to influence the marriages of her children, her influence may have to rest on a power base other than that of property. A study of these matters is among my present interests.

To return to the farm households to which husbands and wives have contributed about equally. It must be clearly understood that formal authority even about household and farm management rests with the husband and father. It is in the informal organization of the household that the very real power of the women is felt.

But to say that women have informal power over household economic decisions and over the economic and marital future of their sons and daughters is not a trivial statement. To repeat what I said at the outset, the family is the significant unit of social and economic structure in the Greek village community, and therefore power within that unit must have important consequences for power distribution in Greek society as a whole.

There is another sense, a negative sense, in which women have power in Vasilika. This does not operate in affecting decisions or actions affirmatively. It is a check upon the power of men through women's ability to disrupt orderly relationships in the men's world. Insofar as men's honor depends on the behavior of their womenfolk, these women exercise a real measure of control over them. It is the women's willingness to behave chastely, modestly, and becomingly that is a prime necessity for the maintenance of men's self-esteem.

But it is not only by the implied threat of misbehavior that a wife or daughter influences her husband or father. This indeed is probably always latent rather than expressed. What is expressed by the women to the men in the privacy of the household is a constant reminder of the lengths to which the women go in the toil and the trouble which they take in the performance of those household tasks which enable the men of the family to preserve their public honor. The effect of these complaints, which are culturally sanctioned, is to keep the men aware of their dependence on their womenfolk, of how they must in their turn and in their own way uphold the honor of the family by reciprocating all the women do for them. For the weaker partner in a social structure, the ability to create and maintain such a sense of obligation in the stronger is a real exercise of power, and one in which Greek village women are past masters.

NOTE TO CHAPTER TWO

1. Friedl (1962:chaps. 2-4).

THREE | Servants and Sentries:
Women, Power, and Social
Reproduction in Kriovrisi

MURIEL DIMEN

RECENT feminist theory about women in the state contrasts their confinement in a domestic role with their exclusion from the public domain of economy and politics (Rosaldo 1974).[1] This theoretical work also examines the functions that the household performs for the public world of work and power (Kuhn and Wolpe 1978). It can be inferred from this thinking that the role of women in the household, though privatized, may also bear on public life in the form of articulating the private and public spheres. To the extent that this is true, the role of women may become internally contradictory, and women may become ambivalent about themselves.

This paper explores, through the concepts of private/public, hegemony, and social reproduction, how women in Kriovrisi, a small mountain village in Epiros, both resist and capitulate to certain forces from the public domain that threaten to fragment both the village and the households in it. These forces are the centrifugal power of the economy and the centralizing power of the state which create alienation and anomie. As a consequence of trying to mitigate the effects of these forces on others, women themselves develop ambivalent feelings about their work, experience, and selfhood.

In Kriovrisi, nuclear and extended family households are the basic units of residence, social relations, and personal loyalty. It is on behalf of the household that men produce goods and services for sale and sell their labor for wages. Through the work of women, the household also performs the task of "social reproduction" (see Rapp, Ross, and Bridenthal 1979); that is, women in the domestic domain enable men to do their work and the young to grow up to be men and women who as adults will do what their parents did. Women make it possible for the young to mature and the mature to be regenerated daily, for social relations to be learned and re-created, and for spirits to be shaped and renewed.

However, women's task of social reproduction is "contradictory," because its tendencies are necessarily in opposition to each other: the household binds up the psychological and social wounds that people suffer when economic interests divide them from each other and state power (hegemony) draws people's loyalties to itself. But the household binds these wounds so that people may return to the very place from which they received them—the public world of work and power. In other words, the domestic domain and its women must make people strong enough to endure in a public world that will chip away at them so that they must return home again for nurturance. On the one hand, the domestic sphere generates a preserving stability for individual psyches and interpersonal relations in the face of economic and political changes. Yet, on the other hand, even as the household is a safe harbor, it must send people out to the politico-economic sea where changes in fortune and power reduce their self-esteem and increase their sense of isolation. Although I do not intend to portray the household as an entirely peaceful harbor, a discussion of its inner storms is beyond the scope of this paper (see Zaretsky 1976 for an analysis of family life under capitalism).

Rather, I intend to focus on how women become internally rent because it is their job to ensure that the household's contradictory task is performed. In word and deed, in social position and demeanor, and in their socially constructed psychic life, women in these households must re-create the social structure (and its contradictions) by simultaneously symbolizing, communicating, and actually reliving it.

Women accomplish this re-creative task in such a way that the young and the old whom they nurture become sufficiently integrated to keep on marching, yet not so integrated that their doubts about whether the trip is worth it lead them to resist domination. Still, women preserve the germ of social change, if only because they remain both proud of and discontented with their lives, if only because their priceless/thankless task splits their role internally and makes them ambivalent about themselves.

The following discussion is only suggestive in its illustration of this argument. It is not definitive because the data on which it is based were collected with other hypotheses in mind (see Schein [Dimen] 1970, 1974, 1975). Therefore, the ideas presented here have the status of hypotheses, which others may apply and test elsewhere.

ETHNOGRAPHIC AND HISTORICAL SUMMARY

Kriovrisi, lying 1,450 miles above sea level in the Pindus Mountains, is located in the geographical province of Epiros and the prefecture of

Ioannina. Although its people are slowly emigrating, it contains some young growing families in its summer population of 400. The village is accessible by motor vehicle from June to October only. That it has a dirt road and telephone at all is due to its former military importance, lying only a few kilometers overland from the once-closed Albanian border. Its summertime, Orthodox inhabitants speak both Greek and a dialect of Roumanian. The members of about half of the 100 house-holds are transhumant shepherds, who winter in Epiros, Macedonia, and Thessaly. They leave behind, from 1 November to 1 June, about 120 people whose incomes are derived from small-scale farming, wage labor, and pensions. Many men are often absent from the village in the summer as they seek weekly, monthly, even yearly wages from coastal towns in Epiros, lowland towns in Macedonia, and factory towns in West Germany.

Village Structure

Kriovrisi's political and economic structure demonstrates a funda-mental contradiction. On the one hand, its administrative structure is corporate; on the other, the village shows a degree of political fragmen-tation and economic heterogeneity unusual in a small, rural Greek community. Although the reasons for this contradiction are explained fully elsewhere (Dimen 1981), I will summarize them here.

The village owns and administers all the land on behalf of its resi-dents. The village council controls the use and taxation of the land. Only official residents, that is, those who are born in or marry into Kriovrisi, as well as their employees, may use the land; nonresident em-ployees pay double the stock head tax paid by official residents. Arable land and house plots are held in usufruct and inherited in family lines, but they may not be sold. Arable land that lies fallow for over five years reverts to common pasture. Forest and pasture take up most of the vil-lage's territory, and the council repartitions pasture annually to stock owners. Residents may collect firewood from designated parts of the forest.

Within this corporate structure exist tenuous political and social re-lations. The village council initiates no independent action; the only so-lidary community activity results from those practices required of the people by a higher level of organization, first, the eparchy and, ulti-mately, the Greek state itself. Kriovrisi lacks religious, as well as secu-lar, village-wide structures. The population congregates as a whole only for the 15 August celebration of the Assumption, but it is too brief a period to do more than remind people of their shared community membership. One might expect Easter to foster solidarity, but trans-humance has removed over half the population until summer.

It would be reasonable to speculate that the community's inactivity in 1967 to 1968, when this research was done, resulted from fear of the recent military *coup d'état*; the junta of 21 April would have created mutual suspicion in the most solidary of villages. However, other ob-servers reported lighter spirits and a more substantial public life in nearby villages at that time (Sivignon, personal communication 1968). Furthermore, on a return visit to Kriovrisi in summer 1981, I found that the anomie continues.

Economic Fragmentation

Diverse rules and values regarding the connection of people to each other and to natural resources and technology create a divisive hetero-geneity that is extraordinary for such a small village.[2] The major means of production—capital in general (for example, construction materials and agricultural implements) and money in particular—lie both physi-cally and organizationally outside Kriovrisi. The nexus of exchange is not in the village but in the economy at large. These facts, together with the twentieth-century economic decline of the always marginal Pindus region, make it difficult for the villagers to survive, and patterns of scrambling scatter lives and loyalties.

Kriovrisi's economic heterogeneity is represented by half a dozen dif-ferent occupations (and combinations of them); two or three different seasonal "patterns of assemblage and dispersal" (Arensberg 1961); and a division into two endogamous, class-like groups. (This economic diversity is amplified by the existence of three sub-dialects.) The con-temporary differences in wealth and power, and the mutual antago-nisms between the two "classes," are not rooted locally but derive from urban financial and governmental power structures (see Dimen 1981, Schein [Dimen] 1974). Differently patterned organizations of produc-tion militate against the commonality in behavior, experience, and in-terests that shared space and time might generate.

Political Fragmentation

State power amplifies the centrifugal effects of occupational hetero-geneity.[3] The state holds the economic and political keys to household survival, reinforces differential access to resources among village classes, and exacts individuals' compliance by ordering the details of their everyday lives. The state facilitates exchange by organizing labor

and capital markets. Governmental programs of structural and ideological incorporation into the polity (Diamandouros 1985:34, 38),
part of twentieth-century Greek nationalization, force individuals to
interact personally with the state. The state views individual males as
the major political units and the nuclear family as the unit of reckoning:
the village secretary-treasurer records births and deaths and registers
men for conscription; the public school socializes children from ages
six to twelve; and the national government issues pensions and food al-
lotments to heads of nuclear families.

THE WOMEN AT HOME

Slowly, quietly spinning amidst this economic and political fragmentation, however, is the stabilizing domestic center. All year round, the
daily domestic routine creates a village-wide commonality among the
women and, through them, the men, because the women have similar,
if internally contradictory, productive and reproductive roles. Domestic work is essentially uniform in its material and labor requirements
and in its spatiotemporal patterns; it thus cuts across economic and political differentiation. Its repetitiveness creates a centripetal pull against
the centrifugal one of the public sphere.

Yet, like the latter, the domestic sphere is filled with contradictions.
As the agents of the domestic domain, women are on the threshold of
public and private. Their position in relation to the public world is contradictory, their role in the public world internally split, and their attitudes about themselves ambivalent. Although they are overtly resentful
of their restriction to the domestic sphere, and of their limited access to
the power and self-esteem available from the economic and political
worlds, they are nevertheless proud of their ability to keep households
orderly and to do so alone. They take pleasure in doing their hard work
without complaining; they even seem to make it more difficult sometimes. They also take pride in and derive self-esteem from the achievements of their relatives—fathers, sons, husbands, brothers, and mothers-in-law—even though they dislike being under the others' collective
thumb (see Schein [Dimen] 1972 for a fuller discussion of women's resentment and pride).

The three concepts used here to make sense of women's ambivalence
about themselves and their contradictory roles come from feminist-anthropological and marxist theory about women, the household, and
problems of superstructure.

A distinction has been drawn in feminist-anthropological theory between two spheres or domains of culture, referred to variously as "domestic" and "public," "private" and "public," or "personal" and "political" (Ortner 1974; Rosaldo 1974). It is likely that the two domains exist universally but in different proportions in each culture; however, the division between them is most sharply drawn and experienced in the state (Rosaldo 1974; but see criticism and revisions in Ortner and Whitehead 1981). The domestic/private/personal domain is located concretely in the household and organizes the particularistic tasks of procreation and socialization. Women and children are always assigned to this domain. The other side of the dichotomy is the public/political domain. This sphere links separate domestic units and is the arena for institutions of social control, political action, and universalistic interests. Men, though attached to specific domestic units, always have some public role, and this grip on the public domain makes them socially dominant. In some societies, women also have access to the public sphere; to the extent that they do, they also can acquire power.

The second, marxist concept is hegemony, which refers to the system of domination characteristic of all twentieth-century nation-states. *Hegemony* means that the state is sufficiently powerful to reach through our most intimate institutions into our souls, to "dominate" us through its organization of things, social relations, and consciousness (Gramsci 1971:261-262 and passim). This domination of people through public institutions may have so permeated home and psyche that private life has been almost eliminated (Aronowitz 1974; Ewen 1978). In the face of the power of the state, all that people can do, if they act as isolated individuals or households, is to dig in their heels and say no.

Hegemony is the means by which the state bridges private and public domains. Greek women, as mediators between private and public (Ortner 1974), both resist and capitulate to this enormous power. They are both servants, bearing an invasive public culture into the domestic domain, and sentries, trying to keep it out of private, personal life. Their job is to transmit a dominating culture of hierarchy to their children while teaching them to have self-respect, that is, to struggle against hierarchy. Their job is also to help adults, especially those who work for wages, to be parts of the public domain and yet to retain their integrity. They enable both children and adults to make their ways in a world they did not create. In other words, women cultivate the compliance on which the modern state depends, while the state maintains its monopoly on coercive force, using it as a threat against disobedience (Horkheimer 1972:47-128). In the course of this process, women create themselves.

Women's work is embodied in social reproduction, the third concept used here. As previously noted, *social reproduction* is the reproduction of social relations through the creation of the new generation and the daily biological and psychological renewal of the present one (Rapp, Ross, and Bridenthal 1979). It is carried out by diverse, often noncoercive institutions: the family/household, kinship, schools, the military, religious organizations, corporations, the media, the bureaucracy. The state can use all of these instruments to reach people's minds and hearts and to construct their elementary social relationships.

Among all institutions of social reproduction, especially in economies in which relatively few years of formal education are required, the domestic sphere, usually in the form of the household, is the most important. In Kriovrisi, as elsewhere, the household organizes biological reproduction because it serves as the cultural locus of kinship, marriage, procreation, childbearing, and early socialization. It also sees to the daily bodily maintenance of the labor force on which depend the livelihoods of both the household and the workers' employers (Mitchell 1971). Usually, men leave the house daily to labor, but they return there to eat, sleep, and share company. The nurturance and the intimacy organized and produced by domestic life, as we shall see, absorb the shocks of daily labor and public relationships and soothe psychic skins sandpapered by the state's constant shaping of individuality.

The domestic scene is therefore the locus of a process that reproduces the social relations and contradictions of state and economy (Kuhn 1978). This process of social re-creation takes place through the enactment of social relations (especially those of kinship and marriage), through the handling of material objects (like brooms, looms, and money), and through the symbolic commentary (in the form of speech and nonverbal communication accompanying other behavior) among those involved about what they are doing. As such, this re-creative process structures the relationship of people to each other, to material objects, and to values and ideas, and it informs the way people communicate to one another about the social structure itself. It is a process that shapes the young and reshapes the adult: the young are enculturated, learning about and influencing their social environment in turn, and these communications, which are absorbed by adults, elaborate what adults already know and what they absorb from all other instruments of social reproduction—the media, religion, and the workplace, for example. All together these transmissions re-create daily life in the minds of adults, in the reality of their social interactions, and in the relationship between the domestic and the politico-economic worlds.

The household communicates not only by demonstration and example, but also by the more subtle processes which Levenson (1978) says transpire in psychoanalytic sessions. He describes them as a sequence of interactions over time that constitute an unspoken discourse which both analyst and patient hear but cannot verbalize. I suggest that the parties to a household communicate in the same way, and, since women run the household, they are pivotal to the communication process. The relationships of parents to children, of sibling to sibling, of adults of both genders to each other, of youngsters to elders, and of kin to kin and to strangers communicate to the young and to adults a comprehensive picture of how people are supposed to behave in these relationships and the cultural meaning of these bonds. In communicating intangible meaning and values, domestic relations also re-create invisible social structure, as well as the tangible persons organized by that structure. This is because domestic relations, like all social relations, are simultaneously behavioral and symbolic: they are what they are, as well as what they represent. They re-create not only the structure as it is supposed to be, but also its hidden contradictions; thus, what child and adult absorb from the domestic process of social reproduction is both social compliance and social criticism.

This discussion has focused on the details of daily domestic life, details often regarded as trivia, but trivia that each day re-create, in matter and in social structure, and thus in every person and in all of social ideology, the materially and psychologically rooted relations of state and economy. I choose four specific details of the lives of Kriovrisi's women to illustrate this process: (1) their isolation, (2) the restricted scope of their work, (3) the severity of their work, and (4) the submergence of their social selves.

First, women work alone much of the time. Proudly accustomed to bearing the domestic burden by themselves, women do all but the heavier, occasional work, such as making structural repairs to the house or chopping wood in the forest. Although a second pair of hands, like those of a mother or a daughter-in-law, helps (see Schein [Dimen] 1972), one female can, with effort, do most of what is necessary, especially if her husband has a profession like construction worker or tailor. Only in the minority of households, those structured by the extended family and therefore sufficiently equipped with personnel to undertake farming or herding, which depend on women's occasional labor, do women frequently work together, sharing the domestic and other work as mothers-in-law, daughters-in-law, or sisters-in-law.

A housewife's major, ongoing task is to love and tend her co-resident kin, both children and adults. She performs this task daily, although, since formal education became compulsory in 1967, the school provides some of the care of children. Each day, the woman also fetches water, sweeps, cooks one main and two minor meals, and, depending on need, sews, weaves, spins, gardens, or collects brushwood for the bread oven. Every ten days to two weeks, she bakes bread. Once a month she may wash clothes and split wood in the courtyard. Every couple of months, she washes and beats the rugs at a village tap. Occasionally, either alone or, more often, with a sister, mother, or mother-in-law, she travels to Konitsa to purchase staples in bulk.

Women in separate households help each other out, but they share technology more than labor. Most sharing takes place within each of the four informal neighborhoods into which the village is divided. During both work and leisure periods, the women in a household have most contact with the women in the four or five households immediately surrounding it. Wealth and occupation are not barriers to this contact (except, of course, during the winter, when transhumant women are absent). The women borrow utensils, share ovens and wash houses, exchange food, sell wool, and transmit gossip. Each day around sunset, women from all households gather at one particular spring to fill cooling earthenware jugs with water for the evening's drinking; this assembly provides the opportunity to learn village-wide gossip. Occasionally, women go to the village's center or to other neighborhoods to buy something or to make a request of the secretary-treasurer.

By working alone, and by feeling both proud of doing so and lonely while doing it, women symbolize, as social figures, communicate, as social participants, and re-create, as social actors, the social and economic isolation of the household itself. The effect is the creation of images of people as both autonomous and isolated. For example, women go alone to the forest to gather brushwood for bread ovens. This work makes them feel lonely. They look forward to their old age when they will be permitted to socialize, to share gossip in the afternoon with friends while daughters or daughters-in-law interrupt their lone labors only to serve them coffee. My seventy-two-year-old widowed informant said of her life in her isolated winter home that it would be like living in "the jungle" were it not for her battery-operated radio.

Perhaps women could gather brush together, perhaps not. Whatever the material reason for their solitude in their work, it takes on a meaning in its social context: the lone woman returning from the forest with her back bent under a load of brushwood mirrors and communicates the self-protective isolation of the household in the public sphere, for each household depends, ultimately, on its own labors for its own livelihood, even though each may hire or exchange labor occasionally. The woman's isolation communicates the necessity of autonomy to herself, to her children, and to her kin; it thus creates people who are oriented toward independence, straining toward self-employment. But, by the same token, it also creates people who are potentially isolated from each other.

This sort of isolated individualism is symbolized and communicated also in the careful closing of doors when all the cleaning is done and when the family wants its mealtime privacy. It may represent the last-ditch struggle to preserve traces of an autonomy that once existed; in the nineteenth century, Kriovrisi's geographical isolation afforded it, like all mountain fastnesses and *millets*, semi-independence from the Turkocracy (see Schein [Dimen] 1970). But such apparent freedom from the state is illusory in the face of industrial capitalism and the modern state, for households are increasingly dependent on the corporation for wages and the state for all manner of care.

The second detail of the lives of Kriovrisi's women that illustrates the process of social reproduction is the restricted scope of their work. The drawing of material and symbolic lines around the household both closes it off to external sources of power and opens up a domain of power within it. This contradiction is manifested in the lowering of voices during an evening's conversation as footsteps tap on the path outside; low tones not only keep outsiders from overhearing, but also assist the speakers inside in eavesdropping on the passers-by. A man's home is his castle, and, as Hoffman's film *Kypseli* (1974) demonstrates, when he is away it is the woman's, his wife's.

For both woman and man, then, the domestic domain is a means to pride, self-esteem, and security. For him, the esteem it produces complements that provided by the wages he receives. Yet in the public domain, his power, like hers in the domestic sphere, is limited. However he is classified, as peasant or rural proletarian, he is part of a lower class, subject to his employer's needs. He is also subject to the state's commands, because he depends on it for schooling, emergency food and feed, loans, and the general infrastructure of everyday life. The daily and long-term requirements of state and economy can be psychologically draining. For example, worrying about whether sheep and goats will produce enough milk and therefore enough income to support the family or to repay advances or to cushion emergency purchases can make a man uncertain about his ability to live up to social and personal expectations. Such uncertainty can wear down self-esteem and one's sense of self. The household's job is to reconstruct such damaged selfhood, especially that of the adult worker, so that he can return to work the next day.

Since this reconstitution and re-creation is a wife and mother's primary social and symbolic assignment, it restricts her to the household. However, this limitation on her world weakens as well as strengthens both her man and her. Her job is to make every effort to ensure that within these boundaries, if nowhere else, the husband and father has control. The form these efforts take furthers her goal: as the woman, in her subordination to her husband, becomes the weak one, he becomes stronger; the limits on her power and esteem simultaneously announce the condition that the domestic domain is meant to muffle—the politico-economic limits on the man's energy, money, and public power—and pretend to erase it. Yet, by transforming his public impotence into her private impotence, her work also obscures their shared class-based weakness, preventing them from acknowledging and resisting it.

The third detail of women's lives is the severity and apparent inevitability of their labor. Women bear heavy burdens, lauding their own efforts and strength; they work unceasingly and boast of their fatigue. Claiming that only old, weak women need long-handled brooms, they sweep the floor with brooms that are only three feet long. And so their bodies become accustomed to bending, which helps them as they cook over open hearths and as they stoop to use the low cupboards in what are often cramped kitchens with low ceilings—kitchens that the men rarely enter. They serve and then eat later; they eat the food the children will not finish. They take pride in this deprivation because their depleted energy will be transformed into good children, well-fed adults, a clean and attractive house, and an ample table.

Even as household pride makes for straight backs, women's sweat makes for bent ones. Their stouthearted exhaustion communicates to the young not only how to suffer well, but also how to struggle well; how to cope with the need to work hard in a hard world; and how to resist the personal erosion that comes from grappling with hard work. Their merry resistance encourages the young to become hard workers for themselves and their families. Yet the women's perhaps over-determined suffering may secretly teach that some suffering is unnecessary. The use of the short-handled broom, for example, is possibly an excessive burden; its effectiveness ("It cleans better," say some when asked why they do not use long-handled brooms) is probably due not to its construction but to the force transmitted to it by the bent back and gained at the cost of aching muscles, aches that a longer broom handle might obviate. The pride that women take in doing something hurtful to themselves also contains their unspoken anger at their burdens and their unvoiced visions of unburdened work.

And the women's drudgery parallels the men's burdens—the long trudge to the pastures; the pain of the winter cold; the sleepless nights during birthing; the long, lonely weeks and months spent by carpenters and laborers in the coastal cities and in other countries' factories; the worry over low wages stretching to meet skyrocketing dowries and aspirations; the insult and rage elicited by lowland prejudice against Aroumani (Koutsovlachi), who are refused employment or the rental of houses and pasture (see Schein [Dimen] 1975). The counterpoint of women's work to men's work shows that drudgery is systemic and spread throughout the society, and it hints that people are not individually responsible for the severity of their lives. It thus may help them to resist alienation.

But although women work hard by themselves, they nevertheless do so not as individuals, but rather as merged parts of social units. This submergence of their social selves is the fourth detail of women's lives that illustrates their socially reproductive work. Women begin as daughters, attain adulthood only as daughters-in-law, get no satisfaction until they are mothers of sons, and become powerful only when they are mothers-in-law. Thus, their lives communicate the inevitability and personal necessity of social connection. The most important connection is to family. All villagers, but women especially, pride themselves on their family lines. An elderly female informant spoke often of "our family line," so that I would know how well connected she was. But, though endowed with social power, it was only one family line in one little village, a fact she acknowledged even as she spun unlikely tales of the village's days of glory when Ali Pasha summered there, or of a distant relative's leap to fame in the Roumanian government. Created to give strength, the nobility of family lines, like the isolation of households, weakens; in effect, both separate people and domestic groups from one another and so prevent the development of strength through unity with others.

The women's connection to family is of a special sort, however, for socially they are not their own persons. Their existence through others' beings is symbolized in their bearing not only the surnames of men, but also the given names of their husbands. For example, after Maria marries Takis, she becomes "Takina" to his family and village; she is called "Maria" only by her family of origin and kin. Women's social prestige and position, then, are functions, not of women's own work so much as of others' accomplishments, particularly the achievements of men in the public domain, but also the renown of their husbands' mothers in the realm of kinship and the domestic domain. If a woman is known for her hospitality, for instance, her daughter-in-law shares in her reputation, just as her husband's family takes the credit for her social esteem because she bears its name. Moreover, women's own achievements are most important when they lead to the creation and maintenance of others' beings. One old woman told me that during the 1947-1949 Civil War she and her eldest son, who was seven at the time, were in great danger; had he died, she said, "my husband would have killed me." In that marital transaction, her own potential grief seemed secondary to her husband's interest in his son's life.

The fact that their social selves are the products of others' beings is a paradigm of the social life of all citizens of the state. Even if this social denial of women's selves teaches them that life is socially lived, that it is the product of mutual dependence, it also teaches alienation: not only can the products of one's mind and body be legitimately ripped away from one's power but also one's selfhood. Thus, this social denial of self teaches that one must seek elsewhere for identity; it prepares the young for, and justifies to the adult, the claims on the self made by the workplace in requiring obedience to superiors' commands, by the halls of state in requiring unwavering patriotism, and by the church in requiring unquestioning piety.

The woman's submergence of self demonstrates that, even if one works alone, one does so as the lower part of a hierarchical unit in which one's powers are diminished. By accepting her secondary place in the hierarchy of male over female, and family over individual, a woman illustrates both the universal dependency on hierarchy and the price paid for it. Since both the gender hierarchy and kinship apparently have biological bases, they seem to be unalterable. By extension, so too do all other hierarchies—of class, ethnicity, religion, and state over citizen—appear to be inevitable.[4] The adult woman's compliance with the hierarchies of gender and kinship teach to children, and reinforce for adults, a lesson of good citizenship in a life embedded in a set of apparently ineluctable loyalties. In this way, conscious acquiescence in all state, economic, and religious hierarchies is secured.

CONCLUSION

The state, the relations of production, and the household create opposing pulls on people and social structure in Kriovrisi. Obedience to the demands of government, obligations to heterogeneous occupations, and loyalty to the household drain the community of cohesive force and tug mightily on individual interests. The state pursues the individual, almost without mediation, into the private world of personal relations.

The household's power to soothe protects a germ of life, but this liberating potential is stunted by its very goals—the return of the worker to, and the entrance of the child into, the dominated life of society. The household's potential to liberate and imprison is both made possible and curbed by the nurturant and self-protective closure which it is women's traditional task, in Greece and in many other places, to construct. What women do, in word and deed, in social position and demeanor, and in their socially created, gender-based personality, is simultaneously to symbolize, communicate, and reproduce the social structure and its contradictions through creating in their children, and mutually creating with adults, a consciousness that both fits with and alters the world in which they must live.

Through women's common pursuit of domestic affairs and their maintenance and renewal of inter-household relations, the household's vitality flourishes in counterpoint to politico-economic fragmentation. In carrying out their hard work, alone and as merged members of social units, women both resist and capitulate to the forces of the public world; thus, they both support that world and chip away at it from within. On the one hand, the female keepers bind up the wounds of public fragmentation. They heal to create personal and interpersonal strength. Even as the state maintains the community's formal existence, through administrative structuring and economic aid, the women in their domestic realm continue to sustain the community's people psychologically. And yet, on the other hand, women do the society's dirty work. The tasks they must perform to enable their men and children to go between private and public make them feel ambivalent about their work and themselves, and this ambivalence re-creates fragmentation in selves, both their kin's and their own. Yet, as long as they love their loved ones, as long as this is the most important work they do, as long as they are the only ones to do this work, they will continue to create and live fragmented lives.

This paper has described how, in one particular Greek village, domestic life is systemically connected to political and economic structure. What now needs to be created is a general theory of how domestic relations interact with political and economic ones to produce and change culture. Marxist theory has analyzed how contradictions in the relationships of proletarians and peasants to production and the state create both anomie and revolution; however, it accounts for neither the similarities between proletariat and peasantry nor, to my mind, the revolutionary consciousness and action of either. Proletarians and peasants are more similar, both within and between cultures, in the nature and dynamics of domestic life than in any other domain. It is the problems inherent in the power balance between the domestic sphere and the state that Kriovrisiotes share with the members of such a seemingly different culture as suburban working-class New Jersey (Kuenstler 1978). The household supports and so capitulates to the state, but it also guards a spark of and struggle for life, thereby preserving anomie and promoting revolution.

NOTES TO CHAPTER THREE

1. The field research conducted in 1967 to 1968 was supported by Predoctoral Research Fellowship No. 5 F01 MH 32834-03 and Grant MH 13, 622-01, CUAN from the National Institute of Mental Health. I thank Peter Allen and Jill Dubisch for constructive criticisms of an earlier draft of this paper.

2. Most peasant villages reported in the ethnographic literature have been economically homogeneous (for example, Tzintzuntzan [Foster 1967]) or internally integrated by structures that catalyze village-wide action, such as the Latin American fiesta system (Cancian 1965). Indeed, the subject of heterogeneity within communities, ethnic groups, and cultures has drawn anthropological attention only in the last ten years (Pelto and Pelto 1975). Cancian (1965) and DeWalt (1975), criticizing assumptions of homogeneity, maintain that we should expect to find diversity in a range of areas in peasant life, particularly along socioeconomic lines. Given an ingrained anthropological expectation (*pace* Lewis 1960) of peasants' cultural uniformity in economic behavior, religion, and ethnicity, and of the politically binding power created by such uniformity (Foster 1965; Redfield 1960; H. K. Schneider 1977:11); our theories for explaining a case like Kriovrisi are weak. Perhaps we can find a clue among industrial peoples.

3. Silverman's (1968) dissection of Banfield's (1958) prejudiced construction shows how local agrarian economic structure and the national distribution of power inexorably fragment communities. Rationally grounded self-interest draws people's loyalties toward their own households, away from concerns that might unite them with other households. The political fact that only a few can succeed economically sets each household against the others in principle, if not in action. This is as true in Kriovrisi as in southern Italy and much of the rest of the world, but it remains to be specified just how processes and events actively pull people and groups in different directions in any village, town, or city.

4. See Attalides (1976) and Loizos (1976) for descriptions of hierarchies in Greece and Cyprus.

FOUR

Women's Roles and House Form and Decoration in Eressos, Greece

ELEFTHERIOS PAVLIDES
AND JANA HESSER

RURAL villages in Greece characteristically are compact settlements, with houses and yards immediately adjacent to one another. Houses are clustered together forming residential islands separated by narrow cobblestone streets. These residential islands surround a large open space, the public square, or *plateia*. Often, an enormous plane tree stands in the plateia and provides shade over a large part of it during the summer. The edges of this space are occupied by shops and public offices and by cafés that serve customers on outdoor tables when the weather is good. The public square is always teeming with men and also may be frequented by children at play, usually boys. When not working, men spend as much of their time as possible in the plateia and in the cafés. There they find entertainment, exchange information, conduct deals, seek employment, or hire laborers.

Women only timidly venture into this public space and only as a last resort. They recognize the plateia as the domain of men. Rather than enter the plateia themselves, women will send children to do errands or to deliver messages to their husbands. If they must enter a shop or office on the plateia, they will not cross the plateia to reach it but will approach it via the streets skirting the plateia. Only when public events or festivities such as a wedding celebration are held in the plateia do women freely enter it, but then only accompanied by their husbands and families.

By contrast, men spend as little time as possible at home. For them, the house is a place to wash, eat, change clothes and sleep. Only on formal occasions such as their namedays, an engagement, or a marriage, will men stay home to participate in the celebrations. The house, the yard, and the street in front of the house are the domain of women, their female friends, and children. They are places of work, socializing, and child rearing. With the exception of going to work in the fields and going to church, which women see as an important opportunity for getting out of the house, women spend most of their time in their own homes and neighborhoods. While recently there has been some "loosening" of this pattern in certain rural villages, by and large it characterizes the social structure of Greek village life.[1]

This paper examines the extent to which women's roles in a traditional Greek village influence the construction, design, and decor of the houses in which they spend so much time, and how recent economic changes have altered the relationship of women to their houses.

One aspect of the recently developed interest in the relationship between women and their environment (see Wekerle, Peterson, and Morley, 1980, as a statement of this field) has been the examination of "women's roles (or lack of them) in the personal, communal, and institutional processes that create built environments" (Wekerle, Peterson, and Morley, 1980:9) and, in particular, examination of women's roles in and control over the domestic environments they predominantly occupy. Most of this recent research has focused on women in highly developed societies. These studies are concerned primarily with the fact that built environments in developed societies are almost exclusively designed by men, and that "control over allocation of resources to create domestic environments and other micro-behavior settings occupied by women still resides in a male-dominated public system that views women as passive clients" (Hayden and Wright, 1976, quoted in Wekerle, Peterson, and Morley, 1980:7).

Women's role in the creation of "vernacular" built environments has not been addressed directly, but examining this role may help to answer an important question. Is women's lack of control over their environments, especially domestic ones, a recent phenomenon, or is it characteristic of "traditional" as well as industrialized urban communities? This paper is an initial effort to answer this question.

WE WILL EXPLORE the issue raised above using information collected in the village of Eressos on the Aegean island of Lesbos. Lesbos lies seven miles from the west coast of Asia Minor (Turkey). Eressos, located on the northern side of a fertile valley, lies on the slopes of three hills which command a view of the Aegean to the south. Like other settlements on Aegean islands, Eressos is several miles inland, away from the sea which, in the past, was a source of pillagers. Most of its fifteen hundred inhabitants engage in pastoralism and agriculture, producing primarily for commercial markets but also for partial subsistence. A small percentage of men are in "white collar" occupations (for example, the civil service or teaching), and some run small businesses (for example, stores, taxi services, *cafeneions*, or metal-smithing). The village is ninety kilometers from Mytilini, the major port and city of Lesbos, and is connected to it by a road paved in the early 1970s. Taxis make frequent trips to Mytilini, and there is a daily bus between the two places. Electricity was introduced into most homes in the 1960s, although some houses still exist without this amenity. Although interior plumbing is now being installed, most houses still obtain water either from a neighborhood spigot or from a spigot in the yard.

We studied Eressos during a continuous residence in the village from October 1977 to August 1978.[2] The basic goal of the research was to identify the visual variability in house form (including design, structure, and decoration) and to test the hypothesis that the visual form of a house encodes meaning that is socially significant to the inhabitants of the house.

We spent the first three months obtaining census data and walking through the entire village, identifying and making notes on a map about the visual diversity of houses. We frequently encountered residents and solicited from them information about village life and social structure, building practices, and the history of particular buildings and people. We documented visual observations with photographs and sketches, and we recorded and later transcribed the conversations and interviews we had with people who invited us into their homes.

During the next five months of our stay, we studied thirty houses intensively. Although the sample was gathered by convenience, we attempted to include in it the full range of visual variations identified in our preliminary work. In a subsequent survey of house types in the village, we found that our sample did contain representatives of each type in roughly the same proportion as they occurred in the village. We systematically documented these house types with photographs, sketches, and drawings based on detailed measurements of all features of the house, including, for example, the dimensions of grooved moldings, the components of double hung windows, and the size of door hinges. It usually took us two days to complete documentation of a single house. Throughout these months, we continued collecting information through unstructured interviews and conversations, especially with the families whose houses we measured.

During our last months in Eressos, we conducted systematic interviews with the owners and residents of those houses we had measured. Using slides to elicit information, we showed each family pictures of its

own house, as well as of the variety of house types and features found
in the village. These interviews provided information about past and
present construction practices and uses of the house. Our informants
were able to pinpoint dates of construction or renovation by recalling
either the age of a particular person (deceased or living) or an important event occurring at the time the work was done.

Based on the visual and verbal information collected, we were able
to distinguish three periods of house construction and renovation in Eressos. Period I, from 1850 to 1889, is the earliest time for which we
could gather any information about houses, either from oral accounts
or from reliably dated existing buildings. During that time, Eressos was
part of the Ottoman Empire, and a small Turkish minority lived har-
moniously with the predominantly Greek population of the village. A
great earthquake in 1889 caused considerable destruction in Eressos
and stimulated extensive construction and renovation. The earthquake
now serves as a convenient marker of time, since the villagers still refer
to it in their conversations, pinpointing events as having taken place before or after it. Period II bridges the time between the great earthquake
of 1889 and World War II. During the last decade of the nineteenth century and the first decade of the twentieth, the idea that Greek political
authority should replace Ottoman rule spread through the Greek populations of the Ottoman Empire, including Lesbos. In 1912, the idea
was realized and Lesbos became part of Greece. In the Balkan Exchange of 1922, Greece and Turkey agreed to exchange the Greek and
Turkish populations within their borders. The Turkish minority of Eressos left and was replaced by Greek refugees who had fled from their
homes in Asia Minor. Period III extends from the end of World War II
to the present. After the civil war, which was fought at the conclusion
of World War II and which ended in 1949, there began a massive de-
mographic exodus from many rural areas of Greece, including Eressos,
to major urban centers. This trend of abandonment of rural villages has
only now begun to wane.

The following discussion focuses on the factors influencing decisions
about when and how to build or renovate a house and how to furnish
it during each of these periods. At the same time, we will examine the
changing involvement of women in this process.

PERIOD I: 1850–1889

Between 1850 and 1889, villagers in Eressos erected new houses or
renovated older ones for the purpose of using them as part of dowries.

While women and men had some input into the choice of their mate, a marriage contract was settled primarily through family negotiations (*proxenio*) that often involved a third party acting as an intermediary. The dowry provided by a girl's family figured prominantly in these negotiations, and its size and quality were instrumental in determining whether she could secure a desirable husband. It was the responsibility of the girl's family to provide her with a house and its furnishings as part of this dowry.[3] Thus, the father (or a girl's brothers if the father had died) either constructed a new building or renovated the house in which the family lived, securing another, smaller building for himself and his wife in which to spend their old age. He was assisted in this task by his sons or by other men in exchange for produce or labor. Only wealthy villagers had the cash needed to pay for the construction of grand houses for their daughters.

Both rich and poor houses on Lesbos in this period had a total absence of furniture. This characteristic was also shared by the houses of Asia Minor, with which Lesbos, as part of the Ottoman Empire, had cultural ties. Houses were also characterized by a use of space that divided them not into "public" and "private" areas but into "formal" and "informal" areas. A variety of activities such as sleeping, eating, and entertaining, could take place in any part of the house.

The absence of furniture and the multiple uses of space largely determined the features of the house and the kinds of items required to equip it. Without furniture, it was necessary for all activities to take place on the floor or on built-in benches. Villages used a variety of portable items for the various activities which today require pieces of relatively immovable furniture. For example, they used a thin mattress for sleeping and a small, low, round or square table for preparing food and for eating. These were stored away when they were not being used. The floors served as surfaces for both sitting and sleeping, so they had to be well covered to provide insulation and protection against dampness. Since they were highly visible without furniture, they also became a significant visual element of the house.

The absence of furniture also affected the appearance of the walls, since all storage was accommodated either in niches or other cavities embedded in them or on protrusions from them. Because all the house was in some sense public, all areas were "on display." Consequently, cavities were frequently "closed" with a diaphanous cloth drape, not only to protect the objects stored inside from dust and sunlight, but also to visually enhance them and sometimes to attract attention to their contents. Horizontal surfaces of wall protrusions and cavities were invariably draped with a decorative cloth and shelves edged with crochet work (*dandeles*). The process of covering and decorating the floor and wall surfaces was referred to as "dressing" the house (*to spiti ine di-meno*) and constituted a major part of the furnishings.[4]

The construction of a house entailed not only the building of walls, roof, ceilings, doors and windows, built-in benches, and cupboards, but also the production of items necessary to furnish it, since these were part of the dowry. The design and size of a house depended primarily on the need for storage and display of these items, which included the material accouterments of daily life, such as clothing, bedding, food, utensils, and rugs, as well as prestige and decorative items, such as embroidery and crochet work, photographs, and handwoven rugs. All of these material and decorative accouterments, except for food and utensils, were produced exclusively by women as part of their dowry.

Through her contributions to her dowry, the woman's role as a craftsperson was integral both to the process of preparing the house[5] and to the vital transaction of an arranged marriage that would link two families socially. Thus, a woman's labor was needed, recognized, esteemed, and ultimately rewarded in the successful arrangement of a marriage.

A young woman and her mother invested many years of labor in producing the items that covered all the interior surfaces of the house. Since they were usually the only items of value in the house, they were highly visible. In the photographs that follow, we will look more closely at the detail and significance of some of these items during the first period.

Carpets

Carpets were an important part of the female-produced dowry, and a number were woven, depending on the anticipated size of the house for which they were destined. Some were made with dazzling patterns and colors, even though they were meant for everyday use; others, even more magnificent, were intended for formal and special occasions. Mothers and daughters shared the tasks of spinning and dying the wool and weaving it into broad strips (*lourides*), which could be sewn together to make a carpet of any desired width. Although wool carpets sufficed on wooden floors, some houses had compacted earth floors; these required a mat, woven with grasses, that would lie under the carpet to provide additional insulation and protection against dampness.

Carpets most often were woven before the house for which they were intended had been built. They thus provided the exact dimensions for the rooms, since complete covering of the floor surfaces was desired and perfect fit considered optimal. Minor errors in either the size of the room or the squareness of the corners—errors which allowed small slivers of bare floor to show—elicited vociferous complaining from women that was feared by every construction worker. Thus, while men built the house, its size was determined by the size of the carpets women made.

Coverings for Wall Cavities and Protrusions

In addition to carpets and grass mats for the floors, the women spun and wove wool, cotton, or silk cloths, which they then decorated with crochet or embroidery and used to cover wall cavities and protrusions of a variety of sizes and shapes. Each had its own name and specific storage function,[6] and each required a specific kind and size of drape or covering.

Every house had a fireplace, which was located in the room used for the widest range of activities (for example, food preparation, informal socializing, child rearing, and sleeping). In the poorest houses, this room was the entire house. In addition to serving as a focal area for many activities, the fireplace also provided a central visual element for the room and for the house as a whole. Thus, the *phari*, the area above the fireplace, was frequently decorated with an elaborate plaster construction containing "niches" and adorned with decorative reliefs (Figure 1). Photographs and precious objects belonging to the family were always displayed on the phari, and its horizontal surfaces were always covered with embroideries or crochet work. The upper portion of the fireplace opening commonly was covered with a piece of material (the *pharopani*), which prevented smoke from escaping into the room. In some houses, this covering was simple and utilitarian; in others, it was quite elaborate and enhanced the visual significance of the fireplace.

Symmetrically placed on both sides of the fireplace were either two open niches (*theridas*) or two wooden cupboards (*armaria*). The openings of the theridas were covered with a piece of material, and both theridas and armaria had doilies covering their shelves.

In addition to these features, the large houses of the wealthy had several other types of wall cavities used for storage. The contents of these storage areas needed to be protected from dirt and sunlight, but it was also desirable that they be visible to visitors. Thus, the openings of the cavities were covered with diaphanous materials or lace. Included among these cavities were the *bedine*, a small, open display niche with a wood frame and single shelf draped with an embroidery placed on the diagonal, and the *messandra*, a large storage niche in the wall of the room(s) where people slept (and also socialized). The messandra was used for daily storage of the rolled sleeping mattresses and linens (Figure 2). (In poorer houses the bedding roll was placed in a corner of the

1. A *phari* decorated with a plaster construction incorporating Byzantine motifs. It has a *pharopani* draped from the mantel, and the fire chamber is filled with a trunk used for storage. On one side of the fireplace is a *raf* edged with plastic *dandela*. An *armari* on the other side is covered with patterned paper. A bed crowds the space in front of the fireplace. The floor is covered with a hand-woven rug of western motif.

2. A *messandra* filled with bedding and draped. A raf runs above it and is decorated with dandela.

room.) The messandra also was used to store the carpets being pre-pared as dowry. These large houses also had a *jamdoulapi*, a wooden cupboard with two or three glass panes in its door that allowed the dis-play of valuable imported silver, crystal objects, and the very finest cro-chet or embroidery work (Figure 3).

Wall protrusions existed in all houses, and they were always covered or edged with decorative embroidery or crochet work. Among these protrusions were the *lampotheke*, a decorated plaster wall protrusion for the oil lamp, and the *raf*, a long, narrow, wooden shelf found in the room with the fireplace and used to store and display plates, utensils, or decorative objects. Under it ran a strip of wood with pegs which sported brightly covered hand-woven towels when the house was dec-orated for a formal occasion.

A wall protrusion found in all the Christian houses of Eressos was a religious shrine (*iconostassi*), where the sacred objects and votive lamp were kept (Figure 4). It was commonly located in the same room as the fireplace and, like the phari, was constructed either with plaster relief decorations or with a simple wooden shelf. Doilies covered its shelf or small embroidered curtains hung in front of it. The iconostassi was the only feature not found in the homes of the Turkish Muslim minority.

Curtains generally were found in the windows of wealthier houses, as well as at the exterior door in the summer. They allowed a flow of air but helped keep insects out of the house.

Floor and wall coverings and decorations, each with a specific func-tion and tailored for a particular feature of the house, were often pro-duced in duplicate, a set for everyday use and a set for formal occa-sions. A third version of these items was produced for use during mourning. On these occasions, old, used, and worn-out items that draped structures in the house were dyed black, along with dresses and kerchiefs.

In Period I, it was the woman who defined the appearance of the house interior. The best linen, embroideries, needlepoints, and carpets all were proudly displayed on the walls and on the floor, not only on the wedding day but subsequently on the big festive days such as name days, New Year's Day, and Easter. Anything of value that was found in a house, especially in the less affluent houses, was produced by a woman.[7]

PERIOD II: 1889 TO WORLD WAR II

During the period from 1889 to the mid-1940s, a fully equipped house was still a primary part of the dowry, and house construction

3. A *salone* with a *jamdoulapi* on either side of the window, its shelves draped with handmade lace. The pillows on the *sentir* have embroidered covers. The table is covered with tablecloths of commercial manufacture, while the television is draped with a hand-crocheted mat. The room is crowded with furniture.

4. A plaster *iconostassi* with embroidered cloth.

and renovation continued to be stimulated by the presence of a daughter approaching marriageable age. Because a great earthquake in 1889 damaged and destroyed many buildings in Eressos, the renovation or total reconstruction of these buildings provided ample opportunity to include new stylistic elements. Stylistic changes in house features and in the products of women's crafts during this period reflected changing tastes and ideas about the characteristics of a dowry most likely to be attractive to potential grooms. The two factors that had the most influence on tastes were a shift in orientation from East to West and perceptions of "modernity" as it existed in distant urban centers and became "felt" through the expansion of world trade.[8]

Orientation to the West

At the turn of the century, there was a rekindling of Greek nationalism both in Greece and in parts of the Ottoman Empire inhabited by Greeks, including Eressos. This nationalism aspired to an enlarged Greek state centered on the Greek mainland and including those areas of the Ottoman Empire containing large Greek populations.[9] With this new nationalistic orientation, Eressos became more influenced by the West than by the East. Inspiration for prestigious visual form was derived from the Greek mainland and Western Europe rather than from Asia Minor, with which economic and cultural ties had been maintained for centuries. These stylistic influences and changes anticipated and accommodated the new political, economic, and cultural order that followed the incorporation of Lesbos into the Greek state in 1912.

A new national identity and orientation to the West were manifested in the interior domestic space in a number of ways. Some elements were derived from neoclassic architecture that had developed in Athens and other cities on the mainland earlier in the nineteenth century under the influence of nineteenth-century Greek revival architecture in Europe. For example, plaster decorations of the phari and iconostassi began to incorporate neoclassic motifs such as triglyphs, Corinthian columns, and dentils, while Eastern decorative motifs, such as the heart shape and Byzantine floral and leaf shapes, were eliminated[10] (compare Figures 1 and 5). Neoclassic influences were also evident on the house exterior. Triglyphs and dentils appeared under the eaves of some houses,[11] and because of the way the tiled roofs were framed, forming triangles, there was the suggestion of pediments on the frontal façades of several houses. In one house, pilasters were actually suggested by the stucco treatment of the exterior corners. Another expression of this

5. A phari constructed in neoclassic idiom and showing Western influence in its "stage" motif. The fire chamber has been filled with a built-in cupboard and drawers.

new sensibility was the precise symmetry of windows and doors on the exterior, a detail that was not a concern in earlier buildings. Other elements, in addition to the neoclassic ones, also were borrowed from the West. For example, the round arches that were found in earlier fireplace decorations and that reflected an Eastern influence were replaced with rectangular openings framed with drapes made of plaster, imitating a stage set.

The iconography of women's handiwork underwent changes paralleling those in the architecture of the house. New patterns representative of Greek national identity emerged in the carpets and other cloth coverings. Figures inspired by Greek folk tales and the meander motif associated with ancient Greece replaced abstract Eastern designs. Greek flags were woven in anticipation of changing political authority.

Economic Changes and Images of Modernity

In addition to the unification of Eressos with Greece, there were other large-scale events that stimulated change in the house interior. An expansion of world markets in the early twentieth century increased Eressos' involvement in a cash economy. The building of a road connecting Eressos with Mytilini, the main harbor of Lesbos, facilitated both the export of local products and the import of novel ideas and new materials for house construction. For example, cement was imported at the end of this period and was used in a limited way both to stucco existing stone walls and to cast cinder blocks, which began to replace stone for construction. Wood became much more available, thereby enabling more people to increase the size and number of wooden house features and to construct wooden ceilings.

As trade with the outside and involvement in a cash economy increased, more manufactured goods and furnishings became obtainable. These, in turn, required increased storage space, and this need was reflected in changes in the size, proportions, distribution, and location of house features used for storage. Men began to construct armaria, jamdoulapia, and bedines with larger dimensions. More of them were constructed in houses and more houses had them. The most significant innovation was the construction from wood of whole wall units consisting of a jamdoulapi flanked by wardrobes with wooden doors and drawers. In wealthier houses, beds, tables, chairs, and wardrobes were introduced. However, the introduction of furniture did not have village-wide impact until after World War II.

In addition to changes in the style and dimensions of interior and exterior house features during this period, there were also some innovations in spatial layout. However, the use of space in these new house plans was basically unaltered. For the most part, this period saw a continuation of existing patterns of architectural features with the addition of new stylistic elements.

Stylistic changes did not affect the fundamental relationship between a woman's productivity, house form, and the way the house was equipped. Radical innovations, such as furniture or the use of new materials, were introduced into only a few houses, those of the wealthy. The carpets, crochet work, doilies, and embroideries that were the products of years of women's labor still helped to determine the dimensions and character of the house interior and still constituted a vital part of the dowry. Women's roles remained substantially unaltered, although in some houses imported items began to take their place with women's handiwork as objects of value and prestige.

PERIOD III: POST–WORLD WAR II TO THE PRESENT

At the end of the civil war in 1949, Greece experienced enormous population migration from rural villages to large urban centers and abroad. Eressiotes were part of this migration, and the village which had had a population of thirty-five hundred before World War II was reduced to fifteen hundred by 1978. However, the maintenance of strong ties between villagers and their departed relatives and neighbors, which includes frequent visiting back and forth, has resulted in a massive infusion of values and goods from urban centers into Eressos. This infusion has been reflected in dramatic changes in house form and furnishings and has altered significantly the importance of women's activities to the character of the house.

The institution of dowry has remained strong and is still the primary stimulus for renovation and stylistic modification of existing buildings, as well as for the occasional construction of new ones. The pressure to provide an attractive dowry, including a "modern," fully furnished house or, even better, a condominium apartment in Athens, has increased since the pool of young women now competing for Eressos grooms has expanded to include young women in Athens, and since families have been trying to attract urban men as grooms. These patterns have become increasingly evident as more and more single men leave the village, either for work or education. Although young single women lack the freedom and opportunities to do likewise, unless they leave with their immediate or extended families, the potential exists for Eressos women to marry with urban men because of the presence of relatives in cities. These factors, along with the aspirations of young people to leave the village, exert pressure on families with daughters to provide either an apartment in Athens or a totally modernized house in Eressos, even though the possibility exists that the house will not be lived in or might be abandoned after several years when the young family emigrates to Athens.[12]

Buildings are modernized in keeping with standards set by the architecture and life style of Athens or other large cities. While in earlier times the form and decorative motifs only of pre-existing elements such as the phari were inspired from distant urban centers, now totally new elements and new spatial arrangements are introduced and old elements eliminated. Modernized houses are primarily older buildings that have been renovated after being purchased from families that have emigrated. The few new houses that are built incorporate all the features that are the products of renovation in older houses.

During Period III, the Eressos house has undergone major transformations both inside and out. The two factors that are largely responsible for these changes are the concern with an image of "modernity" and the more universal involvement in a national and world market economy.

Concern with an image of modernity means incorporation of new stylistic criteria, again adopted from distant urban centers where international modernist architecture has become preeminent. The international modernist movement in architecture, which rejects decoration on both the interior and the exterior of buildings, has influenced architecture in Athens, which, in turn, influences all of Greece. In the context of Eressos, the modernist movement translates into a desire to simplify and smooth out the house surfaces and remove features considered old-fashioned, such as narrow rectangular windows and wall cavities and protrusions. "Modernity" also means equipping the interior with furniture and appliances. Involvement in a market economy makes available these manufactured goods, as well as the cash needed to purchase them. Indeed, bringing furniture into the house has had a major impact on both the exterior and interior of the house.

Changes in the Exterior

The introduction of furniture and appliances into the interior of the house necessitates the removal of windows to provide sufficient wall space against which to place the new objects. Sometimes windows are removed by simply bricking up several window openings. The more costly but also more desirable renovation is to remove two narrow rectangular windows in a single wall and replace them with one modern square window in the center. In addition to replacing the old windows, the exterior batten door is removed and a metal one installed. The façade, or at least just the "public" façade, is also modernized by stuccoing the rough masonry of the exterior walls. Exterior paints have become widely available, and exterior walls (whether stuccoed or not), windows, and doors (whether modernized or not) are often painted. A wider selection of colors can be used for house exteriors that are not modernized than for the stuccoed exteriors. While in earlier times only whitewashing with lime was possible, today the stone surfaces often are painted colorful yellows and blues.

Changes in the Interior

The house interior has been radically redefined since the introduction of furniture and appliances. Beds, tables, chairs, sofas, a refrigerator, and a bottled-gas stove are crowded into the small rooms which were built to accommodate only a few small movable implements (see Figures 1, 3, and 6). The storage functions of the built-in cupboards and niches are now served largely by furniture, thus eliminating the need for these structures. At the same time, the removal from the walls of the old storage features frees up wall surfaces, making it easier to place furniture against them. In the Eressos interior, protrusions such as the raf, the lampotheke, and even the lovely plaster decorations of the phari are removed. Sometimes removal of the phari is justified by the alleged unavailability of skilled labor to do minor repairs or because it is a nuisance to clean. More frequently, however, the pharis that are torn down are in perfect condition, and it is clear that they are removed because of their "old-fashioned" connotation. In addition to eliminating the wall protrusion, families also brick up and plaster over the wall cavities such as the armaria, the bedines, the theridas, and the jamdoulapia. Hairline cracks due to shrinkage provide evidence of where these wall elements used to be. The only small wall element that is not removed is the iconostassi.

Larger wall cavities are not removed but are renovated and modernized. The messandras are often turned into closets with the addition of a pair of doors. The fire chamber can be renovated in one of several ways. It can be turned into a cupboard by adding a set of doors (see Figure 5), or it can be covered with a curtain to conceal its contents. In some cases, the fire chamber is enlarged in height and a *vitrina* inserted. The top of the vitrina has sliding glass doors, its back and sides are surfaced with mirrors, and it has one or two glass shelves. The bottom (the old fireplace cavity) is filled in with drawers. (The vitrina is found not only in older houses but also in newly built houses of this period; its function is to display valuable objects and photographs, thereby replacing the old phari or jamdoulapi, and to store linens.) Sometimes a fireplace is used "as is" by inserting a gas burner and a bottle of liquid

6. An "everyday room," extremely crowded with furniture, as well as with stacked rugs and linens. It is decorated primarily with manufactured cloths, although a large framed embroidery hangs on the wall.

7. A modernized "kitchen" used primarily for informal socializing and for making coffee. A hand-woven rug partially covers the floor.

gas. Finally, the fireplace can be closed off with a light brick wall and plastered over in order to remove any sign of it.

Another built-in feature that has been introduced in this period is a unit built along an entire wall. It consists of kitchen cupboards on top and, on the bottom, a counter top with cupboards beneath it. On one end there is an enclosure providing a place for a gas stove (Figure 7).

Changes in the Use of Space

Changes in the appearance of the exterior and interior of the house, together with the introduction of electricity and piped water, have been paralleled by changes in the division of space in the house. The widespread introduction of furniture has resulted in the identification of particular rooms with specific functions. Previously, a wide range of activities could take place in a particular space, as circumstances dictated. For example, inhabitants slept in various locations in the house. When the weather was cold, they unrolled their thin mattresses near the fireplace. When the weather was hot, they unrolled them on built-in ledges in the courtyard. When the house had two levels, a new mother and her baby slept upstairs separate from the rest of the family who slept downstairs. The introduction of beds, however, has defined one or two rooms as bedrooms (see Figure 1). Entertaining a guest used to take place in different rooms, depending on the status of the visitor or the formality of the occasion. In the modernized house, tables, chairs, and sofas define dining rooms and living rooms, rooms specifically associated with entertaining. Nevertheless, the patterns of space use have changed only modestly. The floor is still used on occasion for sitting, sleeping can still take place in various locations in the house or the yard, and cooking and dishwashing primarily are performed in the yard. The kitchen, which is rarely used for cooking or dishwashing, is the site of other women's work, of informal entertaining, and of child rearing, activities that have always taken place in that space.

These changes in the division of space, the establishment of rooms with specialized functions, undoubtedly will be followed by changes in use patterns. C. E. Clark has discussed a similar transformation, the assignment of specific functions to specific rooms in the use of space and design of houses in mid-nineteenth century America. He attributes these changes to larger social changes, specifically to those accompanying industrialization, which transformed male and female productive roles. Middle-class women became more narrowly specialized as homemakers and caretakers of children, and "the family [became] . . .

an organization which was not an end in itself but rather a vehicle for promoting the development of each of its members" (Clark 1976:52).

Changes in Women's Activities

The interior of the house continues to be adorned with carpets and fabrics; embroideries and doilies draped over wall surfaces are now draped over furniture and appliances. However, increasingly these items are of the manufactured variety and are bought with cash rather than handcrafted by the women. Women's contributions to the dowry in the form of handiwork have diminished both in amount and significance. A decline in skill and interest in handiwork among younger women is commented upon by older women, but they also say that learning the skills of weaving, embroidery, and crochet is not as vital as it was in the past. Women now can buy either finished products (rugs or linens) or materials that simplify their creation of dowry items. For example, although dyes have been available since Period II, now colored wool and cotton thread are readily available, as well as commercially produced textiles and fabric printed with designs for embroidery or needlepoint. Using paint on the walls and the woodwork to enrich the interior decor also has become prominent during this period. In addition, commercially available sheets of colorfully designed paper, plastic, and oilcloth are used to cover the walls and sometimes even the ceilings (see Figures 1 and 8). The ambiance of the interior space is determined by furniture and appliances, and the rooms are decorated more with paints, colored paper, and plastic than with handcrafted items.

The interior of the house no longer derives its finished appearance and its dimensions from women's productivity. At the same time, male-generated cash income has become more important as the furnishing of a house increasingly depends on manufactured items rather than on items crafted at home. The value of the house is increasingly defined in terms of furniture and appliances, and sums of cash have become an ever more important supplement to the dowry. Whereas women once were the creators, provisioners, and guardians of the interiors of their houses, they are now only the caretakers.

CONCLUSION

In examining the Eressos house and women's role in its construction and decoration over the past 135 years, we discovered that the neces-

8. A "utility" room where most of the cooking is done. It is decorated with patterned paper and oilcloth.

sity of providing a furnished house as part of the dowry has been and remains the primary stimulus for house construction and renovation. As the type of house considered most appropriate as dowry has changed over the years, in accordance with concepts of modernity, so have the appearance and furnishings of the house also changed, gradually at first and dramatically in recent years. We also found that over the past century some conditions in the lives of Eressos women have changed drastically, while others have changed little. Most important, women's vital contribution to the house—her production of furnishings as part of the dowry—has diminished because of changing perceptions of modernity, which are strongly influenced by a changing economy.

The sources of inspiration for modernization have been and remain the urban centers of Greece and abroad. However, the magnitude of this influence has grown as the frequency of direct contact with these centers, the availability of nonlocal materials, and the ability to buy these materials have increased. Most recently, changes in concepts of modernity have resulted in changes not only in style and decorative motifs but also in the configuration and use of space, in building materials, and in furnishings.

In this process of continual construction, renovation, and modernization of houses, the role of women has decreased in significance. In the first and second periods, the goods produced by women—rugs, linens, curtains, and embroideries, for example—were an essential part of the dowry; they complemented the men's construction work, since, in most houses, they were the major furnishings and the only objects of value. These goods have now been superseded by furniture and appliances. Families have come to regard these manufactured items as the most significant "furnishings" of the house, and they are able to purchase them through the male wage-earning capacity.

Not only did the introduction of furniture diminish the importance of handcrafted items, but also the house features for which crafted items were considered essential disappeared to make way for furniture. Thus, although some women continue to weave and embroider items for the dowry, such skills are no longer regarded as necessary, and many young women do not learn them. Handmade items are no longer considered valuable or distinctive decorations for the interior of the house. Instead, the "home decorator" now can choose from a wide array of manufactured materials with which to decorate the walls and drape furniture and appliances. In most cases, these purchased items are preferred to handworked pieces.

The decrease in value and significance of one of women's major productive activities has coincided with the increasing importance of men's role as wage earners. Thus, women's status in the village has diminished, and they experience a sense of confinement and frustration. The declining contribution of women to the house in Eressos is part of a major transformation in the structure of Eressos life and in the structure of life throughout the world. This transformation occurs when societies move from a basically self-sustaining subsistence economy to a cash or market economy. In the former, "most people had access to much the same work roles and their success in filling those roles did not vary greatly. Women's and men's roles in the domestic subsistence economy were complementary and differential control over scarce resources limited" (Davis 1980:109).[13] As women have become little more than caretakers of the house, however, men have become provisioners of the house in almost all respects. At the same time, few new activities for women have been introduced (watching television is one of them), few modern-life roles are available to women, and opportunities to earn cash are extremely limited. In addition, the restriction of women to their homes and yards—the public square is still the men's domain—has not changed. While it is true that there remains an air of conviviality in the small neighborhoods where women spend hours at work or relaxing with one another, they are exposed through television to images of an alternative world in which women have expanded domains and greater freedom. Such images reveal to them their own restriction. The resulting discontent is most evident among female teen-agers who complain about their confined lives and whose strongest desires are to leave Eressos for the city. Among older women, discontent, although verbalized by a few, is more widely reflected in the frequent consumption of prescribed tranquilizers for "nerves."

The impact of modernization and development upon the lives and status of women in different parts of the world has been examined by a number of researchers (see, among others, Boserup 1970; Rubbo 1975; Blumberg 1981; Davis 1981; Bossen 1979) and has been the subject of a theoretical treatise (Illich 1982). Most of these studies accept that "the economic role of women is a fundamental factor in determining over-all social position" (Bossen 1979:99). These researchers have focused on the shift that occurs in women's roles and work when traditional or subsistence cultures become involved in market economies or become dependent upon wage labor as the predominant form of "productive" labor—when "labor-intensive products . . . [are] supplanted by capital-intensive products [and there is] an increasing dependence on cash income" (Bossen 1979:108). With great consistency, these studies find that modernization, rather than improving the status of women or bringing about greater role equality, tends to further restrict women's lives, increase their dependency upon male wage earners, and devalue their labor. These conclusions are the same as those that emerged from our study of the house in Eressos.

According to the studies cited above, a general pattern consisting of the following sequence of developments, emerges when a traditional society is modernized. (1) Wage labor opportunities develop or are imposed—in the form of either factory jobs or agricultural production of cash crops. (2) Males tend to become the laborers in either situation. In agricultural settings, the growing of cash crops is often more capital-intensive than is subsistence agriculture and requires more technological expertise. Both capital and technological training are more available to men. In Eressos, subsistence crops have in large part been replaced by commercial crops, and much of farming has become mechanized, although women and men still grow small gardens and produce most of the vegetables and fruits consumed by their families. But women do not participate extensively in commercial agricultural endeavors, except possibly at harvest time. (3) The larger market structure favors men with financial, educational, and training opportunities. In many traditional societies, young women are still much more confined and restricted in their mobility, both within and outside the local community, than are young men. Thus, existing cultural sanctions deny women the chance to take advantage of those same new educational and training opportunities. For the traditionally restricted Eressos women, then, very few opportunities exist to earn cash income; a few manage small neighborhood stores, one makes rugs to sell, and several are schoolteachers, but by and large most women are homemakers and caretakers of children. In addition, Greek laws make it impossible for women to invest money or own a business without their husbands' consent. (4) As opportunities for wage labor grow and subsistence activities (formerly shared by men and women) decline, cash becomes increasingly important as the means for acquiring the basics of life—food, clothing, and housing. Men are moved out of the domestic and subsistence sphere and the "household [has] to be run on what the paycheck [buys]" (Illich 1982:50).

Ivan Illich makes a distinction between the kind of work performed by women in the traditional subsistence-based society, and the unpaid activities of women keeping homes for married wage earners. He sees it as the difference between a "gender specific assignment of culturally defined concrete tasks generating subsistence" and the "unpaid toil that adds to a [marketed] commodity [and highly capitalized production goods] an incremental value that is necessary to make this commodity useful to the consuming unit itself" (Illich 1982:45, 49). Polarization of the unpaid labor force occurs as unpaid economic activities are disproportionately imposed on women. Furthermore, when "women generally lack the training, capital, or cultural permission to enter new occupations, this means that they must accept a condition of partial or disguised unemployment" (Bossen 1979:112).

The economic transformation Eressos has undergone since World War II, and the concomitantly reduced contribution of women to the dowry and to furnishings for the house, signals not only the narrowing range of productive activities available to women who remain in the village but also their diminishing status. The only recourse for young women in Eressos is to find a way to leave the village for urban centers where opportunities for education and wage labor exist. Although this kind of mobility is difficult for women, parents increasingly recognize the limitations of the changing village environment and increasingly seek ways for their daughters to leave under the "chaperonage" felt to be necessary for unmarried women. Sanctioned departure from Eressos can be achieved by sending a daughter to live with relatives so that she can receive special training or higher education; more commonly, however, it is achieved by buying or building a condominium in Athens as dowry. In either case, the ultimate goal is to attract an urban groom who will provide a home for the daughter in the city.

Thus, the important role played by women, directly and indirectly, in determining the character of the houses they occupied has been fundamentally altered as their society has undergone the transformation from a subsistence economy to a market economy while retaining both dowry and traditional restrictions on women. Construction of a house and domestic environment in earlier times could be viewed as a subsistence activity, shared by men and women performing complementary tasks. In recent times, the house and domestic environment themselves have become marketed commodities (produced and purchased by men) made useful by the housewife's unpaid labor as caretaker rather than as producer. In this change, perhaps, lies the transition to the minimal influence wielded by women over the creation of built environments in developed market societies.

NOTES TO CHAPTER FOUR

1. A similar division between male and female domains and places of activity has been described as existing in other parts of Greece, for example, in Va-

silika (Friedl 1962:12), in northern Greece (du Boulay 1974:31), on Tinos (Dubisch 1976:321-322), on Ios (Currier 1976:309-310), and on Kalymnos (Bernard 1976:295). It has been the subject of extensive analysis and of a film by Hoffman, who was doing fieldwork on Thira (1976:331-382).

2. One of the authors (Pavlides) is a native Greek and has maternal relatives residing in Eressos. Linguistic fluency and established ties with inhabitants through the network of kinship greatly facilitated entry into the village, access into people's houses, and flow of communication.

3. The process of arranging marriage contracts and the role played by dowry in Eressos is similar to that described for other areas of Greece. The father everywhere bears the primary responsibility, but he is aided by his wife and sons. The wife's major contribution is the weaving and decoration of carpets and linens for the house interior (Papaharalambos 1968:43; Friedl 1962:53-54; du Boulay 1974:95-96; Bialor 1976:232). However, the house is not invariably a part of the dowry. Although it is mandatory in other villages on Lesbos (Zourou 1974:84) and is mentioned as a common part of the dowry by Peristiany (1976:217), Hoffman (1976:332), Dubisch (1976:321), Bernard (1976:296), Allen (1976:185-186), Kenna (1976:349), and Pasadaiou (1973:12), on Cyprus (Papaharalambos 1968:5) and on Chios (personal communication) it is customary for the groom to build the house. In Karpofora, inclusion of a house in the dowry is a recent phenomenon (Aschenbrenner 1976:214). In Vasilika, the family house goes to the sons of the family (Friedl 1962:214).

4. The pattern of space use and of equipping the house that is described here is similar, with some variations, to that described by du Boulay (1974:23-24) for a contemporary village in northern Greece.

5. The heavy obligation and involvement of the mother in the process of producing her daughter's dowry is perhaps best reflected in a folk poem from Lesbos (Zourou 1974:46).

> I have a daughter and I have a bitterness
> I will be weaving night and day
> I have a daughter and I have sorrow
> They will be demanding me to provide a house
> I have a daughter and I have troubles
> I have to get up at dawn and sleep at midnight.

6. These storage areas also have been noted by Papaharalambos (1968:44) in the houses on Cyprus and by du Boulay (1974:23-26). Our experience in other parts of Greece suggests that building of houses with a similar variety of storage features was typical in rural areas and probably reflected an absence of furniture. That people today, even when they have furniture, commonly sit on the floor for informal gatherings or for work is indicative of the significance of furniture as objects of prestige and show, rather than as totally utilitarian and necessary parts of the house.

7. Sinos (1976:15) reports that in simple houses on Cyprus the only items of

value were those made by the women for their dowries. These items were used not only in daily life but also for decoration of the walls and doorways.

8. The introduction of new traditions into rural areas of Greece through the "emulation" of urban ways has been discussed in depth by Friedl (1968:94ff.).

9. Campbell (1976:19) writes, "The attempt to unite free Greeks with unfree Greeks was enshrined in the 'Great Idea'—a nationalism mixing secular with religious elements, with the redemption of Constantine's city as the ultimate objective."

10. Radford and Clark (1974:67), who have documented a similar shift in motif to neoclassicism on Thira at this time, also see it as the introduction of forms "not direct from ancient Greece, but by way of Genoa, Venice and Germany."

11. Tzakou (1975) has documented a similar transformation of the house exterior on the island of Siphnos.

12. Village life and village "ways" continue to become more heavily stigmatized, or at least the negative value attached to village life continues to become more pronounced. Du Boulay's statement (1976:252) about a village in northern Greece seems applicable to Eressos: "The low esteem in which the village is held means that prestige through the marriage alliance is no longer achieved through the linking of the honour and wealth of two families but by casting off forever the bounds of village life." Friedl (1976:367-375) has documented the process of migration from Vasilika in Boeotia and found, as we did, that the first families to leave were those of the upper strata; these were the families that had the means to provide the daughter with a dowry sizable enough to attract one of these migrant males or an urban "nonnative" groom.

13. House construction could be considered part of the traditional subsistence economy; the male's construction of the house was complemented by the female's production of its furnishings.

FIVE

Introducing the *Nikokyra*:
Ideality and Reality
in Social Process

S. D. SALAMONE AND

J. B. STANTON

THE CENTRALITY of the family unit in both the social and economic sphere has long been noted in rural Greek society.[1] Observers have recognized that, within the nuclear family unit, the woman wields considerable power and influence, if informally, and that in some Greek communities, she may even have predominant decision-making power in household matters.[2] Moreover, there is male acknowledgment of the necessary nature of the woman's work and of her indispensable role in the maintenance of family honor.[3]

Jill Dubisch has argued further that a Greek woman's domestic power, which can be equal to or greater than her husband's, is dependent neither on her economic status per se nor on the size of her dowry specifically. Dubisch discusses several variables that may affect an individual woman's status and power. These include the amount of property relative to that contributed by her partner, her character, the prestige and wealth of her village, her village of origin, and whether she owns her own house (Dubisch 1974:28, 32). Thus, a woman's status is relatively flexible, depending on marriage and circumstance, rather than being formally prescribed. This condition reaffirms the distinction, introduced by Ernestine Friedl, between the "appearance of prestige" and the "realities of power" (Friedl 1967:97).

The views stated above present women's status and power as essentially informal and circumstantial and limited to the private sphere. We would like to take this analysis of power and prestige one step further, using our fieldwork on the island of Amouliani, a village in Halkidiki, Greece that was settled in 1926 by refugees from Asia Minor. We will argue that women's power and prestige is *formalized* in an institution that spans both private *and* public sectors of Greek life. This institution, which historically has dictated the "balance of power" between men and women in rural Greece, is the *nikokyrio*, "household economy." The ideal nikokyrio is a corporate, self-sufficient, family-based enterprise; both men and women derive public prestige and social equality from the success of the nikokyrio itself. Moreover, the nikokyrio is a fundamental organizational construct in both "public" and "private" economic sectors; as an ideal, it has historically taken precedence, whenever realizable, over other forms of rural Greek economic organization.

By adopting this fundamental concept of the nikokyrio as the wellspring of personal power and prestige, we believe that we more closely approximate the Greek understanding of public and private. The nikokyrio—its perpetuation and aggrandizement—is the organizational focus of the nuclear family. Once observers recognize that women are indispensable to the economic organization of the nikokyrio, they will understand that women's social prestige, like that of their husbands, rests on the public recognition of the household's success.

In Amouliani today, women's economic power is neither discrete nor delegated. Moreover, ritualistic displays of male prestige (church rites and hospitality customs, for example) and the traditional obligatory relationships between subservient wives and their husbands must be distinguished from the reality and public recognition of womanly economic power. Appearances of male power, whether within the public or private context of village life, should not be confused with the actuality of shared and commensurate power and prestige of the husband and wife in the fundamental organization and functioning of the nikokyrio. Thus, the concept of public prestige, as realized through the ideal of nikokyrio, is no longer applied exclusively to males, thereby affirming the real influence of women in village life and the fact, especially recognized in the small community, that women too gain public prestige which is often equal to, and sometimes greater than, that of their husbands. The support for this thesis is in part found in the village vocabulary which clearly bestows public prestige on men and women as husband *and* wife in recognition of their roles as *nikokyris* and *nikokyra*, male and female "householders," respectively.[4]

Both terms are logically derived from the term nikokyrio, "household." The nikokyris and nikokyra are, as we will suggest here, "partners." The concept nikokyris/nikokyra is perhaps the most ideal and normative concept in village life, defining the specific roles of man and woman in relation to each other, to the community, and to former and succeeding generations. For the people of the repatriated refugee com-

munity upon which this analysis was based, the concept of the nikokyrio had strong historical and traditional roots in the life style and
socioeconomic conditions of the Asia Minor communities in which the
people lived before the Balkan Exchange of populations in 1922.

While the concept has changed over the last half century of socio-
economic transformations, the ideal has persevered. We can differentiate between the concept and the ideal of the nikokyrio by regarding
the ideal as a corporate, family-based, moneymaking, self-sufficient enterprise and regarding the concept as being dependent upon the changing roles and expectations of the essential constituents of the nikokyrio,
the nikokyris and nikokyra. Both roles continue to evolve, in concert
with economic conditions, in an ongoing opposition between man and
woman, child and elder, individual and community, and personal and
community prosperity.

Thus, rather than distinguishing between the ideal, or formal, position of women and their real power and prestige (Friedl 1967), we suggest the distinction between the *ideal* of the nikokyra (and the nikokyris
for men) and its *functional* realization on a personal level in community
life. This approach may necessitate replacing abstract concepts such as
"superiority" or "inferiority" with those of personal and public success
or failure. A woman's happiness, sense of self worth, and effectiveness
will depend as much on her acceptance of the ideal of nikokyra as on
its public realization. The following statement by a woman of Amouliani illustrates this idea.

> If a woman has her own household, her man, her children, if her
> children are healthy, it's her whole life. Those are the most impor-
> tant things to her. What kind of life would she have if she went out
> merrymaking alone and came back to find her husband had made
> some great mistake and her daughter was out who knows where?

The concept of individual (that is, non-familial) personal accomplishment is alien to the women of Amouliani. When the same woman
quoted above was asked what she thought of American women with
grown children who find themselves asking what they have accom-
plished for themselves or what they will do now that their children have
left home, she replied:

> They have agony inside of themselves. Agony and worry. And if
> they work outside their homes they'll still be that way. They don't
> have steadfast characters.

A woman derives her status in community life from her approxima-
tion to a specific community ideal grounded traditionally in an under-

standing of male-female partnership and the functional equality of men and women in that partnership. It is the economic and social success of the partnership that guarantees the prestige of both men and women and their respective rights. While economic and social factors differ from marriage to marriage (as do individual personalities), a woman's domestic power is not essentially circumstantial. She has prescribed rights and prerogatives inherent in her status as nikokyra—a role that she may or may not live up to in the eyes of the community, her husband, and her family.

Through the study of the women of one Greek community, Amouliani, we will explore the most enduring aspect of female partnership and equality with males—the reproduction of traditional community life through the establishment of future households and the socialization of future nikokyres (the plural of nikokyra), especially through the continuing institution of the production of *rouha* (trousseau and household furnishings) for dowry. We will examine first the special history and traditions of the community upon which our analysis is based and then focus on the question of what it means to be a nikokyra in Amouliani. We will examine not only the women's characterization of themselves but also the community institutions that sustain their models for self-esteem. Finally, we will discuss the possibilities for the survival of the present cultural ideal of the nikokyra/nikokyris partnership.

HERITAGE AND HISTORY

As a resettled Ionian refugee community, Amouliani has particular traditions with respect to male-female roles and relationships that distinguish it from the more extensively studied non-refugee mainland Greek communities. Thus, it may be instructive to briefly recount the distinctive history of Amouliani's women.

The history of the island community is a story of continuity and change, of major disruptions of tragic dimensions, and of the reinstatement of community institutions in a new land. Amouliani's population of approximately 450 residents are the descendants of villagers and emigrants from the Marmaras Islands in the Sea of Marmara. First forced into exile on the Anatolian mainland as a result of the Greek invasion of the Ottoman Empire during World War I, they were expatriated to mainland Greece some eight years later in the 1922 Balkan Exchange.

Amouliani's settlers had already sampled a number of mainland Greek communities before deciding, in 1926, to recreate their own traditionally sea-based existence on unpopulated island land newly expro-priated by the Greek government from a Mt. Athos monastery. In the succeeding decades of geographical isolation, economic depression, and, in the 1940s, two devastating wars, the small community contin-ued its marginal existence on largely non-arable land. It was only in the early 1960s, following the integration of the domestic fishing industry into the national economy, that the community began to prosper and the island population, after a decade of extensive out-migration, began to stabilize. The 1960s also brought the beginnings of a tourist trade that has since blossomed into a major island industry. When Amouliani received electrification in 1974, the already accumulating profits de-rived from the fishing industry sparked a construction boom, especially in tourist facilities, thereby increasing the island's desirability and wealth several fold.

What effect has the particular history and heritage of Amouliani's women had on their social and economic status and sense of commu-nity? How have their experiences shaped their expectations and views of womanhood and the marriage partnership? The answers to these questions will reveal how history and social structure at the village level may be characterized institutionally as interaction between the sexes: through the nikokyrio, the refugee men and women of Amouliani re-generated the devastated community life and values that might have been lost with the loss of their Asia Minor homeland.

Perhaps one crucial distinction between Amouliani and rural, non-refugee mainland villages is that the Asia Minor communities within the commercial and cultural orbit of Constantinople were, by the turn of the century, already undergoing social and valuational changes as-sociated with "modernization"—changes that would begin to affect life in rural Greece on a comparable scale only after the Second World War. Thus, Amouliani's women, as Ionian refugees, inherited a view of social change already developed in their former "transitional" com-munities of Asia Minor. While women's attitudes in Amouliani today may be much the same as those of women in other mainstream rural Greek communities, their modern orientation may be more deeply rooted and may contribute to a smoother, less resistant view of social change. This view is partly reflected in the sense of "tradition," com-mon to Amouliani's women, that has always included a pride in things "progressive" (*proodevtiko*) and even "foreign" (*xeno*). In the follow-ing passage, an Amouliani woman describes her first impressions of mainland Greece and of the village in Euboea where she and other Marmaras refugees were first resettled in 1922.

Peasants! Peasants! Why their clothing was the cheapest sort. Greek wool, some little silver coins strung on their dresses. . . . Old-fashioned clothing, old-fashioned Greek costumes. While we were progressive [*pnevmatoforites*, literally "bearers of the spirit"].[5] We breathed different air!

We wore the latest fashions. Whatever was in fashion in Constantinople, in *the* City, became the style in our island immediately. In our home, we had a mania for Russian styles.

What is perhaps remarkable about this statement is that the villages of the Marmaras Islands were themselves "peasant" communities of agriculturalists and fishermen, not unlike rural Greek communities found along the mainland coasts today. Yet because of their history, Amouliani's residents may have a distinctive sense of tradition and cultural continuity unlike that expressed by Greeks of non-refugee origin.[6] We believe that this sense of tradition and cultural continuity is manifested in those aspects of life that constitute the focal point of this paper, namely the marriage partnership and family enterprise and the status, prestige, and economic power of the nikokyra.

The Family and the Household Economy

Although community life in Amouliani has become less corporate today, families nonetheless continue to socialize their children according to the customary standards adhered to by the islanders ever since their exodus from Asia Minor some sixty years ago. Up until very recently, marriage was predominantly endogamous (now lack of available partners has broadened the geographic scope), and post-marital residence is generally neolocal except for younger daughters and their husbands, who customarily reside with the bride's parents and inherit their home. As we shall see later, families in Amouliani have not significantly utilized dowry to further social mobility, although dowry is invariably provided in the form of a daughter's share of familial inheritance—sometimes a house, rarely cash, and always an extensive trousseau and household furnishings. The dowering of daughters with a house itself or with property for a house is desirable but not requisite.

The family in Amouliani is still perceived as if it were within a traditional subsistence-oriented framework; it is still understood as the basic unit within the local economy. In Amouliani, material success is judged only in the context of the economic success of the family. The family is regarded as a form of basic capital to be invested to its greatest advantage in some type of familial enterprise. This view is manifested in the recent boom in tourist enterprises that are frequently initiated and generally managed by the women of the family, and in familial decisions to emigrate and do wage labor abroad for a number of years for the purpose of accumulating sufficient capital to establish family businesses that can provide work for present and future generations. Not surprisingly, then, it is being a nikokyra that defines for the women of Amouliani, as it did for their mothers and grandmothers, their relationship to the economic framework of both the family and the community; being a nikokyra also serves as the central focus for self perception and for women's own observations of their changing roles.

Since the concept is an ever-evolving and historically specific one, let us begin our exploration of the nikokyra role by examining its contemporary form in Amouliani. As we have noted already, both terms, nikokyra and nikokyris, as defined by the people of Amouliani, connote the economic responsibility attendant upon the management and maintenance of the nikokyrio. Despite the persistence of male prerogatives, the relationship between the nikokyra and nikokyris is not essentially hierarchical but complementary. The acknowledgment of this relationship by men is not a matter of noblesse oblige. They are critically aware of the fact that their own "male" prestige in the "public" sphere is contingent in almost every respect on the *nikokyrosyni*, the "nikokyra-ness," of their mate. Indeed, no man in Amouliani is even considered a mature adult until after his marriage and the establishment of his own nikokyrio. This attitude also has been recognized in non-refugee communities by Campbell (1964), Stott (1973), Loizos (1976), and others.

This sense of complementarity is evident in the terms that villagers use to describe the ideal spouse; a woman must be *filotimi*, "virtuous and prudent," and *oikonomologa*, "an economist," while a man must be *ergatikos*, "hard-working." Indeed, one of the most frequently suggested attributes of a successful marriage was *prepei na tairiazoun*, explained as "working well together" (*tairiazoun* means literally "to match"). It was this attribute of complementarity which, we were told, while not necessarily implying romantic love, would, with the parenting of children, grow into true, mature love.[7]

The nikokyra is an economic concept because proper household management is crucial to economic success. It is a social and community concept because family honor rests on the perception by the community at large of successful household management (the socialization of females is therefore focused on this goal). Moreover, it is an existential concept because the women's view of themselves—their very self-esteem—is wrapped up in both community perceptions of their success or failure and their personal evaluation of it. Thus, the concept of nikokyra incorporates those values that have been shown to be central in so many researched Greek communities: honor (both personal and familial), patronage relationships (for the woman, an extension of the social duties inherent in her role), and the primacy of the nuclear family unit.

The nikokyris/nikokyra partnership is based not only on a male/female division of labor, but also on a division of financial responsibility that underscores the importance of the woman's economic role. In Amouliani, a couple would normally decide together what capital investments the family would make and what savings would be put aside. Wages earned by the man were customarily handed over to the woman. As it was explained to us many times, "If the husband wants money to go to the cafe and the wife doesn't have any to spare, all she has to do is tell him and he won't bother her about it again."

Wives in Amouliani have been credited for many a man's success. Villagers point out that until recently a man's salary so nearly approximated the necessary expenditures of the household that a family's ability to save enough capital for a new home or a child's high school education may have depended entirely on the economy of the wife. One fisherman's family of four, whose sole source of income was the husband's wages, which averaged less than $2,000 annually, managed to save 70,000 drachmas ($2,300 at the time) in the seven-year period between 1967 and 1974. Through the daily record keeping maintained for us by the couple over the period of one year, it became clear how the wife limited expenditures on food, clothing, kerosene (no more than two small nighttime lamps), personal items (soap, not shampoo), and furnishings (none purchased), while eliminating virtually all purchases that would benefit the parents exclusively. (This tendency to center the household economy on the children and their immediate personal and future social needs has been noted by other authors; see, for example, Friedl 1962.)

> Why do you have money and I don't? A woman and her husband, when a woman is an economist [oikonomologa], they make money.
> Take me for instance; my wife is an economist. She loves money and she doesn't throw it away . . . while Yiannis [his brother] . . . his children didn't come out right; they just sang songs. . . . [T]hat is the woman's responsibility. Take me for instance; my children stuck to me. They grew up by my side at work. And right up till now, just look at my boys!

In this quote from an elderly villager, we see once again that the role of the nikokyra is closely associated with financial management. In a questionnaire we administered to eighty-two villagers, men and women were asked to select from a field of seven attributes what they thought were the most important qualities a woman could possess. These attributes included intelligence, beauty, economy, being a good cook, the ability to work with and get along well with one's husband, skill in handicrafts, and the willingness to listen to one's husband's problems. The three qualities most frequently chosen were those that would most enhance the socially significant role of the nikokyra; all but two women chose *na einai oikonomologa*, "to be an economist" (an even larger proportion of men made this their first choice), while the second most frequently recorded virtue among the women, *na tairiazei me ton andra tis*, "working well or getting along with one's husband," reflected the partnership ideal discussed above. In addition, in follow-up interviews to discuss the questionnaire responses, a significant number of respondents suggested that a woman should be, first and foremost, a good nikokyra, and that this ability was most closely aligned with the attribute of economy, or, as one male respondent suggested, practicality and logicality.

The most recent and visible manifestation of the nikokyrio concept of financial partnership, which has as its goal the increasing of familial wealth, are the tourist enterprises, most notably tourist homes that are run almost exclusively by the women, which have sprung up on the island of Amouliani as surplus capital created by the fishing industry's boom has been invested in family businesses. This development is significant because the women clearly have chosen to work in these family-run enterprises rather than do "stranger's work" (*xeni ergasia*). These decisions to open tourist homes, sweet shops, and touristic stores stem not only from objective economic circumstances but also from traditional values. These values are associated with the economic significance of the nikokyrio, the primacy of the nuclear family unit, and the community judgment of the marriage partnership, based on the couple's ability to care and provide for their children. Because of these values, not all women's work outside of family-run businesses is regarded necessarily as socially undesirable. If, through the woman's wage labor, for instance, the family is able to become *nikokyroumenos*—self-sufficient enough to earn future income from an established family enterprise that may provide work for future generations—this labor outside the household may be viewed positively by both family and community. For example, a number of Amouliani's families emigrated to the United States for the express purpose of creating enough capital to become captains of their own fishing boats back home. While abroad, most of the younger women worked—primarily in factories—often with grandmothers caring for young children. Therefore, although one might expect the community to think poorly of a family whose females must take on work outside the home—a move which reflects the man's inability to properly support his family and the woman's inability to successfully manage the household economy, and which indicates that she may not be able to devote herself fully to her family and household tasks—in fact, that family gains status and prestige if, partly through the women's wages, it achieves a primary village goal of entrepreneurship. The current attitude toward women's work beyond the household is reflected in the following comment by a forty-year-old woman with two teen-age sons.

> When we were in Saloniki one time we met a woman with two children who had worked in Germany for years in a factory. She was bringing back her savings to get herself a husband here. I asked her why she didn't go back to her village. . . . She said, "Go back? I'll never go back. All I left there was hunger. I worked with the tobacco for nothing." Her hands were cut up yet from those years. I told her in Amouliani the women didn't work [*den doulevoun*]. She said, "The women in Amouliani sit [*kathontai*]? You mean there exists a village in Greece where the women don't work? But what work would we do here. There's no work. Could I go to Giorgo's [café] and wash dishes (that's what a lot of women do in Germany but then no one knows what they've done]. Me, wash dishes here? My husband wouldn't let me. Not as long as we had enough money to live.

Since this woman was the wife of one of the island's most successful fishing captains, there was clearly no economic need for her to gain employment as a dishwasher; yet this quote is revealing for another reason. Although she did not mention it at the time, this same woman was running a summer tourist home that had as many as two to three families staying there simultaneously. Therefore, she was making a distinction, as other women have, between wage labor and household work that might also be profit making. In fact, in Amouliani there were no women working in non-familial enterprises, although a substantial number (probably 30 percent by 1979) worked in these types of private entrepreneurships, as well as in family-owned grocery and dry goods stores.

THE SOCIALIZATION OF THE NIKOKYRA AND THE IMPORTANCE OF THE ROUHA

We have suggested that although the strength of the nikokyra concept as a cultural and social ideal may derive from its economic significance, it is closely tied to the understanding that self-fulfillment is to be found within and through the family. Thus, the role of nikokyra acquires special meaning through the parenting of offspring; after all, perpetuation of the family is the primary rationale for the nikokyrio. Not surprisingly, therefore, the virtues of being a good housewife and mother are no less esteemed than that of being a good household manager.

Indeed, becoming a nikokyra is considered a craft involving an apprenticeship from the time a daughter leaves school until the time of her marriage. This apprenticeship is unique to the woman; a young man does not go through a similar socialization for his future role as a nikokyris. On the contrary, in the years preceding a young man's marriage, the community expects that he may well be "irresponsible," that only when faced with the obligations of marriage and children—and most important, when guided by the acquired expertise of his wife, with the sanction of his mother—will he achieve the seriousness and providence required of a proper nikokyris. This, then, is a further source of the woman's power and prestige: her husband must rely on her skill.

The social reproduction of the nikokyrio is achieved through the socialization of young women as future nikokyres. A key element in this process of social reproduction and socialization is the creation and accumulation of rouha, or that part of a woman's dowry consisting of trousseau and household goods—the tools of the woman's trade. Mother and daughter enter into a prolonged and intimate relationship through which the required virtues of household management, frugality, technical skills, and proper wifely demeanor are transferred from one generation to the next. The financial, practical, and aesthetic decisions related to the production of rouha are made jointly by mother and daughter with careful regard for community expectations. An examination of the socialization process, specifically the relationship of mother and daughter in the production of rouha, will help us comprehend the many-sided nature of the nikokyra role and the values—economic, social, and personal—intrinsic to the lives of Amouliani's women. As a traditional custom, rouha production will also provide a focus for our discussion of continuity and change. The preeminent position of rouha creation and accumulation within the economic dimension of the nikokyrio is perhaps the most significant indication of a woman's actual decision-making power within the home, for in Amouliani this part of the dowry may alone approximate or exceed the family's annual wage-earning power.[8]

As previously mentioned, dowry in Amouliani consists of that share of the family inheritance that is passed on to a daughter at the time of her marriage; customarily, it is in the form of property (less commonly a house or the promise of the parental residence) and the rouha of the young woman. Because the agricultural value of most land is negligible and no more than a handful of island families ever have been able to make a living by either farming or raising livestock, this property, including fruit and olive trees, while a significant dowry item, was never one of exceptional value until the tourist boom of the last decade.

Tragedy and disaster have been great levelers of the village economy; few families came to the island with any resources, and government land distribution at the time of the village's inception was based on family size. These factors, together with the tradition in Asia Minor of the bride and groom's contributing equally to the new household, have meant that dowry has not been a means to social mobility on the island. Furthermore, unlike women in the Greek villages studied by Friedl (1962), McNall (1974), Peristiany (1976), Allen (1976), and others, women in Amouliani have never been provided with cash dowries, and neither daughters nor mothers would consider city marriages simply for the sake of finding urban husbands. Moreover, in the life of the village, and particularly in the lives of the village women, rouha has been so central a concern that it can be equated in importance, in the social sphere, with the transfer of inheritance. This view is so prevalent among the women that, as demonstrated in the following quotation, they use the word *prika*, "dowry," to refer exclusively to the rouha.

> When Kristina got married I had been ill and the groom insisted on their marriage within two months of the engagement. So I went into debt for 23,000 drachmas [$767 at the time] to provide the prika. Maria's family just went into debt too. They bought the prika here and in Saloniki and Ierissos on credit.
>
> When I got married during the war I didn't have much prika—some few trees, a little land, an old house. My husband used to tell me about it all the time; he made me cry. So I decided that my daughters would have prika that no man could criticize. My Elisaveta's was the first of the big ones on the island. It started a race among all the other girls—they wanted the same. But when Adonis gets married, I'm going to make sure he gets a prika as big as theirs; it's only right I should collect in return.

(The first two uses of the word *prika* refer to rouha alone, while the third refers to inheritance. The fourth and fifth times the term is used, its meaning is ambiguous, although in fact it could only have been Elisaveta's rouha (rather than her inheritance) that was "the first of the big ones." Although the family history of the mother quoted is unusual in that she and her husband had returned to the island from Australia, apparently without observing the customary island practice of long-range rouha accumulation (which perhaps partially accounted for the financial pinch she reported), the story indicates the value, both financial and social, placed on the rouha part of the dowry.

The continuity of the rouha institution in island history is an important clue to our understanding of the tradition that sustains the role of the nikokyra. Both the rouha of today and that of the village communities of the Marmaras Islands consisted of the woman's wardrobe, furnishings meant for the lifetime of the household, and, up until very recently when these became wedding gift items, kitchen utensils. It is clear from the few dowry agreements (*prikasymfona*) still in existence that in the Asia Minor villages of origin the value of the rouha, carefully enumerated by the mother of the bride down to details of material, style, handicraft technique, and even, in the case of store-bought goods, price of purchase, was often equal to or greater than the value of inherited property and capital, which was also enumerated. Moreover, there was a rough parity between the value of the wealth presented by the family of the bride and the gold—ritual wealth that was the product of years of a young man's wage labor—and future inheritance offered by the groom. This custom not only signified the importance of the rouha institution, but also indicated the economic decision-making power of the woman in this essential domestic concern.

From the recollections of the older women of Amouliani, we know that rouha production in Asia Minor was a major household activity for girls from six or seven on, with those few who briefly attended school learning needle crafts there. Besides doing household tasks, many young women worked at producing lace and fish net handicrafts, which were then exchanged for dowry goods brought from Constantinople or sold for cash which, in turn, was used to purchase materials (linen, cotton, silk, and gold thread, for example) to create personal dowry items. Mothers wove silk and cotton cloth which daughters embroidered to produce bed linens, ceremonial towels, scarves, underwear, table linens, and gifts for the groom and his family. Women who lived in that era proudly explain that many of the items were purely for decorative (ritual) purposes, and that the rouha of that time was exceedingly more valuable than today. (The skill, quality, and artistry of the use of gold thread in the few surviving heirloom pieces bear witness to their value.) Most all of this ritual wealth, considered as capital just as was land or gold, was sold by families, painfully, piece by piece, as they struggled to survive the years of exile during the Greco-Turkish War (1919–1922).

Those families who made their way to the island of Amouliani tried to re-create their former life style. But with virtually no financial resources, a major economic depression, and an inhospitable environment, they found this was essentially impossible to do. During this early period, the rouha necessarily became a shadow of what it had been; the economic activities related to immediate survival replaced quality weaving, and materials (not to mention the money to pay for them) for handicraft production were largely unavailable. Nevertheless, the only trips off the island recorded by most young women of that era were shopping trips to Thessaloniki. They went either alone or accompanied by female relatives, to purchase rouha items, for which a considerable proportion of the family cash was allotted. (It should be noted here that purchasing store-bought goods when they were more economical, of better quality, or more fashionable than those that could be produced at home was an accepted norm in Amouliani as well as in Asia Minor at least as far back as the 1870s.) Considering the extreme poverty of those times, it is nothing short of remarkable that a comparison between enumerated dowries dating from the period 1932 to 1960 with those from the Asia Minor period and today shows, after allowing for differences in the wealth of families and the availability of certain materials, consistent similarities in what was provided, with an increase in the number and quality of dowered items (and continuous adjustments for changed styles of furniture) as we get closer to the present.

In the 1960s and 1970s, as the development of the fishing industry produced greater prosperity and inflation continued to rise, there was another increase in the money expended on rouha goods. However, across-the-board comparisons of different rouha show definite reasonable ranges in value in accordance with the age of the girl at marriage and the economic position of her family. By the early 1970s, when fishing families were just beginning to earn over $2,000 yearly, girls were accumulating rouha with an estimated value of $2,300 (a calculation based on the prices at the time).

The obvious economic importance of the institution and persistent tradition of rouha lies in the acknowledgment by the women that it is an economic necessity and in its centrality to the women's view of what makes a nikokyra. The purchase of each and every item is personally overseen by the woman of the house; it is remarkable that the man, given the extent of his lifetime financial contribution to rouha accumulation, has nothing to do with the choice of items—in fact he would be hard-pressed to describe what the entire rouha included and would not be able to name some of the household items in any but the most general terms. The ability to amass those things considered essential and appropriate through years of scrimping and saving is a credit to the woman's ingenuity as housekeeper and financial manager.

That the rouha is deemed economically essential by the women is communicated by their initial surprise at and skepticism about other societies' being able to do without a similar system of provision. As with every household expense, questions regarding rouha goods are practical matters; therefore, decisions about the appropriate number of summer versus winter nightgowns or linen versus cotton sheets are open issues to be discussed and re-discussed by women, their friends, and their daughters. Superfluity is considered wasteful and is subject to the same community censure at the dowry showing before the marriage as are inadequate supplies. A proper dowry display in Amouliani is set up so that guests can see at a glance how many of each item are provided, as well as their quality. Relatives of the bride are quick to discuss places of purchase, heirloom items, objects of special creativity, and, although quite accurately estimated by guests, sometimes even prices. Thus, the dowry showing is a test of the abilities of mother and daughter as nikokyres and a reaffirmation of the importance of the woman's role and the skill and training it involves.

Although men rarely, if ever, refer to the subject of rouha except as part of the "burden" that daughters represent, the two explicit references they usually make to it when recalling the past underscore its economic importance. The first is the descriptions of the wealth of families in Asia Minor, including the embroidered gold and silk handicraft items and their subsequent currency as salable goods during the period of exile; the second reference is to the black market days of the Second World War when, it was said, whole rouha were sold by desperate families to men with "hearts so black" they would profit by the misery of young women.[9] (More characteristic of the male attitude toward rouha is the joke about the young man who was attracted to a young lady by the rumor that she had lots and lots of *metrita* (literally "something counted"), only to find out, after their marriage, that *metrita* refers not only to cash but also to needlepoint stitches.)

The importance of rouha preparation in the socialization of daughters is equal to that of learning how to properly clean a house or care for children. The trend toward the accumulation of store-bought linens, blankets, and clothes instead of handmade goods has not diminished the rouha's importance—it has just changed its focus. Consumerism is viewed as a skill just as important as handicraft ability. Nevertheless, young women are constantly admonished to work on handicrafts (primarily decorative table mats today) from the time they leave school until their actual marriage. Although changes in social mores and sexual ethics on the island have meant that young women have a great deal more freedom of movement within the village and its outlying beaches and groves, community censure through gossip still is directed toward those women—both engaged and unengaged—who are not perceived as spending an adequate amount of time on dowry preparation. A typical comment was, "*Gurizei, gurizei, oli tin mera, den ehei kedima na kanei?*" ("She wanders, she wanders, all day long, doesn't she have needlepoint to do?")

Observation of the community of women in Amouliani during the 1970s would have revealed much the same routine organized around the performance of household tasks in each home: an allotment of a considerable amount of time during the absence of their husbands to rouha-related activities in combination with socializing, and, particularly in those households with daughters and granddaughters of school age and beyond, intense and frequent discussions about community and personal standards in the areas of household furnishings and handicraft skills. Given the relative leisure of Amouliani's women compared with their counterparts who lived in farming communities or worked in factory jobs, there was considerable more time for the production of dowered goods; thus, the centrality of these items was increased. Not only was the creation of dowry a major part of the daily schedules of teen-age girls, it also clearly helped to sustain a strong bond between generations and, although competitive in nature, a bond between the women in the community. In fact, dowry showings, attended by a large proportion of the women in the community, were one of the few remaining community-wide events, generally attracting even greater numbers than weddings themselves. (This is partly because, largely due to the new trend toward exogamy, weddings are much less village- and more family-oriented today. Also, unlike dowry showings, weddings are generally limited to invited guests.)

The inter-generational and community activity is strengthened by the pride of all the women in creating ingenious and unusual patterns, in matching their skill at intricate needlepoint and crocheted designs with others in the community, and in coordinating color combinations and creating a total effect for the dowries of young women who themselves demonstrate both their originality and understanding of community standards. The importance of the rouha preparation as a test of the virtues, industry, and economy expected from a nikokyra is so great that even the few girls who have left the island permanently to attend high school and technical schools elsewhere have come back, or are intending to come back, for a rouha showing before marriage.

Even in the absence of unmarried daughters, women continue to produce household items. In the last decade, this "superfluous" production has found a place in village custom with the invention of a separate exhibition of the "groom's dowry" (*prika tou gambrou*). This exhibit displays the traditional presents to the bride alongside the groom's trousseau (customarily shown *with* the bride's rouha), together with a nontraditional display of handicraft items previously provided *only* by the bride and now supplied as well by the female relatives of the groom. Included are small rugs and crocheted and needlepoint table mats, doilies, and potholders. Although many women have dismissed these nontraditional gifts as "silly" and not all grooms are given such displays, some mothers of boys are now planning for them. In the newly created tradition of a separate "groom's dowry" showing, a custom without precedent either on the island or in Asia Minor, we find another form of affirmation of those housewifely skills women wish to demonstrate they possess, as well as a prime example of the resiliency and responsiveness of community customs.

Lending even greater importance perhaps to the idea of rouha handicrafts is the interest created by the mass media and Greek commercial concerns in recent years in the older, "traditional designs" (now mass-produced by major handicraft suppliers and displayed widely in women's magazines). Although in Amouliani the few preserved pieces of handicraft from the turn of the century and before were shown in successive generations long before the resurgence of interest in the older, "more genuine" handicraft designs and forms, the new popularity of the older styles has added even greater validity to the notion that women are indeed preparing something of permanent value. The success of the commercial enterprises dealing in handicraft supplies alone, as well as the homogeneity of so much of the handicraft items nationwide, tells us that these items play a significant role not only in Amouliani but throughout Greece. The vitality of the rouha tradition and its commercial manifestation is an indication of the strength of the nikokyra ideal for Greek women.

In addition to the rouha institution, there are other visible aspects of the current role of the nikokyra in Amouliani which, we believe, are also applicable to other rural Greek communities. In the next section, we will examine some of the local communal standards of propriety for women. These constitute the basis for an ongoing definition of self in relation to the local community and to other communities—both urban and foreign—beyond.

THE NIKOKYRA IDEAL AND SOCIOECONOMIC CHANGE

If the nikokyra ideal is to be a viable one for Amouliani women, there must be recognized and accepted guidelines of right and wrong behavior. We have explored some aspects of these "rules" in our discussion of rouha as a personal and community concern. However, this "orderliness" extends into all aspects of the household. The most visually apparent standard is the general agreement about the right and wrong way to organize and perform household tasks and to arrange one's household. As one older woman put it, *Ta kanonika einai oraia*, "The customary is beautiful." Although economic troubles may plague one's household, and concerns about children and their future may cause constant anxiety, a woman is secure in her knowledge of community norms regulating the running of her household, as well as her ability to demonstrate her own creativity and individuality within community constraints. This security is a source of strength and was expressed most clearly by the first village woman to go abroad as a tourist. She and her husband went to Germany as the guests of a German couple who frequently visited the island. Her comments on the differences between life styles and her description of village (and characteristically rural Greek) ways reflect her certainty about the daily management of the house.

German women don't dress like we do at all. Everyone is wearing some thing else. If you have this coat and maybe it's old and you got fat, you wear it even though it's tight; if you lost weight, you wear it loose. We don't dress like that.

And another thing is dressing for your age. My friend is my age, she's 40 years old, but she wears her hair back like this [in a ponytail] with these curls in front. Like a young girl. Now the way it used to be here if you were my age you had to wear your hair back and maybe your head covered. It's not like that today but still you have to dress your age.

The German women don't know how to cook. They had rabbit one night and they didn't season and stew it or cut in vegetables, they just sliced it up, fried it a little and served it. It was raw and tasteless. I wanted to help out with the cooking but by the time my friend started to cook there wasn't enough time before the meal to cook the food properly. She'd be sitting around all morning but she didn't start the food until the last minute. You can't cook right like that. We cook the food in the morning, putting the stews and sauces on the fire as soon as we get up, and then, by late morning, we're done for the day. We rarely cook again for supper, just make some eggs, put out some cheese. But that way you always have time and the food is cooked right.

The houses I saw all had nice furniture, much nicer than ours.

But they don't know how to decorate a house. . . . Like these pillows on the couch here, theirs were just thrown around, they weren't laid out nicely. . . . They don't have handicraft work at all!

Despite the present general security about the ordering of one's life and the style of household maintenance, continuing community support for the nikokyra ideal itself may perhaps be threatened by what the women perceive as a dissolution of community ethics and a burgeoning competition, jealousy, and sense of isolation. Before we analyze these trends and their effect on the nikokyra role, it would be instructive to examine the reactions of the women themselves to these threats. The following comments were selected because they generally represent women's feelings about how their community—and their own lives— are changing.

It used to be that you could just drop in on people all the time. Now you have some friends or relatives who do the same, but you're not always sure you'll be welcome.

Before five years ago, only Maria had a new house. Now everyone is trying to build one. On TV women see the latest fashions and know whether they're in style or not. They won't go out if they don't have the clothes; a few years ago no one cared what clothes you had. If some woman has something in her house, some new furniture, you have to have it.

In the old days we had green beans and chick peas all the time. We didn't have a lot of special foods. Now the kids won't eat that stuff. They want us to prepare meals especially for them.

Back in the old days women worked harder but everyone enjoyed themselves more on holidays. Now everyone has to work harder and harder but it's not just to survive, it's to pay for all the clothes the kids have to have and their [special] foods!

There are fewer village-wide celebrations today because people have more *anhos* [anxiety]. Because they have to get their children off to the high school and make sure they're keeping up with their studies, worry about the money being spent every day and whether the child is going to succeed. No one used to worry if children went to high school or not.

Women don't dress up much anymore for *Apokreas* [pre-Lenten holiday when traditionally men and women would dress up as the opposite sex]. That's because a few years back some people started saying unkind things about married women being dressed up and dancing around.

Increased prosperity, new educational opportunities, and rising expectations have done nothing to dilute the force of the nikokyrio ideal; to the contrary, as with the tourist enterprises, the goal has been more fully realized. On the other hand, community as well as personal expectations of what constitutes financial and social success as nikokyra/nikokyris have been upgraded, creating what Amouliani's residents feel is an increasing climate of competition. The perception of greater competition causes distrust and community disintegration which, in turn, is cited as a further cause of jealousy, envy, and personal feelings of anxiety among the women as they try to live up to what they feel are increased expectations of themselves as household managers and mothers.

Modernization has combined forces with tradition to create the primacy of the immediate family, which, the islanders feel, precludes an economic rationale for much of the shared community activity that once characterized the island. The last decade has seen the economic success of a large number of island families and, with the formation of independent fishing and tourist businesses, the realization of the nikokyrio ideal in many households. This success, in addition to the unionization of the island's fishing industry in the early 1970s, has meant that previous intra-island patronage and other social relationships between the wives of employers and employees, relationships that had previously sustained many work situations, have become less significant—with the result, perhaps, that village relationships generally have decreased in importance. Meanwhile, new businesses and professions for the island's menfolk have presented the women with opportunities for patronage relationships outside the island. While these new relationships have brought social prestige and perhaps economic profit, they also have created different types of work and worries. For example, husbands with business connections outside of the island have cemented patronage relationships with the aid of their wives by inviting urban dwellers to be guests for island summers.[10]

Although the women of Amouliani generally are gaining a more sophisticated understanding of city and country life, those women with the greatest number of patronage ties outside the island are, on the whole, those who appear to be most self-conscious about how outsiders view their community and the individuals within it. One woman expressed her irritation at Saloniki visitors, "acquaintances who drop in for a cup of coffee, a sweet, use of the bathroom, and naps," by stating that

> [t]hese women never offer to help. They think that here in the village we're a little backward, "rustic." They don't expect us to be thinking of things like vacations. They tell us how happy they are to get away from the noise and troubles of the city. When they go on vacation, *they* don't expect to do any work!

The visits are never fully reciprocal; Amouliani's women have far fewer opportunities to visit the cities.

Despite the new anxieties they may engender, experiences of this kind have not appeared to weaken the strength of the nikokyrio; neither have other stresses and tensions (anhos) which Amouliani women see as characteristic of the modern age.[11] The women are already well informed about urban and even emigrant existence—especially through relatives[12]—but this awareness does not seem to have had a negative effect on the self-esteem, prestige, and power they associate with the successful fulfillment of the nikokyra role model.

CONCLUSION

Clearly changes in island social structure are on the horizon. Today, with schooling through junior high school compulsory throughout Greece, many more sons and in particular, many more daughters are going on to high school. The girls will have fewer hours of direct and inter-generational communication with family and community. With education seen as a viable and acceptable means of social mobility, many daughters of the present and succeeding generations will be returning to the island only for summer vacations. After they marry, some will undoubtedly have careers outside their households and will be contributors to the income of those households through the wages they earn. Yet these facts alone should not alter the economic principles of the nikokyrio concept, which are the strength of the nikokyra ideal. Future generations of women will perhaps decide that there is no longer any need for the accumulation of rouha, either as a means of economic preparedness or as a training ground for the skills once needed to be a nikokyra. Certain of the homemaking skills (but not economy or selective consumerism) will give way to technology, and, in what is perceived by some as a step toward "women's liberation," the role of homemaker may be downgraded to the point that some women may come to disdain it.

But at the heart of the speculation about the future of the nikokyra role, there still remains the economic principle of the household economy—the goal of familial entrepreneurship tied to the socially desirable goals of marriage, child rearing, and building for the future of one's children. Thus far in Amouliani, this traditional concept has adapted to modernization and industrialization, thereby strengthening the customary power and prestige of the nikokyra's role.[13] But this cultural ideal can only be sustained as long as the individual man or woman expects to find primary fulfillment within the family. This reality and the continued viability of the nikokyrio as an economic construct are probably the most important determinants of the survival of the ideal of the nikokyra in Amouliani and elsewhere in Greece.

NOTES TO CHAPTER FIVE

1. See, for example, Friedl (1962), Campbell (1964), and Loizos (1976).
2. See Friedl (1967), Dubisch (1974), and Safilios-Rothschild (1976).
3. For a discussion of this topic, see Friedl (1962) and Campbell (1964).
4. The complementary nature of the nikokyris/nikokyra concept is highlighted in this statement by a seventy-eight-year-old widow of Amouliani.

> You see I wear black. But it isn't only the clothes I wear which are black. My man is dead. In the house of your mother, father, sisters, brothers, you are a guest [mousafiri]; you are an outsider [xeni]. You live with them, but you are an outsider. But with your man you are a nikokyra. When you are a nikokyra no one says you didn't do this right, or come and eat this food which was made for you. I don't have my own household. I don't have anything anymore.

The social dynamic revealed by this statement is not dependence on the nikokyris but upon the establishment of a joint household in which a woman comes into her own as a fundamental contributor to family and village or community life. The death of the nikokyris signals the dissolution of the nikokyrio and therefore of independent socioeconomic status; the death of the nikokyra has the identical effect on the male partner: to have community standing, a nikokyris must preside over his own household.

For an in-depth contextual analysis of the historical and socioeconomic role of the nikokyris, both in the transitional *fin de siècle* society of Greek Asia Minor and in the resettlement of rural Greece after 1922, see S. D. Salamone (1986).

5. This sense of *pnevma* implies the same idea as the German *Zeitgeist*, "spirit of the times."
6. This uniqueness of a tradition that bears especially on the position of women was noted by Sanders (1962:127). "Greek refugees who left their ancestral

homes in Asia Minor in the 1920's brought many family patterns new to those whose forefathers had lived in Greece itself. The women in refugee villages of Macedonia for example have more independence of decision than those of non-refugee villages."

7. The concept of marriage partnership, and particularly its roots in the socio-economic structure of the Marmaras Islands in Asia Minor, is examined in J. Stanton and S. D. Salamone, *The Noikokyris and the Noikokyra: Complementary Sex Roles in a Changing Socio-Economic System* (1980).

8. The rouha in Amouliani is the particular focus of Jill Stanton Salamone, "The Institution of Dowry in Amouliani, Greece" (1978). The author presents specific enumerations, comparisons, and evaluations of the rouha as it has existed in the community throughout the past century.

9. In one particularly poetic description of the selling of dowry to black marketeers, a young woman is offered a can of olive oil for her entire rouha. The maiden beseeches the buyer, "This is for a whole dowry? Is this something that can be made in a day—in a year? This is something that takes years of saving and suffering!" The marketeer replies, "Everyone has dowries, but who has olive oil to give?"

10. Although patronage and particularly *kombaros*, "godparent," relationships with island outsiders have been common enough in Amouliani for a number of decades, they hardly compare with either the extent, or we believe, the far-reaching effects of today's outside relationships.

11. In a random survey, forty-three island women were asked if they presently suffered from any physical complaints. Nearly a majority offered the complaint of anhos and related nervous ailments: twelve said they had constant headaches and nine claimed stomach problems, including ulcers.

12. All but five of this same representative group of forty-three women had relatives in Athens and all but four had relatives in Thessaloniki. Over half had more distant relations in the United States or Canada and one quarter had relatives in Germany. The women traveled to Thessaloniki—the nearest large metropolitan center and a four-hour bus ride from the closest point to Amouliani on the mainland—on the average of once every nine months.

13. The goal of familial entrepreneurship implicit in the nikokyrio concept is apparent not only in Greece but also, we believe, in Greek families living abroad and is, perhaps, a key to their economic success.

The nikokyrio, we should emphasize, is not a static cultural concept or ideal. In Amouliani itself, the role of the nikokyrio in community life has passed through at least three distinct phases over the more than fifty years of history we researched. Before the First World War and during the brief period of repatriation to the Marmaras Islands between 1918 and 1922, the nikokyrio was an institution dominated by the wealthiest fishing and shipping families in the village. In this form, it bonded the community together in a hierarchical arrangement of what were described by the villagers as first-, second-, and third-class nikokyria, or estates. It was the nikokyraoi of the first estate who in fact organized and directed the political and economic life of the community within Ottoman Turkey. Once again, in the second phase of Amouliani's history, when the population resettled in Greece, these influential households generated the leadership that both founded the refugee community and initiated its economic and social revival. In both of these phases, the nikokyrio as an ideal bonded the community together in a co-operative, though traditionally hierarchical, social structure. Again, the concept of the institution did not change in the historical transition, but the effect of the nikokyrio on village life, as described by villagers, was to produce more communal cohesiveness than is felt in its present manifestation. The third phase began after World War II, particularly in the 1960s, with the ultimate eclipse of village political autonomy, the penetration of the outside economy, and the equalization of financial opportunity within the community. At this point, the ideal and the concept diverged to the extent that the success of the individual nikokyrio seemed to militate against community solidarity, a fact reflected in the villagers' sense of increasing competition and loss of village tradition that we have noted.

Women's Friendships on Crete: A Psychological Perspective

ROBINETTE KENNEDY

Women's friendships have rarely been the focus of social science research. Psychologists, in particular, primarily conduct experiments in contrived settings, using predominantly white male participants and researchers, to "test" preconceived ideas of friendship.[1] While researchers in other disciplines have studied friendship in its natural context, they commonly view the relationship both as relatively weak when compared with interactions among kindred[2] and as primarily an adult male phenomenon.[3]

Despite the lack of research on women's friendships, most anthropologists and sociologists have assumed that women with strong family ties (for example, women in peasant societies) are least likely to experience close friendships. Such uninformed views of peasant women's friendships are based upon the assumption that women's social and experiential lives are limited to the domestic context. These narrow views reveal more about research perspectives on women than they do about the content of women's friendships.[4]

Implicit in androcentric research assumptions about women's friendships is a denial of women's role as social actors, aside from the functional support women give to their family and kin. My own research on Crete suggests, however, that women's friendships, even in this small, traditional community, are rich, freely chosen emotional bonds that, in intensity, are comparable to—and often surpass—women's kinship ties.

After eighteen months of pre-fieldwork on Crete, I spent one year (1976–1977) studying women's friendships in a small village on the western end of the island. The purpose of the research was to explore, through the study of friendship, the basic, positive bond that is at the core of all freely chosen loving relationships, as well as the role of those relationships in women's everyday lives. I sought to determine the meaning of friendship in *context* and to understand women's *experience* of the relationship.

THE TEXTURE OF WOMEN'S LIVES IN THE VILLAGE

In the Cretan mountain village of Hatzi (population 326), women's lives are dominated by a grueling physical environment—an environment that demands much and provides relatively little in return. Obtaining the necessities for survival consumes the major portion of everyone's time, energy, and mental activity, and other aspects of life in Hatzi must be viewed within this context of physical survival.

The specter of starvation looms within adult Hatzians' memories, since many families lost a member—usually a child—to famine during the German occupation of the island in World War II. Some of the difficulties of life in Hatzi are ameliorated by the terrain; unlike surrounding villages, Hatzi is bordered by hills that are rich in snails (*koklous*), carob trees (*haroupia*), and hundreds of varieties of wild greens (*horta*). These three blessings, together with an abundant supply of water, are the mainstays of life in the village.

Olive and citrus trees, grape products, truck crops, sheep, pigeons, rabbits, chickens, and women's textile work (spinning, weaving, knitting, and embroidery) are the main sources of income for villagers. These products are sold in Chania, the district capital.

In their everyday lives, men and women perform tasks that are strictly defined by gender. Men are assigned jobs that require physical strength or their presumed superior ability to make business decisions and to represent the family in the outside world. Women's overt tasks confine them to the domestic realm, since they include predominantly the nurturing of and caring for children, husbands, parents, and animals, in that order.

Men and women spend relatively little time with each other, know little about each other's domains, and have a great deal of animosity toward each other in general. Women see men, as a group, as simultaneously tyrannical and a source of personal freedom through their ability to bestow permission, money, and esteem. Men see women as mysteriously able to exploit potentially unlimited sexual power to build up or destroy men's honor. The psychological stress of this environment is considerable and contributes to a milieu which, by Western notions, might be described as paranoid. The distrust that men and women feel for each other is evident in the social relationships of both genders, from parent/child interactions to exchanges between neighbors.

While oppressive to both men and women, this atmosphere is experienced differently by each group. Although men are allowed greater individual freedom in all activities than women are, men are in many ways outcasts from their homes and lead relatively solitary—although public—lives. Women, on the other hand, are isolated from the outside world. In their unique position, they have attitudes and values that are hidden from the dominant culture.

Women's Experiential "Underground"

Women's experience is colored by geographical confinement, personal isolation, limited social mobility, and lack of financial power within a dominant culture that excludes them. In this psychological underground, information is both highly valued and distorted. A woman usually obtains information from other women, who are subsequently viewed both as allies and as threats to her well-being, since it is primarily when socially unacceptable information is made public that a woman's (and her family's) honor can be destroyed. In this emotional climate full of paradoxes, there is tremendous potential for jealousy, hostility, quarrels, and gossip, and the aura of paranoia in the surrounding society is heightened.

Women perceive men as their oppressors and their relationships with men as being based upon a hierarchical system in which men's needs are to be met before their own. The energy women expend addressing the needs of men is not, in their opinions, reciprocated.

> They think of themselves first, and they want their needs met first *always*. So they get what they want, and we lose out. Every time.

Women describe a system of *androcratia*, "rule by males," and *autokyriarchia*, literally, "rule by the self of the lord or master."

> Men rule. There are many things we cannot do because we are women. For instance, we want to go to Chania. We have to go and ask our husbands, "Will you permit me?" If he doesn't, we can't do anything—not just go to do something personal we need to take care of there. We have to ask his permission. And if he says, "No," then we can't go.

This imbalance of power extends beyond the limits on women's geographical freedom of movement. Among their other care-taking functions, women take responsibility for men's feelings, believing that the difficulty of life in the village exacerbates men's already supersensitive personalities. Men, women feel, are people who need to be constantly calmed, tiptoed around, placated, appeased. Both men and women told me that if a man says, "Go do that" to a woman, she must learn to do so quietly, without "making a man nervous." The president of the village, a middle-aged man, explained to me the rationale behind this social convention.

> A woman makes a man nervous. If the woman sees that her husband is a little sad or worried, and he says for her to stop doing whatever she is doing, she must stop—not go on, "Blah, blah, blah" and continue and then make her husband have to say bad words and perhaps make her eat wood [beat her].

When I asked women what empowers a man to wield such force, a typical answer was:

> Every kind of strength there is. His physical strength, his mind, the force of his character. And if you don't do what he tells you to, you will have a black life. A horrible life . . . every day. A life of torment, a life without light.

Coping Mechanisms

Women have developed complex coping mechanisms that enable them to exist in this oppressive system and to continue to participate in life along the edge of the dominant culture. The psychological scaffold that supports women's using these coping tools to carve out a place in the margins of village social, political, and economic life is a system of collusion with men.

In psychological terms, collusion in a relationship is an unspoken agreement not to be authentic, not to share one's true feelings about certain issues. In Hatzi, women collude with men and do not verbally express certain emotions to men so that they can avoid facing their own feelings of powerlessness—feelings that are uncongenial to their being able to support their role identification.

There are numerous ways women collude with men. Through extramarital affairs, women often fulfill their needs for attention, excitement, and sexual gratification, which enables them to maintain a marital relationship from which they may receive none of these. At the same time, however, this method of coping with a system that is harmful to women perpetuates that system; although women's extramarital affairs are not integrated into the social structure, the perceived threat of these affairs to men is. Women believe that a man fears his wife's infidelity much more than a women fears her husband's infidelity. Having a husband who fears one's infidelity is a difficult position for a woman, because, women believe, it is the trust a man has for his wife's sexual loyalty that is the basis for his *philotimo*[5] and for her subsequent freedom to participate more fully within the village society. Yet, despite the dangers of doing so, women are drawn to having extramarital affairs. But because affairs involve the suspension of normal social standards, they are often a degrading experience, and many women I interviewed expressed ambivalence about the value of these affairs.

However, regardless of their personal attitudes toward extramarital affairs, the methods women use to cope with men's sexual overtures are the same whether or not they wish to respond to these overtures. The similarity of women's responses is based upon the myth that if a man comes and knocks on a woman's door, she has given him some reason to think she is interested. Women collude with men to perpetuate this myth by preventing their husbands from learning of these incidents.

> When I don't say anything to my husband, the evil stops right there. Nothing happens. But if I tell anyone about it, the bad thing goes on. My husband will kill the man. Then the man's brothers say that I invited the man here. They won't blame him. They will blame *me*. They *always* blame the woman, because she is weaker than the man is.

Within her marriage, a woman colludes with her husband by supporting his domination of her.

> If the man pulls the rope, and the woman pulls the rope, it will break. They will divorce. But if a man pulls the rope and a woman lets go, nothing happens, and the family stays together. If the woman pulls the rope and the man lets go, the man is weak, and the woman will go with other men, and the family will be destroyed. So it is better for her not to pull on the rope.

In this atmosphere, created by men and women's covert contract to avoid authenticity in their relationships with each other, women resort to indirect forms of communication. They use threats, lying, and deception to conceal their true feelings while simultaneously attempting to exercise the forms of power that they *have* amassed.

Women perceive that the consequences of direct expression of personal needs are greater than they wish to face. While they frequently rely upon intricate strategies that involve threats, they rarely act upon these threats. Since what they usually threaten to do is outside social norms, to act upon such threats would disgrace them as well as the people they are threatening—possibly leading to their expulsion from village society. Thus, while women have potential access to this form of control over others' behavior, carrying through on threats renders them powerless.

Lying and deception are considered more attractive forms of indirect communication. Lying is more socially acceptable in some instances than telling the truth, if the truth goes outside social norms. Several women, who shared the rules for village social patterns with me, instructed me in how to lie correctly, and I frequently observed the fabrication of intricate lies by women in Hatzi.

These coping mechanisms maintain women's disempowered positions in Greek society, contribute to the momentum of the culture, and in many ways perpetuate it. Women indirectly strengthen the mainstream culture which excludes them by using the forms of indirect communication noted above. They further support societal structures that are not supportive to them through sexist patterns of child rearing. Naturally, the question arises as to why women would support a society that is uncongenial to them. The answer is that the rewards and benefits offered by Greek society to women who fulfill their social roles are considerably more attractive than the penalties for not doing so; without exception, women in Hatzi strive to be seen as successful wives and mothers.

> When a woman is *timia*, an honorable person who doesn't look at other men and only addresses herself to the concerns of her husband and children and has no interests other than them, and things are going all right between her and her husband, then she has no reason to disturb things. Why should she?

Ideas of Personal Freedom

Nevertheless, despite the rewards and benefits, such as the security of an extended family support system, the prestige and status of successful conformity to norms, and the structural stability offered by the culture to its most loyal supporters, many Hatzian women yearn for a different kind of world.

> Of course we want equality. How could we not want to be equal? My dreams for my daughters are for them to try and educate themselves so they will have their own position in the community, to be able to live through the good and the bad independently. If something bad happens, for my daughter to be able to say, "I have my work; I will be able to work and get through this."
> It is very important now that mothers be able to educate their

daughters. That didn't happen before. If you weren't educated, and you didn't have any knowledge of the way things are in the world, you couldn't do anything; you didn't know anything—only how to give birth and work.

But I think that when she is educated, my daughter will be able to decide by herself what to do. She will be able to judge for herself what is the best thing for her.

While Hatzian women are by no means in the stage of social consciousness or political awareness attained by many women in some Western nations, they do experience themselves as living in a world of traditional oppression. A significant aspect of their awareness, however, is that they see no role models within their own social setting which suggest ways to obtain rewards that compensate for the negative consequences of moving outside their social role. Moreoever, they view their options for personal freedom as tied directly to their marriages and the economic reality outside it.

If I had the 250 drachmae for the boat passage to get to Athens, because if I left my husband I would have to leave Crete, *if* I had the money to get there, which I don't, then where can I go? What can I do there? Nothing.

Which shall I be: a maid or a whore? So I am better off here. I have my house, there is plenty of horta in the hills, fruit on the trees, so I am better off here.

Nevertheless, women express their yearning for freedom through their desire to have geographical and social freedom of movement, to participate fully and directly in family decisions, to be self- rather than other-defined, to experience congruency between their feelings and their behavior, to have more free time, and to be full members of the society they support.

One of the few experiential spaces in women's lives in which they come closest to fulfilling these desires is their friendships with other women. Women's friendships are both a powerful coping mechanism and a unique expression of special energies that are not adapted to the dominant culture.

EXPERIENTIAL PATTERNS OF FRIENDSHIP

The patterns in women's experiences of friendship point to the meaning and value of friendship in their lives. Women distinguish between types of friendship according to both the depth and content of the relationship, thereby indicating that each form of friendship has a specific function.

In obligatory, impersonal, and family friendships, the function is primarily social. These three types of friendship exist in conjunction with a woman's role requirements and are directly related to what is expected of her as wife, mother, daughter, and sister. Two other kinds of friendship—simple (*aplo*) and truest (*eilikrini*)—contain elements of personal choice and equality not present in the other three types or in any other area—besides relationships with lovers—of a woman's life.

With childhood friends, girls for the first time have a relationship that is not prescribed by their role and which they feel is solely theirs. These friendships are often empowering experiences, and many girls receive "comfort and courage" from them. Because I was studying women's friendships, I have little data on children's friendships except what I learned through adult recollections. However, I did arrange for twelve children to write essays on "My Best Friend." The exceptional feature of the essays is that each child wrote that the reason for choosing a particular friend was that she, he, or it (in some cases the "friend" was a book, an animal, or the school) did not tell the child's secrets to others. When I showed these essays to one of my key informants, she laughed and said that the essays had not been written by the children but had been dictated by their mothers to keep the children from revealing the names of their friends to me and, consequently, to prevent my gaining access to information about particular families through their children's friends. Regardless of the authors' identities, the content of the essays and my informant's analysis foreshadowed my discovering how potent was the force of secrets in women's friendships.

When village girls complete primary school, they lose many of their friendships. More than half the girls in the village do not go on to gymnasium; therefore, they lose a daily opportunity to see the friends they made in primary school. Unlike young boys, who are encouraged to get out of the house and not be underfoot, young girls are not allowed to roam freely through the village. This pattern significantly curtails young girls' access to friends and, more important, to relatively neutral places in which friendships may grow.

Nevertheless, many childhood friendships remain intact and those which survive often become an important part of the early adolescent period which some women remember as the highlight of their lives. The issue of marriage and relationships with men begins to penetrate the friendships of young women in their mid to late teen-age years. With assistance from local gossipers, women friends may be pitted against each other for the same future husband, and many friendships do not survive the apparent contest.

When women do marry, they often leave their village of origin—a turning point in their lives which, due to geographical immobility and illiteracy, makes their friendships difficult, if not impossible, to maintain. Friendship is rare in adulthood, and many women do not have friends. These women explain that other women are untrustworthy, jealous, materialistic, and gossipy. They believe that to risk self-disclosure would be naive at best and, at worst, would ensure a threat to their own privacy. However, even when women do choose to entrust each other with friendship, they often have difficulty forming and maintaining these relationships because of incessant physical and psychological demands from family and husbands.

Despite all these obstacles, women can and do have friends, and some friendships not only survive but thrive from early childhood until death. Before women initiate friendships in adulthood, they carefully evaluate their future friends based on psychological factors, including integrity, emotional attraction, and trustworthiness; features in common, including age, marital status, and personality; and suitability for friendship ("For instance, I see if she can take a joke, something like that").

Women also consider the practicalities involved in carrying on a future friendship, for example, the proximity of a potential friend's house and whether it is in the same neighborhood. It is not considered correct social behavior to be outside one's neighborhood for a purpose not recognized by mainstream culture, and visiting a woman friend is not supported by the dominant culture. This proscription means that visiting often must occur in relative secrecy, either in someone's kitchen while men are in the fields or at places like the village springs while women are performing laundry tasks. Moreover, unlike men, who have the social institution of the *kafeneion*, women have no place or time specifically designated for social intercourse and relaxation. Even while gathered under shade trees in the late afternoon to rest before beginning their evening chores, most women and young girls are sewing handwork to be included in someone's dowry or to be sold in Chania.

In addition to location, women also closely examine the status, character, and reputation of their potential friends. Some women are not considered for friendship; these women are most often identified as gossips and troublemakers. Forming friendships with them would threaten women's *philotimo*, and therefore they are avoided.

Once a friendship is begun, the relationship is seen as adding a positive dimension to a woman's life, making it happier and more interesting. The course of friendship, regardless of whether it stays the same or grows, is regarded as a similarly positive experience. The reason, say the women, is because of their deliberate cultivation of the relationship—keeping secrets, trusting, understanding, and being good to each other. Many women explained to me that in their everyday lives they experience incongruency between how they feel and how they must behave in order to conform to social norms. The quality of their lives improves, however, when they have a friend, and they value the unique feelings they experience when they are with their friend, for example, the feeling of being understood and of being able to speak openly and tell their secrets and problems to someone else. Being able to express themselves openly with a friend enables them to experience emotional and behavioral congruency, an experience they claim is rare in their everyday lives.

Women spoke of the transformative quality of friendship—being with a friend changes a mundane task such as baking into one of pleasure and intimacy. After confiding in a friend, women often feel their worries lessen. In addition, their identity is affirmed and they may feel understood, believed in, comforted. For some women, friendship is empowering; they feel stronger and more self-reliant when they have a friendship. These feelings are intensified by the pride they take in having such a relationship.

Some women have a friend whom they call their best friend (*kaliteri mou fili*). This relationship usually transcends the various stages of the life cycle, often lasting at least twelve years, and, on the average, more than twenty-two years. It probably began either before or after the woman's childbearing and early child rearing years, reflecting her relative lack of time for friendship during those years. Best friendships tend to be an intense, loving relationship, the central feature of which is sharing.

> My life with her was always beautiful. We were together every day. My husband used to say that he wanted us to quarrel just once, because we never had, but we never did. She comforted me, because I had so many children and so much trouble with them. I needed comforting, and she was a great comfort to me. We were completely open, we never kept anything from each other, and we didn't gossip: neither about what we told each other nor about other people.
>
> We did everything together. We went to church together, we weaved together, we crocheted together, we ate together, we went to see each other when we were ill. Once, when I was ill and in bed,

and she had cancer, she came up the hill to my house, slowly, slowly, stopping every few meters to rest on the road, and she came and prepared our food. Another time when I was ill we had guests staying with us and she came and cooked the food and served them.

A woman's relationship with her best friend is in many ways unlike her relationships with men, in which, although she engages in parallel role support and fulfillment, she infrequently (if ever) genuinely shares personal information, tasks, time, or space. In addition, best friendships tend to have significantly more psychological depth than many of women's other interpersonal bonds.

My marriage is a simple relationship. We worked together, had children together—he was always helpful and willing to help me with them—but we are not alike. We don't have similar personalities. I am not close to him like I am to my friend.

Unlike many of their relationships with others, women's friendships provide an environment in which they can feel secure about sharing their real selves and telling their secrets and other personal information. Unlike their marital relationship, in which the partners are largely isolated in separate spheres of activity for the accomplishment of family tasks, friendships are based primarily upon the expression of the participant's personal feelings and secrets.

Many women reported feeling obliged to be with their husbands, children, and mothers and often did not wish to spend their free time with relatives except on special occasions, such as holidays. With the exception of two women (with whom I had developed a high level of trust) who said that they would choose to spend their free time with a lover, most women said they would rather be with their friends.

When asked to compare friendship to kinship, only one quarter of the women remarked that they are closer to a family member (usually a woman in a maternal role) than they are to a friend. The remainder of the women felt that true friendship is possible only with nonrelatives—people with whom issues concerning possessions do not arise.

There are problems among relatives dealing with possessions— "My sister got more fields than I did, my brother got a better house"—those kinds of things. You don't have those kinds of problems in friendships, because if you do, it ends the friendship.

Many women said that their relationships with their husband and their friendships are not comparable. Others insisted that while the two bonds may not be comparable, they are similarly strong. Yet others felt that during specific periods of their lives their friendships were the stronger of the two relationships. Whatever the relative strengths of their marriage and friendships, women tend not to disclose certain kinds of information to their husbands. This information usually consists of secrets (*ta mistika*) which reveal either vulnerable aspects of the women that they do not feel comfortable sharing with husbands, children, or relatives or material that is outside the norm of social acceptance. In some women's lives, a friend is the only person with whom they have shared such information. Anna, aged forty-two, explained that "friendship is for personal things," implying that women's other relationships are not. I asked women to tell me what they tell friends that they do not tell husbands.

> That I am going to buy something for me that I don't want my husband or children to know about.

> That my husband hurt my feelings.

> Something about the children that I can't tell their father.

> Something that happened with my family, with my brother or with my in-laws.

> If I have a lover, I will tell her about that.

> Something that someone said that hurt me.

The content of the personal material women share with friends changes over time, but the measure of the relationship (keeping this information secret) remains constant throughout the duration of the friendship. Indeed, a friendship usually ends when its vitality diminishes, or when one or both women are irrevocably displeased with the other's behavior. The majority of the latter instances occur because one friend betrays the other by not keeping her secrets. Friendships that terminate due to internal disruptions are called broken (*spazmeni*) or spoiled (*halazmeni*) friendships.

Because she has enough information to threaten a woman's position in village society, a friend often becomes a powerful figure in a woman's life.

> We are no longer friends. She gossiped—told some things about my husband, who was then my fiancé, which, had I said them, would at least have been her gossiping the truth. That would have been bad enough. But she told some things that I never said. It caused a very big problem, and both my husband and I quarreled with her. Now when I am in her presence I have a broken spirit.

Despite the risk that confiding in a friend poses, many women invest considerable time and energy in various types of friendship. These relationships offer psychological renewal primarily through sharing—sharing tasks, secrets, time, recreation, and gifts, as well as behavior that is sometimes outside the social norm in the dominant culture.

Besides the emotional reinforcement she receives from friendship, a woman can benefit from its various social and functional aspects. Women friends are people (along with one's mother) to whom, for example, a woman can turn for assistance with child care and loans of money or other items that are difficult to obtain.

> The community needs friendship. Of course it does. We can borrow things from each other, the women can, and get things from each other that we don't have.
>
> Like Danae has basil, and she gives it to us. She doesn't say, "No, you can't have any basil." It works like that.

The value women place on friendship varies. Some see it as merely adding spice to their lives while others attach to it a richer, deeper meaning that they describe as "a personal necessity." At this level, the need is not simply for someone to perform the functions of friendship but for psychological intimacy with a trustworthy person. Women told me that one needs such a friend to have

> comfort from. I can go astray; my friend can straighten me out.

> someone to whom you can turn your back and know you won't be talked about when you leave.

> someone to trust—a *friend*—not someone to be with all day long and not do your work and sit and gossip with, . . . but someone you can be with when you have some free time; you need someone to talk to.

> someone to talk to. You can just burst if you keep all your bad feelings inside yourself, you will go insane; you will die. You *have* to have a friend. How else can you get rid of your anxiety?

Most women who do not have a friend experience that as a lack in their lives, attributed to the difficulty of finding a woman whom they feel can be trusted with their secrets. Women who do have a friend specify the relationship as one, if not the only, experiential space where they suspend fear of judgment, exposure, or betrayal to the community through gossip. Friendship seems to be one of the few relationships from which women can expect nonpossessive warmth and understanding. However, within the relatively limited arenas that women occupy in Greek society, true (eilikrini) friendship is a narrow realm in the whole spectrum of their lives. Indeed, some women have eschewed the relationship, dismissing it as unimportant, impossible, or even a social liability.

> Look. Maybe this will explain it to you. Once my husband and I went to a name day party. Many ladies came. To one of them, they all said, "Hello, my golden girl," things like that.
> And the minute she left, they said, "Damn her!"
> In front of them, she was a friend. But when she left? So that is why a person—a sensible person, of course, because there are people who don't think things through, they just act—a sensible person gets closer to herself than she does to anyone else.
> She closes herself up inside and says, "I don't trust anyone else."

For women who do experience true friendship, it is a rare and intense relationship. The rich and profound world women friends share is in sharp contrast to the bleak emotional landscape of the rest of their lives; indeed, the strength of this relationship is evidence of women's striving to transcend, through friendship, the limitations imposed on them by their society's attitudes toward women.

> We can be as we truly feel together, having our outside like our inside. Truth and trust. She lets me know she genuinely cares for me and is not just pretending to be concerned. And if I am upset, I can tell her about it. I don't have to pretend that something doesn't bother me.

As an experience, the phenomenon of friendship is structured along a continuum of sharing/not sharing. Keeping the secrets that are shared outside of role obligations becomes the act of preserving the sanctity of a shared existential space. Friendship becomes a rare oasis in a world of volatile and hostile social interactions. Betraying a friend's trust, telling her secrets to another, becomes an act of psychological exposure which, depending upon what information is divulged to whom, has the potential to destroy a woman's social well-being. Yet, despite the power aspects of the relationship and the crucial importance of keeping secrets, many women do not experience friendship as a form of mutual tyranny but as a matter of overwhelming necessity. Not surprisingly, trustworthiness is more highly valued and more frequently mentioned as a characteristic of an ideal friend than love is. Love, according to women in Hatzi, may grow from trust, but trust is not necessarily a by-product of love. Thus, women distinguish between people they love but do not trust and those they trust and therefore love.

Although women were able to describe what they consider an ideal friendship, their own friendships are not usually valued for how closely they approximate the ideal. Unlike other relationships, which are formed and maintained in relation to a third societal element—the village's interpretation of successful role requirements—the value of friendship is derived from the relationship itself. Friendship is cherished for its intrinsic qualities, not for the secondary rewards inherent in societal recognition and approval. Moreover, unlike their other relationships, in which women are without power, friendship is psychologically empowering for women because it allows them choice, as well as the experience of being supported, recognized, and valued as the people they feel themselves to be. Friendship subjectifies, rather than objectifies, its participants, and through its subjectification contributes to the expression of women's psychological integrity. Although their relationships with men are often manipulative, collusive, and hostile, woman receive through their friendships the nurturing and support from others that are demanded from them in their roles as wife and mother.

Women friends are able to be authentic, that is, emotionally and behaviorally congruent in each other's presence. The desire to break role, which surges like a subterranean force through the rest of their lives, is suspended momentarily. Rather than having to suppress these urges, women find that, in friendship, this aspect of themselves is welcomed in an atmosphere of warmth and empathy. In this environment, women are able to laugh and talk freely and to express their opinions and their identity in a self- rather than an other-defined manner—all of which they feel they are socially prohibited from doing in most adult interpersonal relationships.

While the relationship is primarily personal, friendship also penetrates the social realm. Women turn to their friends as loyal and reliable role stand-ins. Since women's position relative to men requires that only women perform certain tasks, friends are valued substitutes when women, at various times, are unable to fulfill their roles because of illness or absence.

The nature of women's participation in friendship tends to perpetuate dichotomized sexual and psychological needs in the village. While we might expect that women's emotional ties to their friends and sexual relationships with their husbands and other men would generalize to sexually active relationships with women and/or emotional relationships with men, neither adult female homosexuality nor hetero-emotionality were, as far as I could determine, evident. However, women's descriptions of their friendships—including the initiation, course, and content of the relationship—contain elements of courtship; some friendships seem like a second or shadow marriage. But unlike their marriage, which, regardless of whether it proceeded from amorousness or a matchmaker, seems to have been experienced as a shock, women's friendships have an air of continuity, familiarity, and ease. Indeed, the fact that the friendships of those women who have achieved maximum societal rewards and benefits (including the appearance of a successful marital relationship) cannot be significantly distinguished from those of women with fewer rewards and benefits indicates that friendship is not a substitute for marriage.

CONCLUSION

This research has demonstrated that, contrary to the view often presented in traditional research, friendship is not a primarily adult male phenomenon; neither are women's friendships relatively weak ties compared with the ties of kinship. Women's friendships exist, and they are strong, emotionally rich relationships. The fact that women can have best friends who are central figures in their lives calls into question the characterization of such friendships as tenuous, unpredictable, and brittle.

This study's findings on the extent to which friendships are embedded in a lived context supplement M. H. Fried's (1953) study, in which he found that a true picture of friendship cannot be drawn separately from the society in which it exists. The perspective of this study extends beyond Fried's, however, because it takes into account women's position as part of a subgroup within the dominant culture to which they belong. Consequently, their friendships simultaneously articulate women's own cultural perspective and reflect the surrounding world's views of women.

In certain respects, this study differs in its conclusions from Y. A. Cohen's (1961) assumption that friendship in any given society is a microcosm of the total social structure; I found that the content of women's friendships is distinctly different from that of the social relations in the dominant culture of Greek society. While the social climate in Hatzi is rife with distrust, hostility, and paranoia, women's friendships are characterized by trust, empathy, and revelation of personal material.

Absent from previous research on friendship are this study's findings on the paradoxical relationship between power and friendship in women's lives. A woman holds tremendous power over her friend in the village because of the secrets that are shared between them, and yet the relationship is based upon confidentiality and lateral rather than hier-archical exchange of power. These findings suggest that previous con-ceptualizations of friendship may be flawed, because the social science literature has not identified or dealt with women's position as a domi-nated subgroup in most countries. Secrets must be kept among women in this subgroup, because they contain material that is unintegrated into the dominant culture.

Much of the previous research on Greek society has portrayed women in Greece as people who are ruled by their passions, and who live flat, predictable lives riddled with negative feminine stereotypes. In contrast to the observations of many of these researchers, this study portrays Greek women as sensitive, psychologically sophisticated in-dividuals who have a highly developed awareness of their emotions and their positions in society, and who seek to improve the quality of their lives through cultivation of friendships with other women.

Since I have focused on the friendship experience of women in a small island village, it is difficult to generalize the findings, and any cross-cultural implications are purely speculative. However, it is clear that these women need and have supportive friendships despite the fact that these relationships are rare and that the emotions supporting them are often suppressed in everyday life.

The content of women's friendships in this village and the meaning of these relationships in their everyday lives suggest that women have a need to maintain and express a sense of psychological integrity. This need transcends a cultural context of physical deprivation, strict role requirements, and emotional alienation. It is a need which Greek women, as actors in a repressive culture, actively seek to fulfill through their friendships.

NOTES TO CHAPTER SIX

1. Carlson (1972) has documented how these trends have contributed to an im-balanced understanding of personality. The distortion of the primary tools for psychological studies has penetrated research on friendship. See, for ex-ample, Aronson (1966), Kelly (1967), Loether (1960), and Marsden (1966).
2. See Fried (1953), Cohen (1961), Paine (1969), and Allan (1979).
3. See Parsons (1915), West (1945), Babchuck (1963), Tiger (1969), and Gil-more (1975).
4. Brain (1976:46) points out that the ethnographic treatment of women's friendships indicates the extent to which men's negative attitudes toward women have seeped into studies of women's friendships. "Friendship," he

says, "has become another act/feeling which men value and which they project women as incapable of."

Tiger (1969) illustrates this attitude by his hyperbolic assumption that women are not genetically programmed to form friendship bonds. Human male friendships are a correlate of the worldwide political power structure, according to Tiger (1974:43), and they "represent the expression of a core pattern of the human biogram . . . essential for the maintenance and survival of human communities." Women's exclusion from formal political structures all over the world is evidence to Tiger that women do not have powerful heterosocial or homosocial relationships because they do not have access to the "central hierarchy" of male political power (Tiger 1974:45).

Du Bois (1974) notes that in the anthropological literature all types of friendships—particularly relationships between best friends—are consistently found to be both empirically and normatively more significant for men than for women. She attributes this traditional perspective to the difference in men and women, to men's greater social mobility, and to their subsequently greater opportunity to form preferential and voluntary friendships.

5. *Philotimo*, literally "love of honor," is a concept that does not translate easily into English. This is unfortunate, because it is impossible to comprehend the Greek personality without understanding what Greeks consider a core concept in their culture. A *philotimos* person cares deeply about maintaining the *appearance* of honor and lives in a manner that is likely to promote the appearance of honor in every arena of life. Philotimo is not to be confused with the American notion of honesty, since cognitive dissonance may result from the need to lie in order to maintain the appearance of honor. The concept of philotimo also is not the Greek equivalent of *machismo*, yet while it applies equally to men and women, the manifestations of what is required to be *philotimos* (masc.) or *philotimi* (fem.) vary according to gender.

SEVEN

Women—Images of Their Nature and Destiny in Rural Greece

JULIET DU BOULAY

THERE is an apparent paradox in the position of women in Greek villages. This paradox lies in the unequivocal association of women both with symbolic, moral, and physical weakness, and with the role of spiritual guardian of husband, house, and family. The logic underlying these apparently opposed classifications depends, it is argued here, on a single religious vision that sees women in two aspects—as by nature fallen but by destiny redeemed—and that places marriage as the essential means of passage from this nature to this destiny.

The first picture of women, according to which they are essentially weak and thus in all respects subordinate and inferior to men, is well known; for this reason, as well as for lack of space, I present it below in an abbreviated form, as it is typified in axioms that were in common usage by both sexes in Ambeli, the mountain village in the northern part of the island of Euboea from which this material is drawn.[1] "Men are somehow superior. That's why they're men." "Men are other, ordained by God." "Men are intelligent but women are gossips."[2] Men are said to sit on the woman's "right-hand side"—the symbolic position of Christ in relation to man—while women, on the left, are "from the devil."[3] Man in his work is said "to have a blessing," but "the woman with the distaff is cursed."[4] Men are reliable (statheri), while women are credulous (evkolopistes) and fearful (foveristries); men are pure (kathari) in relation to women who are periodically polluted by menstrual blood and by the blood of childbirth; man is Adam, but woman is Eve; men carry responsibility (varytita), but women are "the weak link" (adynato meros), the point at which society is most dangerously vulnerable, the potential destroyer of the family—hence the saying, "Houses, mansions, and cottages with tiny windows are lost by means of women."[5] These descriptions are unambiguous, and they are neatly exemplified in a conversation I had with one villager.

"Men are superior. It's from the first myth, God cursed Eve, that she should be subordinate (*ypo*)."

"Subordinate in what things?"

"Subordinate in all things. Eve was cursed."

This particular logic results in a distinction between the two sexes which may be crudely rendered as follows:

WOMAN	MAN
Eve	Adam
inferior	superior
impure	pure
left-hand side	right-hand side
closer to the devil	closer to God
stupid	intelligent
credulous	strong-minded
fearful	cool-headed, brave
unreliable	reliable
weak	strong
irresponsible	responsible

It is a classification based on a system of complementary opposition, and the relationship it generates is centered on the figures of Adam and Eve and on the understanding of male strength and feminine weakness.

The myth of the Fall of Man will be the subject of a later section, but we can anticipate it here by stating, briefly, that, in village thinking, the sin of Adam and Eve was an act of disobedience that manifested itself as the advent of sensuality and sexuality in the world, and that for this sin Eve is held, in effect, to be primarily responsible. Thus it is not only the physical weakness of women which, in the face of male strength, makes them, literally, the "weak link"; women also are thought to be morally weak, easily deceived, incapable of sustained and intelligent resistance to the advances of men, and, therefore, potentially the root of all evil. It follows that women, when unaided by men, are in a double sense thought to be unable to protect and control themselves—an understanding of women as essentially vulnerable in respect to both their sexuality and their physical strength, which leads inevitably to the conclusion that all women should at all times be subordinated to male authority. Thus a woman in this traditional society can never be her own mistress. Before she marries, she is under the control of her father and her brothers; when she marries, this control is transferred to her husband and his family. Within the family group, women are strictly answerable to and under the control of their men, while in the wider society the behavior of women is, allowing for the changed context of the competitive public world, conditioned by the same cultural attitudes. Indeed, in earlier times, I was told, the women were so modest that they would step off the road if they saw a man coming and avert their heads until he had passed by.

This picture of women in traditional Greek society, familiar as it is, is not the only one that can be drawn, however, for there exists also a contrary set of attitudes that appears at first sight to be in substantial opposition to it. According to these attitudes, woman is typically described as being "in the house" (*mesa sto spiti*)[6]—a definition that has given rise to the following universal sayings: "It is the woman who holds the house together" (*i gynaika synkratei to spiti*) and "Without the woman the house cannot exist" (*choris ti gynaika to spiti den yinetai*). I also heard the following comments, which are derived from the same set of attitudes. "Woman is a second God" (*devteros Theos*); "The woman can become like the Mother of God" (*isa me ti Panayia*); and "The woman is the Mother of God in the church. The woman is the Mother of God, she is the church" (*i gynaika einai Panayia mesa stin ekklisia. I gynaika einai Panayia, einai ekklisia*).

This idea of the woman being vital to the house seems at first to be somewhat at variance with the idea of woman as destroyer of the house through her openness to temptation and her proneness to sin; and the paradox is heightened when it is remembered that the house, in rural Greece, carries a connotation that goes far beyond the normal definition of the place or the home where the family gathers, for the word for "house," *spiti*, is synonymous with the family itself. The Greek word for family, *oikoyeneia*, is a compound of *oikos*, the *katharevousa* for "house," and *yeneia*, "offspring"—the family, then, is defined as "the people who originate from the same house." There is thus an identification between the woman, the house, and the family—an identification that is striking when it is pointed out that the family is the fundamental unit of the community, which, in this society, means that it is the main solidary group not merely in terms of its economic and material life, but in terms also of all those religious and symbolic values on which it is based.

In its material life, the uniqueness of the institution of the family lies in the fact that it is this group only that defines all the villagers' categorical rights and obligations, that commands their total loyalty, and that gives them unconditional support, and it is only identification with this group that enables them to fulfill their own individuality and realize their true potential. The family thus provides villagers with the unique arena within which they can without conflict of loyalty express

1. Woman can become like the Mother of God.

their true identity, in an environment of love, trust, and unremitting service to the principles embodied in it.

The house, however, is not only the basis of material and social existence for the villager, for, as I have tried to show in greater detail elsewhere,[7] before even it is these things, it is an image of heaven on earth, re-creating within the human order the harmony of the divine archetype on which it is based. The preservation of the life of the house, and of the family within it, is a creative act that is carried out not merely in response to the immediate material exigencies of the natural environment and the agricultural cycle, but also in response to the sacred world, according to which there are ordained periods of feast and periods of fast, times to rest and times to work, saints' days and penitential periods—an interlocking pattern of work and prayer and festival. The house, the pivot of these activities, is thus both sanctuary and cornucopia, the point at which the beneficence of God and the fruits of the earth meet and are manifested within the material world. And in the values of hospitality to the stranger and the mourning rituals performed for the forefathers, the gift of life and of food is mediated to the communities of both the living and the dead.

Within the house each member of the family has his or her part to play as a son or daughter, husband, wife, or grandparent. But the phrase characterizing woman as being "in the house" calls to mind the particular centrality of the woman to this human and divine drama that is lived out within its walls. It is the woman who bears and nurtures the children, while, as it is said, "the man is a guest in the house" (o andras einai mousafiris mesa sto spiti); it is she who is responsible for preparing the food and for carrying the water, and thus is associated with the two interdependent sources of life; it is the woman "in the house" who "remembers" (thymatai) the dead, bringing to them the consolation of the memorial food and the forgiveness of the community; it is she on whom devolve the numerous ritual activities connected with the various saints' days—an aspect of feminine endeavor which, when I questioned it, was affirmed for me in these words: "The man goes out with an axe, he cuts wood or he ploughs a field, but the woman in the house must keep the saint's day"; and it is the woman who bears the responsibility for the many fasts, as indicated in this common saying: "Fridays protect your children, and Wednesdays your husband" (Paraskeves fyla ta paidia, kai Tetartes ton andra). To connect the woman with the house, then, is to connect her with the mysteries of birth and of death, with the salvation of the dead and the spiritual protection of the living, with hospitality to the stranger, and with the continued relationship of the house to the sacred world on which all life depends.

It has become apparent that, in the context of the house, women are attributed with qualities that conflict sharply with those attributed to them as inferior beings. Women are the "weak link," but they are also "in the house"; women "destroy houses," but "women keep the house together"; women are said to be "from the devil" and "cursed," but they, specifically, "must keep the saint's day" and are the ritual guardians of husband and children; women are said to be "Eves," but they are also said to be "similar to the Mother of God." And indeed the contradiction does not end with these statements, for while the original classification of women as in all things inferior would lead us to expect them to be servile, downtrodden, and without spirit, the undoubted and often heroic stature of the women of the Greek villages appears to reinforce dramatically the apparent hiatus between this classification and many of the observed realities.

This apparent contradiction between the two views of woman can be approached in a number of ways. First, it is possible to attribute the more favorable classification of women to the existence of a feminine "subculture," by means of which the women of the society attempt to subvert the accepted order and to establish, to some degree, their equality with and their independence of men. Second, it is possible to postulate the existence of a "false consciousness" on the part of women, who see themselves as being exploited at the same time as they assent to the ideology of male domination which makes the exploitation possible. Third, it is possible to say that while the accepted cultural evaluation of women is that they are inferior, on the "left"-hand side of men, and from the devil, nevertheless the realities of daily life in rural Greece make clear that in practice they have a great deal of power and influence. The "appearance" of lack of prestige is contrasted with the "reality" of power; the contradiction remains, but it is explained by feminine manipulation of relationships in the house and the exercise of power in decision making that is granted through ownership of land.[8] In the following argument each of these approaches is considered in turn; however, the conclusion ultimately reached is that the classification of women as "supporting the house" and as "equal with the Mother of God" is indivisible from the classification of them as "destroyers of houses" and as "Eves." The one aspect does not contrast in any fundamental sense with the other; that is, they do not constitute two different world views or an "appearance" and "reality" that are logically opposed. Rather, it is suggested that they are two different aspects of a concept of feminine nature that is rooted ultimately in a religious vision of humanity, a vision that sees the role of women in terms of two allied but ultimately very different ideas—those of feminine nature and feminine potentiality. Thus, a reconciliation is achieved, not by the competition, however subtle, of women with men in the sphere of power and economics, but by a process in which they complement in a totally different sphere of activity the more active and dynamic role of men, and achieve an honorable and respected place as the central element of the house and family, not by denying but by transcending their ascribed inferiority.

THE HYPOTHESIS OF A FEMININE SUBCULTURE

I do not want, at this point, to become involved in the conceptual difficulties surrounding the term *subculture*, and therefore I would like to make it clear that my use of the term here is purely pragmatic, as a way of referring to a certain range of important questions about allegiance to the values of the culture as a whole. Thus in the following pages the word *subculture* means simply a body of opinion held by a group of people within society which in some degree contradicts a value held by society as a whole; and I accordingly examine the acknowledgment of male superiority by society as a whole in the light of four questions, any one of which, if answered in the affirmative, would throw a fresh light on the nature of beliefs about the sexes: (1) Are women as a group in a position to speak with a common voice on subjects about which their opinions might be contrary to those held by the men? (2) Are beliefs supporting the point of view favorable to women denied by men? (3) Are beliefs supporting the point of view unfavorable to women denied by women? (4) Are beliefs unfavorable to men affirmed by women?

Do Beliefs about Female Nature Differ between Men and Women?

With regard to the first question—whether women at any time speak with a single voice and in contradiction to the male ethos—it is clear that two important structural features militate against any division of society occurring along purely sexual lines. The indivisible nature of the family is one of these, and the custom of virilocal marriage is the other, for both set up considerable barriers to the development of any crosscutting affiliation between women as members of a common sex, no matter what their common interest.

To take the structure of the family first: It is a corollary of the exclusive loyalty that is contained within each house that the society at large is severely fragmented, for the solidarity of the individual family involves its members in behavior toward the outside community that is the reverse of the behavior that is the norm within it, and imposes on them the obligation to defend the family at the expense of others, even at the expense of their loyalty to their own kin. The instability caused by tensions generated in this way is evident at various levels in the society, even at that of first cousins. In such cases, because first cousins are said to be "like brothers," the relationship may be very close, yet equally well there may be bitter animosity because, although like brothers, cousins are in fact not brothers and are thus outside the circle of each other's primary loyalty. As kinship weakens, the imbalance between expectation and obligation ceases to be so important, but there then arises the situation in which attitudes of open competition are accepted as the norm.

Relations among the families of the community are thus conditioned by a social situation in which everyone's interest centers primarily on his or her own family, and in which only the strongest ties of mutual interest are able to overcome the natural tendencies to isolation and self-preservation. This does not mean that unrelated families are always fighting and quarreling; unrelated girls frequently go together, for instance, to clean out one of the chapels in the country before a saint's day or to collect wild greens, and unrelated women form little groups to go together to the local market town, while in the cafés the men gather amicably enough. But it does mean that every family recognizes that in any given situation the other families of the community may become a threat to its reputation or to its livelihood, and their relationships with each other are conditioned accordingly.

In the house, then, the family gathers in a mutual affection and trust which is in many respects the antithesis of its external relations, and is reflected in the saying. "You can't trust anyone outside your own house" (*den yparchei embistosini exo apo to spiti*). Thus the family, or the house, is the villager's sole unequivocal refuge, accommodating different generations and sexes impartially and demanding and receiving the total loyalty of each. For women to band against men in any significant way would therefore be an act of betrayal to the group from which they draw their very existence, and would contradict precisely that attribute of being central to the house which has been noted as an essential part of the complex of ideas that assigns women their greatest value.

In addition, though, to this fundamental obstacle posed by family loyalties to the formation of cross-community groups—of either sex—in a common cause, an additional feature militates against any decisive combination of women even in the same house. This feature is a consequence of the organization of marriages in Ambeli, for here, as in many mainland villages, marriage used to be virilocal—it being, until very recent times, the custom for any sons to bring their wives into the parental household, to live as a joint family until such time as it was thought that the inheritance should be divided and the various families go to live separately. When this happened, it fell to the lot of one son, usually the youngest, to stay in the familial house with the now aging parents, to look after them, and, after their death, to inherit the house and a significant part of the land and appurtenances of the farm. This situation thus created an obvious fault line between the mother-in-law and the bride (or brides) who came into her house; for while she was happy for her son to marry and to give her grandchildren, and happy also to have a younger woman in her house to work under her direction, she was also aware that the incoming woman would be a threat, both through her ability to take over the affection of her son and in the fact that by her very youth and strength she was in an ultimately victorious position, waiting only for the older woman to die before she would in her turn become the mistress of the house. Thus the mother-in-law, it was said in the village, would be the greatest threat to the young bride, grumbling to her son about his wife when he came home in the evening and in this way very often being instrumental in the wife's "eating" a blow or two. Thus it is true that while the women of the society dislike the aspect of male domination that results in their getting beaten, it is also true that a certain category of women would consistently exploit this particular feature, using the dominant position of their sons to achieve their own ends. It is plain that in this situation the development of a feminine subculture would face considerable difficulties.

With regard to the next two questions—whether there is a significant variation between men's opinion of women and women's opinion of themselves—it becomes immediately clear that there is very little difference between the two. Although more will be said in the next section about this particular complex of masculine and feminine values, a few comments will serve to illustrate that men acknowledge the positive aspects of feminine nature just as women acknowledge the negative ones. The phrase "the woman in the house" is consistently used by men; and an even stronger version of this remark came from one man who, proposing to ask his wife about something, said, "I must ask the house." Again, it was a man who, having been unable to find, in a room of remarkable confusion, any food to serve his guests, exclaimed, when his wife came in and produced bread and wine, olives, clean napkins, and a piece of cheese, "Look! When the woman is here, the house is a garden!" And finally, an astonishingly explicit statement regarding the value of women was once made in my hearing by a boy of fourteen who, pointing to the work of his mother in preserving figs, said that she was "a second God"—a statement that was enlarged upon by the woman's husband, who explained that what the boy meant was that in collecting the figs, boiling them with herbs, and then laying them out in the sun to dry, she had in a sense imitated the act of creation.

On the alternative problem of the women's view of themselves, it is undoubtedly true that women reflect in equal or even greater measure the cultural evaluation of their inferiority. "Worthless women!" (*palaiogynaikes*) and "shitty women" (*skatogynaikes*) are phrases, often heard on the lips of women, that refer to their accepted propensity for shouting and arguing and for stirring up trouble in quarrels and gossip. And it was from women that I heard the following phrases: "Eves! They have long hair and little sense!" (*Eves, echoun makria mallia kai ligi nou*) and "Eves! What are we? Eves!" (*Eves, ti eimaste, Eves*).

There is no denying, then, that the apparently contradictory picture of women described at the beginning of this paper is held in common by both sexes. There are, however, two particular areas in which women feel that the domination of men is excessive, and in which, because the men's behavior is disliked and resented by the women, we might think that some common view might be taken of it which was rejected by the men.

Do Beliefs about Male Nature Differ between Men and Women?

It is in the realms of violence and sex that the subordinate position of women appears to be most seriously exploited by the men; thus it is in these two areas in particular that any resistance on the part of the women, "muted" or otherwise, might be anticipated and beliefs unfavorable to men be found to occur in women's thinking. Nevertheless, in spite of this, there appears to be little evidence to suggest that the accepted watershed between reasonable and unreasonable behavior in these areas is different for women than it is for society as a whole.

It is clear that, especially in earlier times, it was very common for men to use force as a means of correcting their wives. "Men have woken up a bit now," I was told, "but in the old days it was bullying and grumbling and blows [*grinia kai maloma kai xylo*] for the least thing." A woman who had allowed the food to burn, who had failed in any of her numerous household tasks, or who had answered back, for example, would receive a blow or two. Any suspicion of immodest behavior would always be punished in this way, and there was a girl in the village during the time of my field work who, it was said, was beaten frequently by her husband because, having had an affair with her before they married, and having thus himself received unequivocal evidence of her unchastity, he could have no faith in her subsequent virtue. Women were to be faithful and obedient to their husbands at all times, and the accepted sanction for any sort of disobedience was the use of force—a philosophy expressed quite clearly by one man who said, in the presence of his wife, "A little beating doesn't matter."

It is important to note, however, that in spite of this customary expression of male domination, there were many checks within the society that militated against the excessive use of force, not least of which was the general understanding that a man was despised if he indulged in it. There was a story of a woman in the 1930s whose reputedly very jealous husband beat her for her immodesty when she rolled back her sleeves one day while rinsing clothes at the spring—and this episode is reported to the present day as an example of an unacceptable degree of savagery in a husband. Similarly, a man who is "ill-rooted" (*kakorizikos*), that is, a man who is thought likely to ill-use his wife to an excessive extent, is greatly feared as a prospective bridegroom, and the disapproval, both of the community and particularly of the kinsmen, is a powerful deterrent to any man wishing to behave in this manner.

Thus regular wife-beating was a matter for shame, but to strike a wife on occasion was not—a counterpoint that is neatly illustrated by the number of men in the present day who say that they are intelligent and know better than to beat their wives; for while this statement reveals the community's disapprobation of excessive ill-use of women, it is also a testimony to the frequency of the phenomenon within the culture.

Women react to this violence in two ways. On the one hand they dislike and resent it—a resentment often expressed in front of men in such statements as, "They pretend to be good and gentle, but after that they beat you." And this attitude also is illustrated in the following riposte made by a fellow guest to the old man who praised his wife for making the house into a garden: "Yes, you men! When you are young you boast about the women you have had, and you say, 'Do I pay any attention to what my wife says?' and you beat your wives, and ignore them. But when you get old you need them, and you speak them fair, and realize that you can't do without them, that it is your wife who gets you your pants to put on." And the old man laughed and did not deny it. On the other hand, accepting that women are protected, to some degree, by the limits on force exerted by popular opinion and, as indicated in the preceding quotation, by the fact that the violence of men abates with age, not only do women as mothers-in-law subscribe to the code that sanctions the use of force against women as brides, but also women in general give consistent expression to a system of ideas that basically justifies such behavior. These ideas hold that man is the superior and the more intelligent partner in a marriage, and because of this he is the head of the household, carrying the weight of responsibility for the entire family on his shoulders. If, as a consequence of this burden, a man is "irritable" (*nevrikos*), it is the woman's business to placate him by running an efficient house, having hot food ready when he comes in tired and hungry, appeasing his ill moods, and calming incipient quarrels both within and outside the house. Thus while a woman who is struck by her husband for failure in any of these particulars would feel angry and resentful, she would not find justification for these feelings in any kind of ethos in the community at large, nor would she, in the case of another woman, subscribe to any such ethos. The answer to this problem is simple—if a woman wants to avoid being beaten, she does not burn the lentils.

In conclusion, one final example of the women's view that men ultimately have the right to use force may be given here. A woman, commenting some years ago on a man who had got drunk at a village festival and, because he had done a certain amount of damage, had been drawn into a lawsuit that was likely to cost his family some money, remarked: "What business had he got to go and beat up a stranger? If he gets drunk, let him come home and beat his wife or his child. They won't take him to court."

In sexual matters, the same patterns, both in male behavior and in the cultural justification of that behavior, are evident. The sexual relationship between men and women is, basically, one in which the strength and the desire of the man is the dominant feature, and in which, as in the matter of outright physical violence, there is an unquestionably exploitative element. Women are taken, so they say, whether they are well or ill, "wanting or not wanting" (*thelontas, de thelontas*), whether they are tired or not, resisting only at the risk of blows; and by the age of about forty, I was told by one woman, many of them have passed the age at which the act of sex gives them any pleasure at all. This woman's comment on her own situation was, "I don't want it at all. . . . Never again." And this exploitative element of the relationship is well illustrated in a particular story that is told in the neighborhood. There was a certain villager who one night went into another man's house and slept with his wife without her realizing who he was, and on leaving, he tripped over a water jug and it broke. Not long after, the husband came in, and his wife said, "Where have you been?" He answered, "In the café." "Weren't you here just now?" "No." "Didn't you trip over the water jug?" "No." Needless to say, this story is told as an example of the limits of shocking behavior and does not reveal any sort of norm. But when I expressed my doubt as to whether it could really have happened, the answer came, "Why shouldn't it be true? Of course it can happen." Further discussion of the matter revealed not, as I had thought at first, that one man is literally indistinguishable from another in the dark, but rather that, worn out by the hard work of the day, people fall into bed and sleep very heavily, and that it is not uncommon for a man to require sex of his wife even when she is fast asleep and incapable of waking up.

Nevertheless, in spite of the obvious element of exploitation in the way women are treated by their men in their sexual relationships, and in spite of the continual pregnancies that result, there is strong cultural pressure on men to give way to and even to nurture their sexual urges, and this pressure is imposed as much by women as by the men themselves. I have seen an older woman, for instance, tease a young boy by handling him and talking about his future sexual prowess. Men are thought to be made in such a way as to be "incapable of restraining themselves" (den boroun na syntirithoun), and it is accepted, so I was told, that if a woman's husband does not "approach" (plisiazei) her for three or four days in a row, she may be sure that he has another woman elsewhere. And while the truth of this statement may have been stretched to accord with the cultural concept of male virility, that in itself is proof of the strength of this value. Finally, if further proof were needed, it lies in the present-day attitude of girls who, although they have so much to lose from this situation, apparently believe that a man who does not attempt to sleep with them within a very few days of their first going out together must be a homosexual.

This sexual latitude accorded to, and demanded by, men is occasionally contrasted with a better male nature that, it is said, was characteristic in earlier times when men used to have no difficulty in keeping chaste during, for instance, the eight days before communion or the nights before the many saints' days and festivals; and even in the present era, a man newly back from Germany was castigated as a "monster" (teras) because he insisted on sleeping with his wife on the eve of the Annunciation, saying to her apparently, "Let the sin be mine." But nevertheless, the charter for male behavior, which is that men must be, basically, free and unconfined, is in startling contrast to the code of "shame" and rigorous self-control that is the lot of the women.

This charter has already been shown to lie in the cultural understand-

ing of male nature—men are like that. But this definition of male character, like the previous definition of men as "irritable" and thus as lia-
ble to beat their wives, is related by a logical sequence of thought to the
original classification of man as "superior" and as corresponding to
Adam as women correspond to Eve. First, as the victim of the seduction
of Eve, man is less involved in the sin of sexuality than is woman, but
also important is the fact that man's superiority is indivisible from his
possessing greater strength, physically as well as morally and spiritu-
ally—a strength so important to the protection and preservation of the
family that a prosperous house is one that is said to have "strength"
(*dynami*). This concept of male strength, which also includes sexual
power, must be allowed free reign if the house is to be kept safe, and the
only limitations on this freedom would be those engendered by the
same values. Thus an affair with another woman that involved the
heart and thus risked the involvement of money and time that should
be spent on the house is deplored, as is an affair carried on within the
neighborhood of the village itself, where not only is the man's wife
present, but also the family of the other woman, with all the attendant
risks which that involves. Otherwise, however, a man's sexual life is his
own business.

It is not then, that women approve of sexual promiscuity in men or
think it "good"; neither is such promiscuity related directly to man's
superiority and counted as one of his virtues. Rather, it is that men,
being "superior" and strong, are the protectors of the house, and as
long as nothing interferes with the well-being of the house, they are
"free" in their sexual activity as in everything else. Thus, men can be
"animals" (*zoa*) sexually, but they are still "superior" to women. And
it is this superiority that explains the cultural prohibition against jealousy in women, for even if a man has another woman, it is, I was told,
only if "the devil progresses" (*prochoraei o daimonas*) that a woman
will grumble and complain. Even in such a case, a man has a right to
peace in his own house; and the same woman who told me that "men
are animals" also said, "They are made that way, to go where they
like."

In spite of the context in which it has been cited, this last quotation
may appear to indicate a devaluation of men of the sort that has earlier
been denied. To say that men are "animals," that is, subhuman, is a far
cry from saying that they are "superior" and "on the right-hand side."
To produce an apparent contradiction is, however, not necessarily to
produce evidence of a radical shift in consciousness within the culture,
for what is needed in such a case is evidence that the contradiction has
been correctly understood—that it concerns the same attribute in the

same context—and this is not the case in the present instance. For here the reasoning concerns two different attributes of man: man may respond freely to his physical urges—to be an "animal" in respect of his physicality—but he is at the same time bound to fulfill the heavy responsibilities for the house placed on him by his spiritual superiority. And it is only when the former invades the latter, when man's animal nature threatens the house rather than protecting it, that this superiority is undermined. In that event, the previous latitude given to man's physicality is withdrawn, the woman is entitled to be jealous, and the man becomes the object of widespread condemnation. In the absence, however, of this eventuality, a man may be an "animal" but at the same time free "to do as he likes."

It appears, then, that while there are certain situations in which women feel themselves to be abused by men, this does not amount to a subculture set up in opposition to the dominant ethos, but rather to an intelligent and realistic reaction to the faults of that ethos. The women dislike being abused, and they understand the more negative aspects of subordination to men. Yet it is no part of their understanding to set up, even in a "muted" form, an order of society radically different from that which already exists or to overturn the essential premise of the authority of men, for, as will be seen later, it is on this orientation that the equilibrium not only of the house and family, but of the whole cosmology, depends.

THE PROBLEM OF FALSE CONSCIOUSNESS

I have described as obviously exploitative the approach to physical violence and to sex that is characteristic of village men, and that is permitted them by the charter of their superiority. This exploitation is obvious in the sense that women in village culture dislike becoming, as on these occasions they may easily become, objects in the eyes of their men; yet at the same time, they assent to the idea of the spiritual superiority of men that these actions justify or excuse. The possibility, therefore, that this assent is based on some demonstrable self-deception is one that needs careful investigation, without, again, involving ourselves too closely in the conceptual difficulties and ramifications of what has been called "false consciousness."

First, however, it is necessary to recognize the context in which these exploitative responses occur and to see them in their due proportion, not endowed with the significance that they would have in our own culture, but understood as part of the deeper realities of a village marriage.

It has been shown that the connection between the original classification of men as superior and the latitude they are given for violence and promiscuity is not direct, but occurs rather as a set of logical steps that interpolate the idea of male responsibility as head of a household. There is thus an important point to be made here regarding the duties imposed on men, in the fulfillment of which they come to merit the loyalty and obedience of their women.

Because of the terms in which women are so often discussed—terms set by the severity of the social code under which they live—observers often form the impression that the men to whom the women are subordinate are their opposites—arrogant, willful, selfish, and unthinking. In the context of a rural Greek village, however, the truth is that, except in the case of a man who is a brute or a wastrel, man, also victim of original sin, whose "toil and sweat" on the land is evidence of an environment set against him by the curse of God, is himself not free from a higher authority and from the necessity of obedience and service. Thus while woman is subordinate to man, man is subordinate to the powers of the natural world and the pressures of economic reality. While woman's character is forged by the demands of the heroic code of self-sacrifice and obedience to man, man's character is tempered by an unremitting and often tyrannous service to the house. Food, shelter, and clothing, not to mention dowries for the daughters and inheritances for the sons, neither are nor were won easily from a harsh and rocky land, and when it is said that the man is the head of the house, it means that he bears, quite literally, with only his two hands to help him, the responsibility for the lives of all within it.[9] The protection that is afforded to a woman by a man may not be manifested in niceties of etiquette, nor yet in certain aspects of the manner in which she is treated, especially when she is young, but it is no less real for that. And the fact that men have a certain latitude in their behavior to women is closely related to the fact that it is only by their obedience to the powers of weather and wilderness, and their successful competition against other men, that the women are given the house and its provisions with which to create the beauty and the order by which they live.

This, then, is the nature of the marriage in which the subordination of women to men must be understood, and in the context of their joint struggle to create a family, and the direct and powerful experiences associated with it, the simplicity of the men's demands for sex and their occasional use of violence is not regarded by women as being of overwhelming significance.

Despite, however, this understanding of the pressures on men, it is nevertheless fair to ask whether the women's acceptance of these attitudes involves them in any kind of double-think. It seems plain that subscription to a code of superiority does not, at any rate, involve women in deliberate self-deception about the faults of their men, because, as has been made clear already, the process of reasoning from a concept of male superiority to male responsibility, with its attendant burdens, means that there is room in village thinking for a considerable degree of realism about men's failings. Thus women may be classified, and may see themselves, as gossips, as the source of quarrels within the community, and as being on the "left"—the inauspicious and more demonic side of creation—and yet it is possible also to hear them say that quarrels really originate from men, and I have even heard them say that it is men who are the "further from God" because they are known to curse the Cross, the Mother of God, the faith, and so on with a blasphemy unknown in the women's vocabulary.

There is thus no attempt to falsify the observed facts of men's behavior. But at the same time, because of the logic within which these facts are observed, adverse comments about men do not constitute a direct challenge to the culture. No one believes that men do not quarrel, or that they do not quarrel fiercely, but their quarrels, because they are men's quarrels and because they involve the economic security of the house, are given a value—by all—that is not accorded women's quarrels, which are more often about the minutiae of reputation and the minor irritations involved in the fact of neighborhood. Moreover, while it is acknowledged that men blaspheme and observe the prohibitions of the faith less punctiliously than the women, it is accepted—again by all—that they behave in this way by virtue of their being men, and that the freedom accorded them as the bearers of responsibility allows for an extravagance of behavior that would be by no means proper for women. Thus, while critical comments about men do not in these cases reflect an attack on the basic values of the social order, women's subscription to a code of subordination to men does not prevent them from exercising a sharp and accurate eye on the follies of those men; for the way in which the nature of men and women is ascribed in this culture relies not only on the observed details of the behavior of either— whether women quarrel more than men, whether they are seen to be more or less pious than men—but also, and fundamentally, on the basic classification according to which their nature is construed and, consequently, their social behavior regulated.

Women, then, are by no means systematically self-deceived about the facts of their men's activities; neither can it be said that their knowledge of these facts is inconsistent with men's ascribed nature. It may seem, however, from what has been said about sexual mores, that men are in certain respects self-deceived about women's responses, especially in regard to the way in which Eve in the origin myth is held responsible for sexuality, and in regard to the way in which all women in the social world are made to show extreme modesty, while, in various metaphors of "burning ovens," and "burning fields," the assumed sexual desire of widows, in particular, is joked about in the brilliant double-entendre of village talk. Men are indeed excessively optimistic about their power of seduction, and thus it must be asked whether the culture permits men systematically to project their fantasies onto women and to hold them responsible for impulses that in fact arise from within themselves.

This is a complex question to which only a brief answer can be given here, but what is significant is that although the overall code of feminine modesty is unequivocal, many of the rules that express this code are to some extent flexible and are interpreted contextually so as to achieve recognition not just of the woman's exterior actions but also of her inner intentions. It is impossible, for instance, for women to avoid falling in with men on the long road to the market town, and it is fully accepted that "company" (*parea*) on the way is enjoyable; in addition, no one suspected of immodesty the girls who in earlier times regularly went to and from the herds by themselves. What is noticed, however, is whether, if a chance meeting with a man occurs in the course of work, a proper deportment is maintained.

As a stranger and an anomaly in the culture, I was perhaps in a particularly good position to notice this concern with intention, and even in the obviously sensitive period before I had fully learned their rules of conduct, and when the villagers were trying to interpret my motives, no man from Ambeli ever attempted to take advantage, for instance, of my walking between the villages in the course of my work. Indeed, it became abundantly clear on many occasions throughout my years in Greece that the honor of the men is in fact closely bound up with the value of not approaching a woman against her will. When things go wrong with strangers—as increasingly they must in a country more and more subjected to tourism—it is not because the men understand themselves to be automatically desired by an unprotected women, but because the woman has not correctly signaled that she does not desire a man, and because men believe that since women are weak, they can gain their cooperation if they are given half a chance. Thus a woman, however virtuous in the terms of her own culture, who sets out deliberately to make herself attractive to men is necessarily, in the terms of rural Greek culture, a "prostitute" (*poutana*).

In this way, the emphasis on Eve as a sexual seductress has to be understood not as a statement that women are necessarily and even unconsciously desirous of sex but simply, as one man explained it, as a statement that women are responsible for arousing men's desire because they are physically made to be desirable—"beautiful" (*omorphes*), as he put it. It follows from this that women, aware of the ways they are apt to be desired, are also responsible for taking steps to protect themselves from such desire; those who show themselves to be reckless of this known factor show themselves to be desirous of the consequences, and it is with these women that the men are optimistic of success. This sequence of thought is perfectly logical, and while someone from another culture might quarrel with this assignation of responsibility, there is at least no element of illusion in it, and the code of behavior that it imposes on women is one in which it is in fact possible for a woman to be seen to be "good" (*kali*).

There is, then, in my opinion, no necessary or systematic self-deception involved in village conceptions of male and female nature. However, the doctrine of a male and a female "nature" itself raises certain problems which should be discussed here. Anthropologists have of course learned to treat with skepticism claims that a particular condition is "natural," and feminists in particular would doubtless wish at this point to raise the familiar objection that the biological facts of sex are compatible with a very wide range of cultural prescriptions in which some of the gender characteristics attributed to men in one culture may become those of women in another. However, the people of Ambeli do not argue that gender characteristics are inherent in the biology of the sexes; they argue from the gender characteristics themselves, with both men and women being understood to possess a "nature" and a "destiny" as a direct inheritance from their society. What I have called "destiny" is an ideal pattern that is prescribed a priori, while what I have called "nature" consists of the observed deviations from this destiny that answer to the pattern of temptation in daily life. The villagers themselves, however, do not use the terms "nature" or "destiny" but embody these concepts in images—on the one hand, of Adam and Eve, and on the other hand, of Christ and the Mother of God. In this way, villagers view Adam and Eve in terms of certain observed behavioral traits of their own men and women, while these traits are themselves defined by their failure to approximate to the prescribed ideal. Thus, in this culture, both the "nature" and the "destiny" of men and women remain interdependent outcomes of a moral presupposition enshrined in the sacred stories that create for them a picture of the meaning and purpose of their lives.

It is, of course, possible to suggest to the Ambeliots a different moral presupposition about the ideal relationship of men and women and to infer from it alternative interpretations of the "natural" man and woman that are figured for them in the story of Adam and Eve. But unless that presupposition is embodied in the Holy Family of Christ and the Mother of God, they would see no reason to recognize the picture it implies as "true" or to conclude on such evidence that their own picture is "false." Therefore, it is on the representation of the Holy Family as a primal value that the "truth" or "falsity" of the Ambeliot consciousness depends.

At this point, however, it ceases to be self-evident that a decision about truth or falsity can be made on the basis of academic standards. The Holy Family itself is indeed, within certain limits, subject to varying cultural interpretations; but the dispute between these interpretations, like the dispute over the allegiance to be accorded the sanctity of the family in the first place, is not a question that holds any meaning for the villagers, and neither is it a matter for purely academic debate, since it belongs properly to the realm of faith, or conviction. One can say only that the villagers' conception of the Holy Family is closely related to their lives, and that the failings, in comparison with that Holy Family, of Adam and Eve, which they recognize in themselves, are realistically understood. Thus there is no sense in which a corporate resistance of women to men is a part of this understanding, because the faults of Adam, expressed in acts of excessive violence and inconsiderate sexual demands, do not justify the disobedience of Eve, whose own weaknesses have cursed her also.

"APPEARANCE" AND "REALITY"

Finally, the paradox with which this paper began—the apparently contradictory sets of characteristics attributed to women—has some parallels with Friedl's (1962 and this volume) problem of "appearance" and "reality": the "appearance" of man's prestige and the relatively low status of women compared with the "reality" of power exercised by the women in the house. Here, however, I point to a different contrast—the fact that while in one context women have a low position, in a different context they have a high one. Their position is low in one respect (the respect in which women are "Eves") and during one chief period of their lives (that during which they are young brides and relatively strange to their husbands, and also most intimately connected with sexuality). However, the corollary to this is that two factors, motherhood and age, act over the years not to modify the severity of the code under which women have to live, but to increase the respect which they are accorded within it.[10] In the old days of the joint family, a new bride only gained a real measure of acceptance on the birth of her first child. Furthermore, because of the close relationship in this culture between sons and mothers, a man who customarily ill-treated his wife would, when his sons grew older and began to form independent judgments, become "ashamed of himself" and, I have been told, moderate his behavior. As a woman grew older, took new brides into her own house, and became a grandmother, she undoubtedly gained in stature, and in the present day, when there are few joint families, it is still the case that, as the woman quoted previously, stated, a man realizes the value of his wife in later life. And it is not a coincidence that this decrease in abuse by the husband and the increase in the stature of the wife correspond with the decrease in the woman's sexual power and the increase in her general responsibilities. The conversion of Eve into the Mother of God is not, it appears, an immediate process, but one which gathers momentum as time goes on; and the respect accorded the woman by her husband and by society is transformed with it.

The related question of women's power is not an easy one to resolve. It is certainly true that a woman increasingly exercises power as she succeeds in embodying the maternal ideal that is open to her, and as she gains both in stature and in the value accorded her by her husband. It is also true that in certain houses in Ambeli the woman is so influential in economic decisions as to "have," as it is said, "the say-so" (*kanei koumando*) or to "undertake" (*aiorizei*) the household and farm management. But in these houses, no single condition specifies this particular arrangement, and it is not a matter, as in the case of Vasilika, of the possession of land.[11]

Many women in the village possessed very small amounts of land which, although giving the owners the important power of legacy, did not bear significantly on the disposition of power in the house. It was unusual, though, for any woman to own large amounts of land unless she had a *sogambros*—a man who married "in" to his wife's house and cultivated her land; and of the three sogambri in the village, all were in fact noted for their harshness to their wives. One man reputedly did not allow his wife to go often to see her own family, and he was certainly extremely autocratic toward her in my presence; in the second case, it was said, the wife did not "dare to speak" (*den koutaei na milisei*); and in the third, the woman, who in addition to her land had a small earned income and had achieved a considerable degree of independence, nonetheless had been very ill-treated when she was younger, and even much later would be struck by her husband, she said, if she grumbled too much. It seems, therefore, that in such cases the wife's possession of property could, far from giving her power, merely increase a man's insecurity and feelings of aggression.

The five households in which the woman was said to be the organizer represented every variation in property ownership, from the poor woman from another village who married with "nothing" to the woman whose father died intestate, and who therefore inherited a lot of property which should, properly, have gone to the sons. These five cases in which the women were known to have a considerable influence were explained by the villagers as being the result simply of a particular combination of characters—a wife who was good at organizing and a husband who was willing to accept this ability in his wife. In these houses, the husband would give in to his wife's safekeeping the money he had acquired during the day and ask for sums back again to cover any expenses he would incur when out of the house; and this was accommodated because it was said not to indicate a reversal of roles but merely to reveal the exercise of a legitimate power granted to the woman by her husband—a grant symbolized by the fact that she in her turn would tell her husband of any expenses she had incurred during the day and seek his approval. In the other, more typical houses, however, it was the husband who kept control over the money, recommending when to buy even the children's clothes and supplementary stores for the house, and in such a house it would be unthinkable for the wife to take money for any purchase she wanted to make without asking her husband first.

It appears, then, that in a culture such as that which prevailed, at least until very recently, in Ambeli, a number of factors, besides their gradual assumption of the maternal ideal, could endow women with a specific dominance in the affairs of the family, but that these factors were fortuitous while the respect for mothers was structural. However, the point should be made that although the increasing respect accorded a woman as she matures is undoubtedly accompanied by an increase in power, the real influence of a woman in this society should not be judged ultimately in terms of power and authority, which are the spheres of the man, but in terms of more subtle values relating to the woman's symbolic position as the matrix of life. No matter what her effective authority in the practical running of the house and farm, it is in this other area in which she is unquestionably central, and in which her influence is most profoundly realized. Thus a man notorious for his autocratic behavior was able to say, after the death of his wife, that she had "taken the key of the house in her pocket" (*pire ti klidi sti tsepi*), by which he meant that after her death he had had to close his house and leave the village for good. And the comment, quoted earlier, of the woman who told me of this could not have been a more eloquent testimonial to the value of woman: "The woman is the Mother of God in the church. The woman is the Mother of God, she is the church."

NATURE AND DESTINY

I have attempted, in the preceding pages, to explicate the nature of the thinking that results in the subordinate position of women in rural Greece. The analysis, however, has largely been concerned with the more negative aspects of the subordination and has not concentrated on the possible fulfillment that women find within it. In this last section, therefore, I attempt to show that the more negative consequences of the symbolism of women in rural Greek culture relate to one aspect only of a total spiritual understanding which is much more complex, and that the undoubted stature of women within the culture is, paradoxically, an inherent consequence of the subordination of their role. The analysis relies on the cultural understanding of feminine nature and feminine destiny, and it argues that women not only do not attempt to overthrow their social role, but also do not feel they have cause to, for it is a role that offers, as a reward for faithful obedience to the authority embodied in men, the fulfillment of being linked ultimately with the greatest feminine archetype of their cosmology—the figure of the Mother of God.

It has already been made clear that it is to the myth of the Fall of Man that the typical temptations of man and woman are fundamentally referred. Every villager knows this myth, and as told by them it is similar to the biblical story, except for certain minor folk alterations or additions. As in the biblical story, Eve is the first to fall, and she is viewed as compounding her sin by seducing her husband. But even though woman bears the main burden of the sin, it is plain that man, also, although having, as has been said, "a blessing," is by no means considered to be uninvolved—merely less involved—in mankind's first sin. Thus while this myth engenders relations between the sexes that are in complementary opposition, it is an opposition that does not involve a basic dichotomy of types, but rather a relative differentiation between the two, according to which man is always "somehow superior" and woman always "on his left-hand side." Man, that is to say, is not altogether good, nor is woman altogether evil, and it is this relativity that provides the opportunity for woman to transcend her nature and achieve a marriage in which, though she is subordinate in power, she is equal with her husband in dignity.

This, then, is the natural woman—Eve—a being not evil but prone to evil, less wicked than weak, prone to temptation and triviality. It is into this archetypical nature that woman is born, able to ruin families and to destroy houses, but destined nevertheless to a life involving the redemption of these original characteristics and the re-creation of her feminine nature to become a figure "similar to the Mother of God."

I have elsewhere attempted to trace in detail the way woman as Eve in her natural classification becomes the wife and mother of her ideal role;[12] briefly summarized, this argument holds that, in spite of all her natural defects, woman is thought to possess one quality, that of shame or prudence (*dropi*), through which she not only controls herself and her passions and desires, but also, crucially, puts herself under the control of a man—father or husband—by whom, supremely, she is protected and redeemed from those elements in her nature that threaten always to betray her. Thus, although according to the law of fallen nature woman is characterized by the defects of that nature, she is, in her perfected nature, a being who has transcended these defects and is associated with a range of qualities quite different from those of her original classification.

It is of course possible that these two categories could be rendered as "nature" and "culture," but by using the terms "nature" and "destiny" I intend to draw attention to the fact that there is a temporal dimension to this cultural status, and that women achieve their ideal goal only through incessant effort and the process of an entire life cycle. Even baby girls, minute Eves, are differentiated from baby boys by their being withheld from the sanctuary at baptism; nevertheless, up to the point of marriage, girls enjoy a certain freedom from some of the requirements of society because, as "virgin girls" (*koritsia*), "they have no responsibilities." It is on marriage, with the awakening of sexuality and the serious engagement with the task of life in the form of setting up a household and having children, that women are faced with the real test—whether to give way to the innate temptations of their nature and re-create, in their own household, the catastrophe once and for all initiated by Eve, or to transcend the inertial pull of this nature, and, accepting a life of self-control and dedication to the family, to image in the house the All Holy Mother of God.

The importance of marriage, then, in this scheme is clear, for while from one point of view it might be assumed that the ideal for a woman would be lifelong chastity, the icon presented by the Mother of God is not only one of virginity, but also one of obedience and motherhood, and the saying, "God wants you to marry and become a housewife" (*o Theos thelei na pandrevteis, kai na yineis noikokyra*) is a consequence of this. However, because at the same time motherhood in the fallen world involves an awakening of sexuality and an involvement in the broad range of feminine temptations that unquestionably link a woman with the sin of Eve, it has also given rise to the apparently contradictory phrase "If you get married you damn yourself" (*pandrevesai, kolazesai*). Thus a woman must marry, but she must bring to her marriage a chastity that reaches far beyond sexual fidelity and involves, without exception, all areas of her behavior. She should not only be faithful in the matter of sex but should also be hard working in the house and on the farm, honorable in her dealings with the community, and scrupulous in her ritual life; for since in all these respects she represents a threat to the house, it is only by exercising continuous care in all these matters that she can prove herself otherwise. Finally, though, it needs to be emphasized that this entire redemptive process rests on the overriding concept of deference to male authority requiring an obedience so unequivocal that, as it was said to me, "If a man says water runs uphill, and the woman says it runs downhill, she spoils the whole undertaking" (*chalaei ti douleia*).

It might be thought that the prospect of such unquestioned obedience to whatever man the future holds would be disagreeable to many village girls; however, because of the essential part played by marriage in this society and because of the other face of male authority that has already been discussed, it is not an exaggeration to state that there is no girl in the society who does not wish "to become a housewife." The very duties that were noted earlier, the serving of a husband, the carrying of water, the preparation of the meals, are, in this context, rights as well as obligations, revealing the dignity of a woman and her subordination at the same time. They are symbolic as well as physical actions, for while the man creates the basis for the house, the woman conserves and nourishes the life within it, and without the woman not only does the physical order of the house fall apart, but the spiritual order also. This idea is dramatically illustrated by the story of a little girl who, many years ago when her mother died, neglected to change her clothes as is customary after a death, with the result that she encountered a Nereid and became crippled for life. "A man doesn't bother about such things," I was told. "Her father didn't say anything or pay any attention; it was for a woman to say 'Don't go out like that.' " In carrying out her role, then, a woman gains much more than mere "satisfaction"; she acquires a knowledge of the meaning of her life and a vital place occupied within the total social and symbolic order.

This point having been made, however, the full significance of the feminine role within marriage cannot properly be demonstrated with-

2. Women should not only be faithful in the matter of sex but should also be hard working in the house and on the farm.

out some explanation of the strength, within the Orthodox mind, of the particular archetype—that of the Mother of God—on which it is founded. The Mother of God is, in Orthodoxy, vital to the salvation of the world through Christ, for the teaching of the Fathers of the Church is that without the perfect obedience and submission of the Mother of God to the Holy Spirit, the birth of God into the world would not have been possible. It is in this way that the Mother of God is the prototype of the Church: the vessel of the spirit becomes the bearer of the divine life—the *Theotokos*, or God-bearer. And although the villagers invariably say that Christ is "first" (*protos*), while the Mother of God is "second" (*devtera*), she is nevertheless seen as the gateway through which God entered into the world and redeemed, in the symbolic figures of Adam and Eve, the whole of humanity. Thus the Mother of God stands in direct opposition to Eve; the woman through whom the world was saved is contrasted with the woman through whom all was lost, and she is related to the human situation by a series of explicit parallels. Just, it is said, as a mother "agonizes" (*agonizetai*) for children, so the Mother of God "feels pain" for us; it was the Mother of God, as an apocryphal story has it, who "has pity" (*lypatai*) on the souls in hell, and on whose account these souls are released for a period after every Easter. "We have the Mother of God as our Mother," I was told by one villager, and by another, "Just as one calls 'Mother' when one is in trouble, so one calls on the Mother of God." She is the first to whom the villagers fly in their prayers, for she is Mother to the saints as well as being the Mother of Christ, and she intercedes with them on man's behalf. Thus it is she who is venerated as the great intercessory figure of Orthodoxy who keeps mankind under her protection and she who is celebrated particularly during the long period of penitence and supplication of Great Lent.

Yet these similarities between woman and the Mother of God extend beyond the concept simply of a common motherhood to include the whole redemptive activity of the woman in the house; and the saying "From woman sin was born and from woman salvation was born" (*apo gynaika eyine amartia, kai apo gynaika eyine sotiria*) (in another version, "From one woman all evil comes, and from one woman all good comes") reveals the full nature of the relationship of woman with her sacred archetype. Thus, while women are sinners through Eve, they "became honorable" (*timithikan*), it is said, through the agency of the Mother of God. The implications of this symbolism are far-reaching, for since the Mother of God is the means through which the Holy Spirit became manifest in the world, it follows that woman, modeling herself on this divine archetype, performs *mutatis mutandis* the same function in her family. And it is in this context that the remark already quoted, "The woman is the Mother of God, she is the church," must be interpreted. For the church in this case is not the church but the Church, not the material institution but the spiritual reality through which the Holy Spirit is revealed, and which becomes as a consequence the Bride of Christ.

It is clear, then, that many parallels are drawn between the Mother of God and the ideal figure of the married woman. The virginity that for a village woman is a prerequisite for an honorable marriage is analogous to the virginity of the Mother of God; the prototypical relationship of a woman with her husband is provided by the total obedience of the Mother of God; the care and protection that a mother lavishes on her children and her husband and the constant ritual acts by which she preserves the integrity of the house and re-creates its relationships with the spiritual world represent the role of the Mother of God as the vessel of the Holy Spirit; in giving birth, and especially in giving birth to sons, a woman reflects the divinely appointed mission of the God-bearer; and in bearing the task of mourning with all the particular weight of grief that is the lot of women in this society, she reflects again the figure of the Mother of God who saw her Son on the Cross, and who grieved over his body on the bier.

It is important to state, however, that this notable analogy between the human and the divine worlds, illustrated so clearly in the figure of the woman, is not confined to her alone, and there is a custom in the village which demonstrates that it is not just the woman but the family as a whole which is drawn into a relationship with a divine paradigm. According to this custom, the women refrain from work on the evenings preceding Wednesdays, Fridays, Sundays, and certain saints' days, saying that "just as the family is eating on earth, so Christ and the Mother of God are eating in heaven," and adding, by way of explanation, that, particularly if they spin or weave, the bits of fluff from their handiwork will get into the bread of this divine meal and ruin it. The true function, then, of the earthly family is to be an icon of the Holy Family in which the husband, the wife and the child, are earthly representatives of Christ the man, Christ the child, and the Mother of God.[13] And it is this which accounts for the continued necessity of the woman, however much she may reflect her divine archetype, to be in all things loyal to the man of the house, for although the association of the man with Christ is not as explicit as the association of woman with the Mother of God, this is not because man has, ultimately, a less great or a less spiritual stature; it is because, rather, as Adam in the world of humanity, he is less linked with sin in the first place. And although there appears to occur a type of inversion, according to which woman begins as a character more demonic than man and ends up as one more holy than him, this assessment ignores the fact that the superiority of the man is based on the belief that he is, by nature, in a certain relationship with the divine world that woman has to strive endlessly to create for herself. Thus whatever the stature of woman in this society, and it is undeniably great, it is achieved always on the condition that she remains loyal to her husband and obedient to the spiritual principle embodied in him.

It appears, then, that while the superiority of men, with all its implications, is inevitably a value prominent in the culture, the redemption of women within the terms set by male superiority is a value that is equally important. The dominance of men is emphasized because in power and authority they are dominant. Yet the terms that bestow this destiny on men allow an equal though different fulfillment for women—a fulfillment that lies not in the area of power and authority but in the mysteries of life and death and in the symbolic significance of generation. While it is the nature of women to be Eves and to be vulnerable to the devil, it is their destiny to become figures in the image of the Mother of God, who, as the villagers hear in the liturgy every week, is "more honorable than the cherubim, and beyond compare more glorious than the seraphim." The equation of women with the house and with the Mother of God is neither a coincidence nor a backlash of the dominance of men—it is an intended consequence of the culture.

Thus while it is true that in the imperfect world of humanity the men of rural Greece tend to overstep the bounds of their proper authority and power, and the women to suffer for this, it is true also that the women wish only to modify this behavior, not to reverse the order of reality on which it is symbolically based, for if they were to overthrow their association with the myth of Adam and Eve, they would, in consequence, be forced to overthrow also their association with the myth of the birth of Christ and the honor given to women through the figure of the Mother of God.

NOTES TO CHAPTER SEVEN

1. The ethnography of this village has been described in du Boulay (1974).
2. "Oi andres einai kapos anoteri, y'avto einai andres." "Oi andres einai alli, ap ton Theo." "Oi andres einai logiki, alla oi gynaikes einai koutsombolisses."

3. "Sti dexia plat." "Apo ton daimona."

4. "Echei evchi." "I gynaika me ti roka einai katarameni."

5. "Noyia, katanoyia, kai kataparathyrakia apo tin gynaika chanondtai."

6. This phrase refers to the physical presence in the house of women as wives and mothers. This sense does not conflict with a different and symbolic one in which boys are described as "in the house," referring to the fact that the house and the land are passed down through the male line.

7. See du Boulay (1974).

8. See Friedl (1967 and this volume).

9. The men's understanding of their role as the stronger sex and therefore as the upholders and the comforters of their wives in adversity is sharply described in Loizos (1981).

10. See Campbell (1964).

11. See Friedl (1962:106-108).

12. Du Boulay (1974:107ff.). See also Hirschon's (1978) symbolic analysis of the "closed" and "open" states of women.

13. See Campbell (1964:34-35) on the Sarakatsani: "The family and flock are both forms divinely confirmed, the earthly family being a refraction of the Holy Archetype Family," the Holy Family comprising God the Father, Christ the Son, and the Mother of God (p. 322). The people of Ambeli do not, however, appear to think of God the Father as a parallel with the head of the family; rather, Christ who became man is for them the parallel with both father and son.

EIGHT

The Bitter Wounding:
The Lament as Social Protest
in Rural Greece

ANNA CARAVELI

Very early on a July morning, with the Cretan village of Dzermiades barely stirring to life after a summer night's sleep, I was led by a boy through the winding cobblestone streets to the house of Anthoula Lyraki, a gifted lament performer who had recently lost her sister in an accident. Hearing of my interest in laments, Mrs. Lyraki had reluctantly consented to talk to me. After several days of negotiation, we agreed that I could record her laments for her dead sister in the privacy of her home on one condition: that it would be done without her husband's knowledge. A boy would be sent to me on the following morning to let me know when Mr. Lyrakis left for his work and to lead me to their home. Mr. Lyrakis was reputed to be particularly strict (*afstiros*) and disapproving of his wife's lament performances, because he feared they would upset her. But frequently during my research into death rituals in the village of Dzermiades in 1978, women lamented for their dead in the company of other women, either despite men's disapproval or without their knowledge.

I conducted fieldwork for this paper in two areas of Greece: four villages in the Zagori area of Epiros and the village of Dzermiades in Crete.[1] Being a woman, Greek-born, and a mother helped me gain access to the female circles of these villages. Motherhood, recovery from an illness, and expatriation (I had been living in the United States for years) enhanced my status as a mature woman. I was considered to have had experience with the griefs caused by "exile" (*tous kaimous tis xenitias*) and, in general, to be knowledgeable about the kind of troubles (*vasana*) that are the subjects of women's informal conversations and formalized narratives such as laments.

By following women to their homes, to the fields, on their visits to the cemetery, and as they did their daily chores, I discovered a universe of female activity outside the realm of men. Although based on the village's larger system of values and interpretations, this universe had its own variants of these, while many of the tasks, social roles, and expressive genres were gender-specific, limited to women only.

At first, when hearing of my interest in laments, many women were surprised. In public conversations, they would laugh and tease me about my desire to record such worthless songs, echoing the general devaluation of lamentation practices that one heard from many nonparticipants in the village. Others were shocked by what they saw as a macabre preoccupation on my part. In time, and in discussions among women that took place in more private surroundings, the conversation would turn to critical appraisals of lament performances and fine lament performers. It was through this type of discussion that the women's high regard for both form and acclaimed performers became evident. Indeed, successful compositions are often passed down through generations, becoming valuable learning tools and prized aesthetic possessions for the traditional women in the village.

An important point, then, is that at least while operating within the world conjured up by the lament performances, women use its participants—other women—as their frame of reference. In his recent book, *The Death Rituals of Rural Greece*, Loring Danforth interprets women's prominence in lament rituals as an attempt to continue their relationship with their male kin beyond death—a relationship that gave them their identity in life (Danforth 1982:136-138). Yet in the villages where I did my fieldwork, narratives about female "heroes" (worthy mothers or wives, skilled midwives or healers, talented singers, storytellers, or craftswomen) constituted a female history of the village, a body of women's expressive genres, and a female line of transmission (Caraveli-Chaves 1980:145).

In Dzermiades, as in the rest of rural Greece, ritual laments for the dead are performed by women.[2] It is important to remember, however, that not all village women performed or approved of laments. Thus the male/female dichotomy is not the only framework for understanding lament practices. A rising village middle class, and those with urban jobs returning to the village for brief visits, frequently were embarrassed by lamenting relatives (Caraveli-Chaves 1980:131). Occasionally, younger family members were unaware of the talent of a lament performer in the family or of the reputation she enjoyed among the traditional women of the village. In the villages where I worked, the lament tradition was, with few exceptions, performed by middle-aged or old women.

The performance of laments, however, creates a symbolic female universe that affects in many ways female activity outside of it (Caraveli-Chaves 1980). This paper examines the intricate dimensions of this universe as they relate to the larger context of the village in which lamentation is performed, and it considers the remarkable aesthetic, ritual, and social elements of lament performances and how they interrelate.

The first part of this study focuses on the performance process, concentrating particularly on three elements: the indigenous system of aesthetics connected with lament composition and performance, as revealed through folk criticism;[3] the role of lament as a type of folk religious expression, separate and often antithetical to institutional religion; and the role of lament performance as a vehicle for affecting social bonding among participants.

The second part of this paper examines the point of convergence between the separate world of women involved in death rituals and the mainstream of public life in the village and beyond. It is through the active choices of the lament performers that creative strategies develop and are handed down traditionally, transforming laments into instruments of protest and social commentary. Thus, while they are engendered by the occasion of death, laments become instruments for voicing the concerns of the living, and although they are created in a separate realm of experience and activity that is exclusive to women, they constitute a dialogue between the performers and the disparate worlds around them.

The Aesthetics of Pain

The death of a beloved person is the catalyst for and focus of women's lamentation and the broader universe of activity and experience generated by it. Yet participation in death rituals also becomes an important expressive avenue for the living. A significant aspect of lament performance is its religious dimensions. While male priests perform rituals in church and interpret official church doctrine, women are the leaders in folk religious events that are principally, but not exclusively, performed in the context of the domestic sphere—events such as calendar holidays, name day celebrations on saint's days, and life cycle rituals.[4]

Ritual lament performances are a significant type of folk religious expression in that they constitute a metaphysical communication outside the official church, relying heavily on an extraordinary state of consciousness or emotional engrossment, with the lamenter acting as the mediator between the living and the dead.[5] Employing the expanded definition of possession offered by Vincent Crapanzano and Vivian Garrison (1977:1-40), which considers "extensions" of possession to be important phenomena for study since they are "intimately connected with possession" (1977:10), this paper suggests that there are at least metaphorical similarities between possession rituals and the performance of laments.[6] As in some possession rituals, for example, lamentation uses "a learned idiom" of patterned text and performance "for articulating a certain range of experience" (Crapanzano and Garrison 1977:10-11) and a state of consciousness removed from that of ordinary experience (Bourguignon 1976:esp. 5-14). Both lament texts and folk commentary employ possession-related metaphors, including an entire system of aesthetics developed around the concept of pain (*ponos*)[7] and used to connote the state of emotional engrossment of the performer. In Dzermiades, for example, the consensus regarding the definition of a lament is that it is a song for the dead, produced when one is immersed in and inspired by pain. A lament performed by someone who is emotionally disengaged might be considered for its poetic merit but is not a true lament.

Just as emotional context defines lament aesthetics, a highly refined system of aesthetics is used to judge the degree and quality of the lamenter's "pain." Criteria include depth, authenticity, and style of delivery. The distinction between "in pain" and "out of pain" (*eine pano ston pono tis; den eine ston pono tis*) is, in the villages I researched, among the most significant elements constituting the complex lament aesthetics. *Den vriskome ston pono mou tora; den boro na po miroloyi*, "I am not in pain now; I can't say a lament," was a frequent answer to my request for laments from women in mourning. At times, I would be urgently referred to a well-known performer because *vriskete pano ston pono tis tora; tha sou miroloyisi kala*, "she is in her pain now; she will lament well for you." Moreover, the stronger the pain of the performer, the more value her composition has as ritual communication with the dead. An interesting parallel is offered in Lauri Honko's study of Finnish laments. Stating that the best lamenters in Finland are elderly women, especially widows, Honko cites Volmari Porkka's explanation that older women are considered to "have had time to experience also the shadow sides of life" and thus "do not need to make an effort to reach a sorrowful state of mind; their hearts are already full of sorrow" (Honko 1974:26).

Close observation makes clear that *pain* does not refer merely to the chronological proximity to death, although no one doubts that a recent death produces more intense pain to the living than a death that occurred long ago. The term as used by lamenters, however, has subtler and less literal implications. More than just grief produced by a specific occasion, the "pain" of folk aesthetics refers to an intense and extraordinary emotional state, manifesting itself in specific, structured behavior and achieved by the lamenters either voluntarily or involuntarily.

Artemisia Kapsali, sixty-seven years old in 1978, was born in the village of Asprangeli in Epiros and lived in the city of Ioannina. She was an example of someone who could enter into the state of pain voluntarily. Even though her husband, Yiannis, had been killed in World War II approximately thirty-seven years earlier, she was able to recall, apparently in its original intensity, her grief over his death. The lament she performed in my presence was interrupted by sobbing and displayed the characteristics of laments performed when one is "in pain." The ability to recall effortlessly almost the original intensity of one's grief over the loss of a beloved person who has been dead for a considerable length of time was a situation I encountered repeatedly. A possible explanation might be that bereaved women never completely stop lamenting for their loved ones. Past the prescribed period for mourning (usually the five years between the actual death and the exhumation of the remains—Danforth 1982:148-149), women continue to lament in a variety of contexts. Doing household chores, working in the fields, being present at another funeral—these can all become occasions for the continuation of the dialogue between the living and the beloved dead (Fig. 1). Thus, the channel for symbolic communication and emotional expression is always open.

Performers make use of a variety of methods to induce "pain." First, especially outside the context of funerals, they may use objects that contain rich symbolic associations with the deceased, such as a photograph or personal items that once belonged to him or her. Second, women loosen their black scarves to signal increasing emotional intensity, but also to facilitate it. Finally, narratives about the specific dead person or about topics related to death in general or to vasana—misfortunes or great sorrows—serve to ease participants into the proper frame of mind.

In or out of funeral contexts, the "help" of others is an important factor, contributing to a collectively arrived at emotional climax. Artemisia Kapsali, known as the best lamenter in the area, told me at the end of our recording session, "I could have done it better if I had gathered some women to help me." Each woman's recollection of her own grief serves to remind and intensify the grief of the others. During rituals, a skillful lamenter is judged not only by her talent in poetic composition, but also by her capacity to move others, thus enabling them to reach a charged emotional state.

To move her audience to ponos, and thus, symbolically, to lead the living to the dead, a lamenter skillfully employs the same devices she

1. Women lament at a grave site in the village of Olymbos on the island of Karpathos. (Photograph by Constantine Manos, courtesy of Magnum)

uses to bring herself to the state of pain: melodic conventions in conjunction with signs that are associated with sorrow, such as stylized interjections, gestures, and movements of her body; lyrical images and metaphors; manipulations of shared allusions; and repetition of key elements, such as appeals to the dead by name. It is not the poetic language alone, however, but also the style of delivery that is most responsible for inducing emotional intensity.[8] It has often been demonstrated to me that the audience can be deeply moved even when many of the poetic lines are obscured by weeping or interjection which, in the case of the Zagori lament, breaks words in the middle and leaves them incomplete. Singing itself, then, can facilitate the transition from ordinary to extraordinary experience.

There is, in each area I researched and in each culture group within these areas, a set melodic pattern to which laments are sung. In addition to the main melody, stylistic conventions carry emotional associations and can trigger a sense of sorrow in the audience (Caraveli 1982:138-139). The lament melody characteristic of the Zagori province, for instance, uses microtones, stylized interjections of wailing sounds, and leaps of several intervals at the end of each hemistich (half a line) to induce a state of pathos. Lamenters often preferred reciting texts for me rather than performing them. While reciting a text can be relatively unemotional, singing it produces intense emotion on the part of both performer and audience.

Aglaia Hadzopoulou, aged seventy-six, and Alexandra Tsoumani, of approximately the same age, belong to different culture groups. While both live in Tsepelovo, Epiros, Alexandra belongs to the Sarakatsani nomad group, which is presently settling in villages and abandoning its nomadic lifestyle.[9] Although a good deal of tension exists between the established village residents and the more recent settlers, the two women have been friends for years and have shared many trying experiences in the course of their lives. Talking about their personal losses and grievances moved each other deeply. A story about the death of one of Alexandra's children—an event that had been witnessed by Aglaia—produced weeping in both women. Yet when they lamented in their very distinct styles, each woman's performance left the other indifferent. The Sarakatsani lament uses a completely different melody from the Zagori one, and it is sung in a falsetto voice with many artificial breaks in the words that render the text unintelligible to the nonparticipant (Fig. 2). Conversely, on the occasion of the sudden death of a cousin, Xanthippi Papa, aged seventy-six, from the village of Ano Pedina in Epiros, performed a lament in the presence of family members who were unaware of her talent and reputation as a lamenter. Upon the

2. Lament poets in Tsepelovo, Epiros. *Left*: Aglaia Hadzopoulou. *Right*: Alexandra Tsoumani, a Sarakatsani nomad who has settled in the village. They have been lamenting for the death of their children. (Photograph by Jonathan Chaves)

first notes of the lament melody, the entire family burst into sobbing. Such reactions on the part of diverse audiences suggest that responses to specific styles of lament performance are, to some extent, learned. Not only are the texts of laments symbolic languages unto themselves, but performance components also carry symbolic associations, thus triggering "pain" in the participants and facilitating the creation of an extraordinary emotional context.[10]

There are also cases of women who involuntarily experience a "painful state," which signifies more than the mere accidental recollection of a sorrowful event. Alexandra Pateraki, from Dzermiades, performed in a relatively unemotional tone a lament she had heard from her mother. When asked if she could perform a lament "in pain," she chose a lament for her child Pavlos, now dead for over ten years. This time her performance caused her to weep so profusely that her three-year-old granddaughter ran out of the room in fear. In describing the circumstances surrounding the origin of the lament, Alexandra said, "As I was walking to the cemetery once, it suddenly came to me in its entirety." Statements such as "it came to me" (*mou irthe*) also were used by other lamenters in the region to describe the occasion for the original composition of a lament. Tomais Veringou, also of Dzermiades, whom I recorded performing on her son's grave, related to me how she came to compose one of her best laments. As she was walking on the public road at the outskirts of the village, "it" (the pain) came to her (*m'e-piase*) with such intensity that she could not contain herself. She burst into a lament so passionate that the few fellow villagers who met her on the road were startled.

Folk aesthetics, then, define the lament not primarily in terms of its poetic value but according to its effectiveness as communication with the dead and its role as a vehicle for an extraordinary experience for the living participants.[11] Accordingly, laments fall into the following groups (in ascending order of efficacy and importance):

1. Laments that are simply recited as poetry
2. Laments that are sung, but not on a ritual occasion or in an extraordinary emotional context
3. Laments that are sung in an extraordinary, heightened emotional context, but in an ordinary setting such as one's home or the fields
4. Laments that are performed both in a heightened emotional context and on a ritual occasion (for example, tending the grave, memorial services, funerals)

The relationship between aesthetics and heightened emotional context has several implications. It suggests the existence of an intricate system of folk aesthetics connected to the daily emotional needs of the performers, such as the need for emotional catharsis and for confrontation with fearful aspects of their world. Moreover, it suggests that the performance of ritual lamentation, not only as a form of sophisticated poetic composition but also as an alternative religious expression that functions outside the official church, is open to women only and bears similarities to spirit possession.

In addition to the religious dimensions of lament performances, the social elements they incorporate hold distinct benefits for the living. The existence of a muted, separate women's world creates the opportunities for strong friendships among women.[12] Rituals of shared grieving reinforce, intensify, and negotiate a great variety of relationships that often pass into daily narrative as metaphors of and codes for female experiences. The realm of suffering, for example, is believed to be one in which women dominate over men. Either because of burdens exclusive to women, such as childbirth and child rearing, or because of women's capacity to experience suffering (especially death) more intensely, villagers believe vasana to be linked especially to women's experiences, and they form a frequent topic of conversation. Both informal narratives and formalized events, such as laments, echo these themes and reinforce the sense of bonding "in pain" (Caraveli-Chaves 1980:145-146 and passim). In addition, lamentation provides another sphere for female interaction within the extraordinary context of emotional engrossment, as well as a vehicle for shared artistic expression. Finally, the very processes of performance and of providing mutual comfort (especially in the case of laments performed by women for women) enact and negotiate varied significant relationships among women across kinship and generational lines, for example friendships between the old and young and bonds between master performer and apprentice. These relationships are vital to both the women themselves and the larger world of the village that they inhabit.

Ultimately, then, death rituals, both in themselves and in terms of their impact on women's daily lives, constitute an alternative and exclusive sphere of aesthetic, religious, and social interaction, in which participants vent creative impulses, undergo emotional catharsis, and reinforce their individual identity and group membership. Though less accessible to the outsider than the public domain of men, this female realm is equally complex and complete in that it possesses its own criteria for status within it. These criteria include artistry in composition and performance, capacity to experience and transmit ponos, proper performance of rituals, and observance of social relationships associated with death rites.

LAMENTS AND LARGER SOCIAL EXPERIENCE

Women's laments serve not only to create, reflect, reinforce, and negotiate realms of experience and action that are exclusive to women, but also to mediate between the living and the dead and between seemingly disparate or antithetical types of experience: male and female, traditional and modern, sacred and secular, and ideological and actual, as well as between formal institutions and individual or domestic needs not accommodated by them. It is by focusing on the points of overlap between these sets of antithetical experiences that we can gain insight into the lament's use by and for the living and its fluid, continuously adaptive nature.

In the villages where I did my fieldwork, people with "modern" attitudes frown upon the practice of ritual lamentation, but the dichotomy between tradition and change is not as clear-cut as it appears at first glance. Traditional laments can employ textual conventions to comment on a wide range of topics, from the performers' own social roles to practices in modern medicine and the effects of the changing economy on their families. Thus, age-old thematic conventions incorporate modern subjects with relative ease.

Moreover, there is a frequent overlap between the women's realm of lament performance and men's separate sphere of public activities. For instance, while men in the areas of my research often expressed disapproval of their wives' or mothers' participation in laments, and while most of the women I recorded lamented without their husbands' knowledge, closer examination of men's attitudes revealed a complex and ambivalent view of this tradition. Although they expressed disapproval and the fear that such practices might strain their female relatives emotionally, men also displayed open admiration of laments. Professional male folk musicians in Epiros, for example, admitted to their appreciation of the artistic qualities of laments. A clarinet player, Grigoris Kapsalis, told me of his great fondness for the polyphonic laments of the Pogoni area of Epiros. "Whenever I play there," he confessed, "I gather a few women to sing me some laments."

While it is only women who participate actively in ritual laments for the dead, men tend to participate in more passive ways. A man in his sixties, the nephew of a famed lamenter from the village of Kapesovo, told me of his intimate knowledge of lament composition and performance. He described several occasions on which he was alone, when he would burst into lamentation as the only appropriate vehicle for venting his feelings. He spoke of a recent experience, walking through the abandoned fields that he remembered as richly cultivated in his youth, when he spontaneously began lamenting out loud, singing about the changes he saw and the sadness these changes inspired in him.

Finally, while it is women only who perform in rituals such as funerals, men may sing publicly *about* death. The words, however, are often sung to melodies of other folksongs and not to the characteristic lament tunes of the area. Frequently, a *paniyiri*, or village festival, in Zagori opens with such laments before the dance songs begin. I am told that at times the festival may begin at the cemetery where the performance of male *moiroloyia*, "laments," such as the well known Epirotic lament *Mariola*, takes place before the start of the main part of the paniyiri at the village square (Fig. 3).

Another point of convergence between the women's world as created by lament performances and the larger world is the dimension of social protest. Folklorist Ilhan Başgöz explores the notion of a fifth dimension of folklore in discussing its role in heightening rather than resolving tensions that can lead to social change. "Like other art forms such as literature, painting, music and the graphic arts, folklore functions to

3. Musicians in Tsepelovo, Epiros, starting a *paniyiri* (village celebration) with the lament *Mariola*—part of the *epitrapezia* repertory of songs, that is, songs sung while seated around a table.

dramatize conflict, to encourage dissent, to cause disunity, and to rouse people to activism and even to press for revolutionary changes in the social system" (Başgöz 1982:6). His article goes on to document a historical connection between expressive forms and protest, focusing on contemporary performances of the romance and the shadow puppet theater in Turkey.

A historical connection between lament poetry in the Greek tradition and the expression of grievances is evident both in the subject matter and in the various stylistic and thematic conventions of laments. Characteristically, laments have always taken a wide variety of forms, from grievances against death itself and all its metaphorical extensions (which will be discussed below) to social commentary on political events and individual situations. Margaret Alexiou (1974:55-122) lists several categories of laments in the Greek tradition, such as the historical laments for the fall of cities; the laments for "departure from home, change of religion, and marriage"; the ritual laments of women; and the laments for gods and heroes. Thus, since antiquity, laments have commented on, protested against, and affected social change.[13,14]

In addition to the variety of subjects covered in laments, there are thematic conventions that allow the focus of the song to shift from the plight of the deceased to the plight of the mourner. Since the performers of these ritual laments are women, the grievances thus voiced often relate to the social role of women in the context of the androcentric village and to painful situations (child raising, for example) peculiar to women (Caraveli-Chaves 1980:esp. 138, 146).

Widowhood and emigration are regarded in the Greek folk tradition as metaphorical extensions of death, and they can be used interchangeably, as alternative and equivalent forms of death, within one lament, thereby intensifying the impact of the actual death of an individual through inference to its metaphorical dimensions.[15] The subject of widowhood and the loss of social status a widow suffers in rural Greece[16] become frequent topics in laments, forming an entire category that I term "widows' songs." Protest against widows' social isolation and ambiguous status is frequently expressed in these songs. Stavroula Haralambopoulou, forty-nine years of age when ethnomusicologist Sotirios Chianis recorded her in 1959, articulated the theme of widowhood in the following lament.

The widow stays inside the house—gossip around her all around!

The widow stays inside the house—gossip around her all around!
(Painful exile!)[17]

She can't gaze out the window, she can't sit by the doorstep.
(Bitter widow!)

There are fresh breezes by the window, there is gay chatting by the doorstep.   (Bitter widow!)

Widow, go change your name, don't let them call you widow!
(Ah! Bitter widow!)

Widow, night comes on the mountains, yet soon daylight sets in,
(Bitter widow!)

But so many plumes and feathers as a black hen has,
(Bitter widow!)

So many times must you sit and wait at your front door, my widow.   (Ah, bitter woman!)[18]

> Performer: Stavroula Haralambopoulou
> Recorded by Sotirios Chianis,[19]
> Hrysovitsi, Peloponnesos, April 1959

Sometimes protest is expressed more subtly in the poetic voice that recognizes a "sisterhood in pain" among women, a sense of communal victimization inflicted by either social or natural forces (for example, the death of children). Often, this voice takes the form of an invitation to communal grieving.

> Come women! Let you who are still untried, and us, who've known sorrows,
>
> Join together our tears, shape them into a river;
>
> And let the river turn to lake, to seashore, water fountain,
> (Oh, my love, my eyes!)
>
> Where young beauties can come to wash, young men to groom themselves,
>
> And where unmarried children can have their target practice.

> Performer: Alexandra Tsoumani
> Recorded by Anna Caraveli,
> Tsepelovo, Epiros, August 15, 1978

At times, protest takes the form of an attack against a vast, all-encompassing category of evils, including war, natural disaster, and death itself. However universal the evil being lamented may be, almost always the point of departure is its effect on the female mourner. In the following lament performed by Artemisia Kapsali of Asprangeli, Epiros, in memory of her husband, Yiannis, who was killed at war, the singer bewails not only war, but also the impotence of women who are powerless over the killing of their children and husbands.

> What's wrong with you, miserable crow, wailing and squealing so? (Oh, I can't bear it, Yianni!)
>
> Are you that thirsty for blood, that hungry for young flesh
> (How awful, my fate!)
>
> Go beyond Gribala mountain, go to Gribala peak
> (I can't bear it, Yianni)
>
> To find proud, young bodies there all bathed in dark blood
> (Oh, I can't bear it, Yianni!)
>
> To find their poor mothers singing laments for them.
> (Oh, my luck is awful!)
>
> How bitter the wound! How poisonous the gunshot! Damned be the war! Damn it a thousand times! (Oh, what horrible fate!)
>
> It takes children away from mothers, brothers away from brothers (Awful, awful fate!)

And it tears man away from wife, though they love each other.

(My fate is awful!)

And on the spot on which they part, no grass can ever grow.

Performer: Artemisia Kapsali
Recorded by Anna Caraveli,
Ioannina, Epiros, August 17, 1978

Ritual laments also protest against a variety of situations that may not be directly connected to the position of women but which are, nonetheless, spoken out against in the voice of the "weak, marginal, or downtrodden." The traditional lament theme of the journey of the deceased often involves an explanation of the manner in which he died— either a mythical account of death (the conventional battle between Charon and the deceased, for instance) or an actual description of his illness. In this portion of a long lament performed by Tomais Veringou on her son's grave, the recounting of her child's treatment for kidney disease clearly conveys her sense of impotence in the face of medical technology, as well as her disapproval of questionable medical practices.

Ah, my beloved child, my only son!

They were practicing their craft on you, my darling!

They were practicing on you and learned their craft, my child.

They learned about medicine my golden, my glad boy.

Oh, they thrust their machinery inside your belly, child,

And more machinery in your hand, my glad son, my king.

They put tubes of oxygen through your nose, my darling,

And fed you blood through the other hand, my king, my good son.

Ah, how can I bear all these now, my child?

Performer: Tomais Veringou
Recorded by Anna Caraveli,
Dzermiades, Crete, July 15, 1978

Indeed, protest against doctors and practices of modern medicine, especially in the case of the death of a small child, as in the following portion of a long lament, is a frequent theme.

Ah, deeply pained child, I have loved you so much!

They tore your belly open with their knives twice,

Looking for the sickness in your guts, my white dove.

But the medicines were drained, the healing herbs were lost;
So they left your pain uncured, my small child.

> Performer: Alexandra Pateraki
> Recorded by Anna Caraveli,
> Dzermiades, Crete, July 15, 1978

Implicitly, in terms of subject matter alone, laments comprise a "protest" against the official church and the Christian doctrine of death. The very notion of death expressed in laments is contrary to the Christian views of a rewarding afterlife for the pious. The Hades of the laments is marked by darkness and despair, and it retains its pagan name. Christian attitudes toward death preach patience, acceptance, and perseverance. Laments express despair, fear, and anger toward death and the deceased. The laments that follow convey the physical terror of dying, the despair characterizing the underworld, and the frustration felt, in the first one, by the deceased and, in the second one, by the living.

All lies! All fables you hear in laments!
People don't meet, people don't talk here in the underworld.
They call this "place of rot," where bodies rot away.
I saw them and was frightened. My heart turned to ice.

> Performer: Xanthippi Papa
> Recorded by Anna Caraveli,
> Ano Pedina, Epiros, August 16, 1978

Rise and cast away Charon's sheet.
Wake up to see springtime and people's joy.
I'm left alone again—a desolate bird!—
Singing instead of crying to soothe my bitter pain.
I want to let out a shrill cry and see if you still know me
And see if you can welcome me, my sweet, beloved sister.
Rise on the twenty-first of May! Rise on your name day,
Rise and give out flowers, and give out white lilies—
But slowly, and carefully—body upright with pride;
Oh slowly and carefully—the wound is not yet healed.
A wound is nesting in my heart and when we meet again
I'd like an hour for us to talk, beloved; one short hour!

Up, my love, rise! Rise and talk to me

So I can rest awhile in peace before I come back to you.

> Performer: Anthoula Lyraki
> Recorded by Anna Caraveli,
> Dzermiades, Crete, July 15, 1978

Perhaps in part because of such expressions of protest, a historic antagonism has existed between the church (and, at various times in antiquity, the state as well) and the women's performance of laments (Alexiou 1974:14-24). Alexiou explains the phenomenon of restrictive legislation against laments in antiquity, aimed particularly at women, in terms of the social power inherent in the expressive and symbolic roles of lamentation practices. "If the family, based on father-right, was to be established as the basic unit of society, then the power of women in religious and family affairs must be stopped, and they must be made to apply a more secondary role in funerals" (Alexiou 1974:21).

The use of the lament as an instrument of protest depends greatly on the role of the individual performer as an active manipulator of conventions and as an agent of change. Most studies on the expressive culture of Greece underemphasize the role of the performer. To ignore the lament singer as conscious creator and articulator of the lament tradition would be to lose sight of the lament's use as a creative strategy for coping with change, conflict, and social limitations, as well as to devalue the sophisticated aesthetics of its composition and performance and the skills of its creator. The lament performer's active role, as evidenced by her manipulation of stock poetic units during composition, her use of diverse, often everyday settings for ritual performance, and her incorporation of everyday communication and immediate concerns into the traditional idiom of lamentation, illustrates both the complex skills involved in composition and performance and the superb artistry of actual laments. Clearly, the dynamic nature of the lament in terms of composition, performance setting, and usage endows it with the potential for becoming a potent instrument of protest in the hands of a skillful lament poet.

Laments, like other types of Greek folk poetry, are composed according to formula.[20] Improvisation is possible, depending on the stock patterns of composition and stock individual poetic units, which are dictated by tradition and which vary with the region. In the fluid *mantinades* tradition of the islands, a greater degree of improvisation is possible for the performer. Even with the relatively "set" and less changeable laments of Epiros, however, individual control of traditional poetics is considerable, though more subtle.

In the following lament for the death of her brother Loni, Aglaia Hadzopoulou employed the conventional subject of the encounter and ensuing battle between Charon and the dead man. She was aware of both the mythical dimensions of her subject and the additions that she made. "I heard the lament from my grandmother," she said. "She sang it for someone else, but because my brother was a hunter, I added the line about the sword and gun." She also added the date of his death and the detail of its coincidence with his birthday.

> A young man was roaming on a high mountain slope—
> > (I'll burst with pain, Loni).
> Hunting gun in hand, sword dangling by his waist.
> > (I'll burst with this pain, my soul!)
> And Charon was waiting in a hollow canyon.
> > (Oh, my brother!)
> —Please, Charon, let me through; let me cross this canyon
> > (Ah, poor man!)
> Because I'm young and green, because I'm a young father.
> > (Oh, Loni!)
> And Charon did not let him cross, and Charon snatched him then,
> > (Oh, my brother!)
> On the Virgin's holiday, and on his birthday
> > (I'll burst with this pain!)
>
> > Performer: Aglaia Hadzopoulou
> > Recorded by Anna Caraveli,
> > Tsepelovo, Epiros, August 14, 1978

The state of "pain" does not diminish a singer's control of conventions and compositional techniques. Asked how one could compose such intricate songs when immersed in a seemingly agitated emotional state, Sofia Papakonstadtinou, daughter of the famed Thia Hrysa and a good lamenter in her own right, answered, "It is because the pain concentrates you [se syngedtroni]; it does not let your mind wander."

As mentioned earlier and quoted in part above, Tomais Veringou performed a long lament of approximately twenty minutes on the grave of her son who had died a year and a half before of a kidney disease. This lament was part of a weekly ritual for her that involved changing the oil of the oil lamp by the grave, replacing the faded flowers with fresh ones, and censing the grave with incense—all without ceasing to lament for one minute. One day, my husband and I were at the grave site when Tomais entered the cemetery. She made a dramatic entrance—armloads of fresh flowers, black scarf loosened, and already lamenting at the top of her voice, even before leaving the public road to enter the cemetery. During the entire performance, she did not acknowledge our presence once, even when—her grief having driven her to a seemingly uncontrollable state—we tried to raise her from the grave and stop her lamentation. She did, however, acknowledge us within the lament text itself.

Even the strangers grieve for you, child, my only son.

The most obvious difference between this performance and others recorded in more everyday settings was the rapidity and facility of Tomais's composition and delivery. Whereas lamenters who sang relatively "out of pain" paused in an attempt to remember and made mistakes in syllabic count per line, Tomais's lament flowed effortlessly and was metrically flawless, even though it was one of the longest laments I recorded in this area.

Manipulation of textual and performance elements can render a lament applicable to a variety of contexts. Kleoniki Kodtodimou was introduced to me as the greatest living lamenter in the area. She spent her winters in the Epirotic city of Ioannina with her children and her summers in her family home in Kapesovo, which she managed capably by herself for the duration of the season. Though eighty-six years of age, she struck me as a woman in full possession of her intellectual—and even physical—powers. The incidents of her life, which she related to me, were marked by a strong love for life and the desire to survive. In telling me of her husband's death, for instance (he died in his sleep next to her), she said that upon discovering that he was dead, her first thought was for the living, not for the dead. Since her grown son suffered from a heart condition, Kleoniki suppressed her own fright and grief in order to soften the blow for her child. Paralleling the tone and style of her narratives, the lament that follows uses conventional lament subject matter to express, ultimately, Kleoniki's life-affirming message.[21] The usual journey to the underworld taken by the mourner—normally a grim experience—has a different resolution for her. Her dead relatives, both husband and son, receive her kindly but only to heal her and return her to life. She handles the guilt she feels as the bereaved person who is alive when a beloved person is dead by making her own dead loved ones give her permission to rejoin the living. Not only does Kleoniki (through the voice of her dead) allow herself the gift of life, but she also cleverly finds a justification for it: to keep the old family home open and to keep alive what has been left behind.

> Listen to that great roar! What is all this confusion
>
> Heard from the earth below, heard from the underworld?
>
> Are they slaying oxen there, or hanging wild beasts?
>
> They're neither slaying oxen, nor hanging wild beasts.
>
> It's only my son, Alcibiades, my husband, Kostakis.
>
> They're waiting for their mother, the mother they had loved.
>
> They're sending servant boys for doctors, servant girls for fresh herbs.
>
> For she must heal and become well, and they must send her back,
>
> So their home won't close down, their old family home.

> Performer: Kleoniki Kodtodimou
> Recorded by Anna Caraveli,
> Kapesovo, Epiros, August 12, 1978

The fact that the lament is considered a communication with the dead by the lamenters themselves enriches the possibilities for conveying everyday grievances to the living and to the dead. When Kleoniki Kodtodimou refused to subject herself to the "pain" of actually performing laments, she merely recited fragments of those laments which she considered her most successful. These informal recitations and discussions of laments revealed the performer's view of laments as communication above all else. Like other lamenters who sang "out of pain," for instance, she would introduce a lament with the words "Then I told him," "This is what I told my mother when she died," or even "This is what I will tell my friend, Victoria, when she dies" (*tha tis po*). Kleoniki said of her husband who died in his sleep, "I remember I turned to him and told him . . . I told him a lot of things, I can't remember them all . . . but I remember I told him":[22]

> It was a bitter evening, a heavy winter night
>
> When Charon put me to sleep to take you in secret
>
> Without time for us to talk, without a message from you.

> Performer: Kleoniki Kodtodimou
> Recorded by Anna Caraveli,
> Kapesovo, Epiros, August 12, 1978

Laments also are used to communicate news and other urgent concerns relating to the daily life of the mourner. Tomais Veringou, for example, uses portions of the long lament cited previously to convey all the latest news to her dead son—from his cousin's wedding to Tomais's grievances over the restrictions her family imposes on her visits to the cemetery.

I'm going, child, my young king; evening has come already,

The family will look for me, they'll come here to find me,

And I'll create trouble home, my tender plant, my son.

I'm leaving you now, my boy.

> Performer: Tomais Veringou
> Recorded by Anna Caraveli,
> Dzermiades, Crete, July 15, 1978

These interactive elements in laments allow for links to be created between convention and everyday experience, and they expand the possibilities for the lament's use as an instrument of protest.

CONCLUSION

Most studies of laments tie its performance to a specific setting, mainly cemeteries (for example, see Danforth 1982). My own fieldwork has suggested more diversity in performance contexts and, therefore, this paper offers an expanded definition of lamentation that includes singing, reciting, even silently composing a lament, in contexts as diverse as visiting the cemetery, doing housework, working in the fields, and walking (Fig. 4). Indeed, the laments presented in this paper were recorded in a wide variety of performance situations, in addition to formal funerals. I heard women lament at cemeteries during their weekly visits there, at their homes, in the fields, alone, or in the company of other women. I recorded performances that occurred spontaneously, and I recorded women who performed at my request. The latter were not artificial, in the sense of being emotionally disengaged performances. The women would arrange their weekly visits to the cemetery at a time convenient to both of us, or they would bring themselves, through narrative accounts of the deceased or through the handling of objects that had once belonged to the dead relative, to the heightened emotional state necessary for lament performances. All these performances, in other words, were regularly occurring events in the context of everyday life, but they were occasionally manipulated for the sake of a recording.

Such variety in performance situations and in the motivation of in-

4. Stamatia Biri of Vrisohori, Epiros, one of the best lamenters of her village, performing a lament for all of those recently dead in her family—some of her children and sisters—in a room in her home. (Photograph by Jonathan Chaves)

dividual performers provided important insights into lamentation practices and revealed relatively unexplored aspects of the folk aesthetics associated with laments. Women described to me performances of laments that served them as intimate conversations with their dead and as the means for airing their own grievances. These took place in a great variety of secular settings. An appropriate line for a lament might be conceived and hummed during the performance of household chores, while an entire lament might be performed while walking on the way to an errand or working in the fields—either alone or in the company of other women.

Viewing lamentation beyond formal "genre" categories and performance settings has important implications for our understanding of expressive culture, traditional rural Greece, and gender roles. By examining the continuous interaction between formal event and everyday life, we can understand the process of change and adaptation that gives contemporary meaning and relevance to age-old traditions. Women's sphere of activity and influence is also expanded considerably.

Lamentation, then, is a process that is not defined by its setting but instead symbolically demarcates space as mediating ground between the living and the dead, the ordinary and extraordinary experience. Such extension of performance contexts not only suggests an expanded definition of laments, but also an expanded use of them as instruments for airing grievances on an everyday basis. It is the performer's role as creator and actor that allows her to transform everyday into "extraordinary" space and to utilize conventions as means for personal expression in the same way that she transforms the fact of death into an extraordinary artistic expression and experience of religious significance.

Ritual laments for the dead in rural Greece today, far from being part of a static tradition antithetical to the mainstream culture, are dynamic, ongoing creations that allow for the integration of textual conventions handed down by tradition and topics of immediate relevance to the universe of the performer. Thus, lamentation becomes for the singer an avenue for social commentary on the larger world, rather than an instrument of restriction and isolation.

Performance, as well as the folk aesthetics used to judge performance, suggest still another dimension of protest in the lamentation ritual: its role as a form of folk religion outside, and often in protest against, the practices of official Christianity. In this capacity, laments serve as vehicles for "extraordinary" experience outside both official institutions and the confines of ordinary reality, and they reveal connections between aesthetics and emotional texture.

It is the individual performer who shapes age-old conventions into instruments for the personal expression of grievances, transforms ordinary into extraordinary space, and expands the context and setting of lament performance to suit her everyday needs. Attention to individual performances and their relationship to the performer's life story can illustrate clearly how the singer adapts traditional forms to the immediate concerns of her community, to her personal situation, or to the moment of performance.[23]

Ultimately, it is the role of the individual within the tradition that expands the definition of the lament to include the realm of the living in addition to that of the dead, the everyday experience in addition to the extraordinary experience. It is this interplay between fluid tradition and active performer that enables the lament to serve as a vehicle both for airing grievances and for creating a continuous dialogue between the singer and the larger world. Focus on human dynamics, then, reveals another important dimension in women's role—as creators of coping strategies, artists, critics, articulators, and manipulators of one of Greece's most important verbal arts in continuous existence.

NOTES TO CHAPTER EIGHT

1. Fieldwork for this article was conducted mainly during the springs and summers of 1974, 1975, 1978, 1980, and 1981. For my work in the area of Zagori in Epiros, I am deeply indebted to Mrs. Frosso Ioannidi of Tsepelovo. A member of an old, esteemed family, Mrs. Ioannidi has worked relentlessly for over six decades to collect, interpret in public presentations, and write on the folklife of this region. In recognition of these efforts, the Zagori residents have bestowed upon her the honorary title of "Mother of Zagori." Even though she was in her eighties at the time, Mrs. Ioannidi accompanied me to many locations that were nearly inaccessible. Her work and example, as well as her hospitality and support, were of enormous practical and moral value to me. Especially during the summer of 1978, she became a friend, a teacher, and a window to the private world of the Zagori households.

2. See Loukatos (1978:esp. 205-225) for a discussion on rituals and beliefs related to birth, marriage, and death in rural Greece, within the larger context of the history of Greek folklore. Alexiou (1974) provides a comprehensive study of Greek ritual laments, emphasizing continuities between ancient and contemporary traditions. Both books contain rich bibliographies consisting of Greek and non-Greek sources. For examinations of laments in social and performance contexts, see Caraveli-Chaves (1980:129-157) and Danforth (1982). Herzfeld (1981a) discusses Greek laments in relation to taxonomy.

3. For a discussion of Greek folk aesthetics, see Beaton (1980). For studies on the same topic, which consider folk commentary and indigenous interpretive systems, see Herzfeld (1981b:113-141) and Caraveli (1982:129-158).

4. Du Boulay (1974:131-133) discusses the woman's role in the home as both "physical and metaphysical, for it is she who makes of the house a sanctuary for the living and a memorial for the dead" and it is she who "is thought to hold the house together" by overseeing both physical and ritual activity in it.

5. In discussing the beer-drinking ritual among the Iteso people of Africa (near the Kenya-Uganda border), Karp emphasizes the "heightened form of social experience" associated with it (Karp 1980:93). "Increasing engrossment" of the participants in beer-drinking parties was evidence of the success of these events (pp. 105-109) and contributed to the role of beer drinking as "Iteso social theory" and an important social experience (p. 83 and passim). This emotional framework, termed by the Iteso "much understanding," is equivalent to the concept of *ponos* in laments and *kefi* in the ritual *glendia* per-

formed in the Greek village of Olymbos on the island of Karpathos (Caraveli 1982:82 and 1985:263-264, 277-279 and passim).

6. For an important study on the relationship between possession and social marginality, see Lewis (1975). In their study of spirit possession, Karp and Karp (1979:22-25) maintain that the trances encountered in their fieldwork were genuine but served, simultaneously, as strategies for relieving women of responsibility for inappropriate behavior. Kessler (1977:295-331) draws relationships between possession and the low status of widows and divorced women. Danforth (1983) links the expression of submission in a Greek possession ritual to women's strategies for power, while Crapanzano and Garrison (1977:17) link spirit possession and its cure to issues involving identity. This connection between possession and strategies for coping with conflict or ambivalence and, in the more general sense, issues of identity, parallels the central thesis of this paper: the use of lamentation for airing grievances and obtaining power. Thus, the similarites between lament ritual and possession link the two to literal or metaphorical social protest on many levels.

7. Danforth (1982:142-147) cites ponos as an important concept in folk commentary and poetic metaphors, and he notes its desirability and conscious cultivation among lamenters.

8. For an important analysis of the relationships between expressive style and culture and between style and social marginality, see Lomax (1968).

9. See Campbell's (1964) study on the Sarakatsani.

10. For the relationship between style and content and an examination of the role of "meta-textual" factors, such as performance, community world view and history, and symbolic associations contained in music, in the creation of "meaning" surrounding a song, see Caraveli (1982, 1985).

11. In the ritual speech event called the *glendi* (sing.), whose performance in the village of Olymbos and in the Baltimore, Maryland settlement of Olymbos emigrants is especially vibrant, the ritual specialists, or *meraklides*, are judged by criteria similar to those used for lamenters. A good *meraklis* (sing.) is not judged by poetic excellence alone, but rather by a number of social and interactive elements, one of which is his capacity to move the audience to a state of heightened experience, or kefi. A complex set of aesthetics, similar to those defining pain (ponos), differentiates between the various levels of kefi one enters into, while the success of a glendi depends on the existence and quality of kefi in it. See Caraveli (1985).

12. See Kennedy (this volume).

13. See Caraveli (1982:129-157) for an examination of textual conventions in laments and their effect on social action.

14. Alexiou (1974) provides a comprehensive analysis of ritual laments in Greece, including a historical overview and a thematic and stylistic analysis.

15. Danforth (1982) cites emigration both as an important element in shaping the social context of death rituals (for example, pp. 16 and 23) and as partial metaphor for death (pp. 33 and 90-95).

16. For a discussion of widowhood in rural Greece, see du Boulay (1974:122).

17. In this paper, the stylized interjections known as *tsakismata* are set apart in parentheses. For a discussion on the stylistic and symbolic meaning of this type of digression in Greek folk song, see Caraveli (1982:129-158).

18. All the translations in this paper are by the author.

19. State University of New York at Binghamton, collection of field recordings by Sotirios Chianis.

20. For an important study of the formulaic nature of epic poetry, see Lord (1965). For varying approaches to the relationship between improvisation and textual conventions in oral poetry, see Finnegan (1977) and, with regard to Greek folk poetry in particular, Beaton (1980) and Caraveli (1982).

21. Danforth (1982:144) observes that "many Greek villagers subscribe to what can be called an indigenous theory of catharsis," and he cites in the same book examples of anthropological interest in "ritual systems of psychotherapy," including Danforth (1978:312ff).

22. Danforth (1982:127) notes that "the social relationship that continues to link the bereaved to the deceased is in effect a conversation between the living and the dead." On a similar note, Danforth observes that "a mother who has lost a child does not say 'I am going to my son's grave.' She says, 'I am going to my son' (*Tha pao sto pedhi mou*)" (p. 133). Also, on lament as communication, see Caraveli (1982:127, 117-152).

23. Başgöz (1982:27, 29) stresses the need for close attention to individual performances and the personality of the performer. He also discusses the process of functional transformation, or changes in the function of the folklore form *during* performance for the purpose of social protest.

NINE

Culture Enters through
the Kitchen: Women, Food,
and Social Boundaries
in Rural Greece

JILL DUBISCH

IN GREECE, as in other societies, strong beliefs regarding the polluting power of female sexuality and female bodily processes often are interpreted by ethnographers as both indicators of and reasons for wom-
en's subordination and inferior status. This interpretation parallels
Ortner's observation that women are everywhere "more involved most
of the time with 'species life' " and thus more closely associated with
"nature," an association that accounts for "the pan-cultural devaluation of women" and for the control of women by men, themselves
equated unambiguously with culture (Ortner (1974:73). This paper
takes a somewhat different approach to the oppositions of male/fe-
male, culture/nature, and purity/pollution.[1] Rather than examining
concepts of female pollution in terms of women's status and their
greater closeness to "nature," I wish instead to analyze the ways that
women function as *controllers* of pollution, both their own and that of
others, and as transformers of natural products and processes into cultural ones. Beyond this, however, I wish to take up Strathern's idea that
"[i]n many cultures notions about differences and similarities between
the sexes (gender constructs) are put to use, not just to order actual relations between men and women, but as a kind of language for talking
about other things as well. . . . Such a usage of gender draws upon sex
differences as a source of symbolism" (Strathern 1980:49; see also
Herzfeld, this volume). Specifically, I suggest that, rather than being
just "about" women, body symbolism, especially the symbolism of
pollution and boundaries, is "saying" something about Greek society
generally, and I propose a relationship between the body (particularly
the female body), the house, and social order. To analyze this relationship, I will explore the connections between pollution, boundary main-

tenance, the house and kitchen, the role of food, and the symbolism of the body.

GREEK POLLUTION BELIEFS

That women's engagement in natural processes, and the products of such processes, are considered polluting in a number of societies seems to support Ortner's theory that women's natural functions place them closer to nature than men are thought to be. Certainly the ethnographic literature on Greece records a number of such beliefs. Menstruating women are believed to spoil wine and rising bread. They are also ritually unclean and not allowed to enter church or take communion. Women who have just given birth are also in a dangerous and vulnerable condition and, for the sake of themselves and their children, must remain secluded in the house for forty days, following which they undergo a ritual purification and ceremonial reentry into normal life (see, for example, Blum and Blum 1970). Because it threatens family reputation, female sexuality is viewed as a danger to society, and it must be kept under strict control by male guardianship, both before and after marriage, as well as by women's own sense of modesty and "shame" (*dropi*) (see Hirschon 1978; du Boulay, this volume). Susannah Hoffman speaks of Greek women's "intrinsic taintedness" and the threat they pose to social order (Hoffman 1976:338).

These beliefs suggest at first that rural Greece does in fact conform to Ortner's model, that women are devalued, and that their being closer to nature accounts for their subordinate status. However, such an interpretation is misleading, for it considers such beliefs only in terms of gender roles and sexual subordination. As Olivia Harris suggests, "[t]o restrict oneself to the analysis of the ways that male and female *as symbols* are brought into relationship with the categories that most closely approximate to Ortner's use of nature and culture is to miss out on some of the most interesting questions"; instead, we ought to consider how men and women "as *social beings* stand in relationship to these categories" (Harris 1980:90).

In Greece, it can be argued, pollution is not limited to women. The bodily processes of both sexes are a potential source of danger, and male as well as female sexuality can be viewed as potentially destructive.[2] Thus, pollution in and of itself is not an attribute of femaleness alone. However, it is upon women that the burden of controlling pollution falls, and this control is part of their larger responsibility for preserving the essential boundaries that support social and cultural life. To understand how women's roles are related to the symbolism of pollution and boundaries and to demonstrate how this symbolism reflects wider social concerns, we first need to examine women's relationship to their most crucial domain—the house.

THE WOMAN AND THE HOUSE

The house is the focus of Greek family life.[3] In certain areas of mainland Greece, the family may, for part of its domestic cycle, be an extended one (see, for example, Campbell 1964; Friedl 1962); in other regions, such as on many of the Aegean islands, the practice of neolocal residence places each nuclear family in its own dwelling (see, for example, Casselberry and Valvanes 1976; Dubisch 1976; Kenna 1976). There is in all areas of Greece, however, a sharp distinction between the inside of the family dwelling and the outside (cf. Pavlides and Hesser, this volume; Herzfeld, this volume). Within the walls of the house are carried out the daily activities that sustain family life in all its physical, social, and psychological aspects: the preparation and consumption of food, the socialization of children, adult sexual activity, the discussion of private family matters. The house is also a spiritual center, for each dwelling has its own icons and regular rituals associated with them (see, for example, Campbell 1964; du Boulay 1974; Dubisch 1983). Moreover, the family itself has a sacred aspect, for it represents the Holy Family, which it seeks to emulate (see du Boulay, this volume). On the occasion of certain ceremonial events, such as name days, weddings, baptisms, and memorial services, the house is opened up to the community and, in its public face, displays the family's hospitality.[4]

The house is the special responsibility of the woman, and she is both functionally and symbolically associated with it. In the area of Greece in which I did fieldwork, the Cycladic Islands, a house is the preferred dowry for a woman at marriage (see also Hoffman 1976; Kenna 1976). But even when she does not actually own her dwelling, a woman is viewed in terms of the house and the house is viewed in relation to the woman.[5] It is a high compliment to say of a woman that she is *tou spitiou*, "of the house," that is, that her time and attention are devoted to the house and family and their care (cf. Hirschon 1978:80). Once, on the occasion of a wedding, I heard several village women discussing the bride. They all agreed that while she did not have much of a figure, she was definitely *tou spitiou*, and the phrase was repeated several times with great approval, with all those present agreeing that this was a much more important feature in a wife than looks. Juliet du Boulay

1. Icons in the household shrine, or *ikonostasi*.

2. An elderly grandmother performs a disappearing female task—spinning. (Photograph by Harold Shapiro)

notes that in the village where she worked a man might refer to his wife simply as "the house" (du Boulay 1974, this volume). Ideally, a woman should be confined to the house, leaving its boundaries only as necessity demands and never for idle or frivolous reasons. Within the house, she busies herself with cooking, cleaning, airing or washing the linens, watering the potted flowers, sweeping and scrubbing, and then, if all else is done, with mending, embroidery or knitting.[6]

The opposite of the house, which is the realm of cleanliness and order, is the "street," a place of both dirt and immorality. Here, order and control are, to some extent at least, absent. In the village, the street is the place where trash is thrown, where humans and animals defecate, where strangers pass by. The street and the fields that lie beyond symbolize "the wild," the outside, the realm of competitiveness and danger (see du Boulay 1974). In this outside world are forces that threaten order and family life. A common euphemism for adultery is to say that a woman deceives her husband "in the street."[7] By spending too much time outside the house, a woman is not only neglecting her domestic duties, but also may be engaging in polluting and destructive behavior, such as illicit sexual activity or gossip (the pollution of words), which can disrupt social relations and damage a family's reputation (see du Boulay 1976; Hirschon 1978:92). Of course, this does not mean that a woman never leaves the house, for there are a variety of legitimate duties that may take her outside. She works in the fields when necessary, she feeds the chickens and the pig, she attends religious festivals.[8] But these are all activities connected with her role as maintainer of the house in both its physical and spiritual aspects. A woman who is not in her own home when her husband and children return and need her is neglecting her most important duties. Only when her day's work is over and her family provided for can she enjoy a little leisure, socializing on porch or doorstep or taking a short stroll (*volta*) with other women.

For these reasons, the state of a woman's house reflects her moral character. If she has tended it properly, she has not had time to engage in mischief and her house is in order. If, on the other hand, she has engaged in improper behavior, she has neglected the house. Once, several village women questioned me about the interior of the home of a woman who was noted as a gossip and troublemaker. Although they had never been in her house themselves, they assumed that it must be ill-kept, and they were quite gratified to find their suppositions confirmed, for it supported their own conviction that moral untidiness and an untidy house go hand in hand.

It was also appropriate that this particular woman was a poor cook (a rarity in the village), since cooking and the kitchen have an impor-

tant place in the symbolism of gender and house. The kitchen is preem-
inently a woman's realm and the locus of some of her most important
functional and symbolic activities. Renée Hirschon found that even in
the crowded conditions of Piraeus, where several elementary families
might live under one roof, a separate kitchen area symbolically mark-
ing "the existence of an independent household" and "the woman's
primary role in providing sustenance for her family" was a priority for
each married woman (Hirschon 1978:82). The kitchen is also the locus
of the everyday intimate life of family and friends, the area in which
most informal socializing takes place. And it is of course where the
tasks of preparing and serving food are carried out.[9] The kitchen is
also, as I intend to show, an important location for the control of pollution, for the transformation of natural objects into cultural objects,
and for the maintenance of the boundary between inside and outside,
culture and nature, order and chaos.

Intermediate or transitional between the kitchen and the outside is
the porch, or courtyard (avli). Usually opening off the kitchen, it is
more public in nature, for it is attached to the house yet outside it.
Whether it fronts onto the street or faces other porches to the rear of
the house, it serves as a means of connecting the house to public life.
Women sit on the porch to clean vegetables or do mending or knitting,
or they throw bedding over the porch wall to air. Sometimes, they socialize here as they work, carrying on conversations with women on
neighboring porches or with passers-by in the street. The porch is also
an area where certain types of dirt can be controlled so that they need
not enter the house. Laundry is usually done on the porch, and a man
coming in from the fields removes dirty clothes and washes on the back
porch or doorstep before entering the house.[10] Women may also attempt to extend their control into the street, sweeping up trash and animal droppings from the narrow space in front of their houses. Village
women sometimes apologized to me for the state of the streets, pointing
out as they swept that, after all, it was only a village (horio ine) and
what could one expect? (The extension of the whitewash used on the
exterior walls of the houses into the street to outline steps and paving
stones may be an aspect of the effort to extend control and order—cf.
Hirschon 1981.)

HOUSE, BODY, AND BOUNDARIES

There is a parallel between ideas about the house and those about the
body. Just as there is a contrast between inside and outside the house,

3. The front steps become a public gathering place on a Sunday afternoon. (Photograph by Harold Shapiro)

a distinction is made between the inner and outer body,[11] and it is important that the boundary between them be maintained. It is here that we can begin to understand Greek concepts regarding pollution, for they are connected to ideas of boundary maintenance.[12] Once we view them in this light, we can move away from the notion of women as polluters and begin to see that what pollution beliefs reflect is not gender status so much as more general concepts of control and order. Certain substances, whatever their source, must be kept under control, for if they are out of place they pollute (see Faithorn 1975). It is women's task to assure this separateness and thus to create and maintain the order that is the foundation of culture. And it is within the house, especially in the kitchen, that much of the activity associated with this task is carried out.

This control involves several kinds of substances and different areas of the body and the house. Contact must be prevented between that which goes into the body and that which comes out and between things associated with cleaner and dirtier areas of the body. To this end, women must keep objects in contact with dirty substances separate from items that are clean. Thus, laundry and personal washing are done in basins, not in the kitchen sink, even when the latter is the only source of running water. And these basins—made unclean by dirt from the body—are not used for food. In addition, activities such as laundry and bathing are often performed outside, on the porch, thus further assuring separation. As noted earlier, a man coming in from the fields will often wash in the yard or on the porch, leaving dirt outside where it belongs. The towel used to dry the feet (which are closer than the rest of the body to the dirt of the outside) is not used to dry the hands and face, which are clean areas of the body.[13] The chamber pot, as the repository of bodily excrement, is particularly dirty or polluted (*magariasmeno*)[14] and is handled with special care. In this manner, pollution of the body, of the house, and of household objects is prevented.

We see, then, that rather than viewing women simply as sources of pollution (for men are also polluting), we need to examine their role as controllers of pollution, both their own and that of others, and thus as guardians of order. But this view is more complex than it appears at first, for women are not just concerned with the "negative" task of preventing pollution. They also have the positive task of transforming natural products—things grown in the "outside," in the fields, in the realm of nature—into a cultural product, namely food. Before examining this process more closely, we need to discuss the relationship between food and culture and to analyze the importance of food in Greek society.

CULTURE, NATURE, AND FOOD

Claude Lévi-Strauss has called to our attention the relationship between cooking and culture, proposing the analogy raw:cooked :: nature:culture. The act of cooking is an act of mediation between the realms of nature and culture (Lévi-Strauss 1969). In the Greek village, men bring food from the fields (the wild) to women, who transform it. This transformation is a necessary one, for agricultural products must be acted upon if they are to be considered food. By the act of cooking,

4. A basin in the courtyard for personal washing.

women perform "a vital humanizing function" (Paul 1974:289). Rather than speaking of a "hot meal" as being a "real" meal, Greeks emphasize the quality of "cookedness" (the actual temperature of the food when it is served is not of particular importance). These two ideas express the same thing—the necessity of cooking, a cultural transformation, to turn produce from the fields into food.[15] Even fruit eaten raw is always peeled or otherwise modified before it is consumed (a point also noted by Hirschon [1981]). I remember that once my landlady picked a large bowl of fresh strawberries, and then, after she had me "clean" (hull) them, to my dismay she sugared them heavily before she served them. Although to me their more "natural" state seemed preferable, for her this was a necessary transformation to ensure their edibility. The only produce consumed in its "natural" state is that picked in the field (the wild) and eaten on the spot.

For a village woman, the tasks revolving around food and the preparation of meals consume a significant portion of her day. Little is stored in the house, so meals usually require a trip to the store, an inquiry among the neighbors to see if someone has eggs or extra potatoes for sale, and at least one trip to the garden. Bread baking used to be a twice-weekly task that could take up a significant part of the day. (Today bread is usually purchased.) There seems to be little long-range planning of meals, and the topic of what to serve is often discussed and worried over as meal time approaches. If a man is working in nearby fields, he may come home for a cooked midday meal, or one will be taken to him by his wife or child.

Food is intimately related to the family and is a general area of concern and interest in Greek social life. Every household has at least the ideal of self-sufficiency. If the ideal is seldom realized today, it is still presented as a much-admired feature of the past. The family takes pride in its food, whether in the products of its own household economy or in the fact that its village produces the best wine in the region, and locally produced food is always considered superior to any purchased item. A considerable part of casual conversation consists of discussions of past meals—where they were eaten, what was served, and the quality of the food.

Family meals are generally consumed in the kitchen, the center of a woman's domestic efforts. Preparing food and serving it to her family reflects a woman's relationships with them and her fulfillment of her role as wife and mother. Moreover, cooking demonstrates not only love and nurturing but also good character. As mentioned above, a woman who had a poor reputation in the village where I did fieldwork was also a bad cook. Hirschon reports that among Asia Minor Greeks, quickly

5. An elderly couple on the island of Tinos. (Photograph by Harold Shapiro)

prepared foods were referred to as "prostitute's food" (*tis putanas to fai*). After all, what else could motivate a woman to take shortcuts with her food than the need to free her time for other, presumably immoral, activity[16] (Hirschon 1978:83).

We might add another dimension here, drawing on Lévi-Strauss's suggestion that noise and food are incompatible with each other (Lévi-Strauss 1969:294). Given the negative evaluation of a woman who is known to have a tongue (*glossa*—Hirschon 1978), we might suggest that, ideally, a Greek woman should cook, not talk, and that the more time she devotes to one, the less time she will have for the other.

Food also has a spiritual aspect. A family meal is a sacred event (du Boulay 1974; Hirschon 1981). Food figures prominently in any holiday, and the major ones (such as Easter) have their own special foods which are cooked only for that occasion and require elaborate preparation. Food is also an important part of family hospitality, itself important to a family's (and community's) reputation. When guests are present, it is the woman's products that represent the household to the public world. Food also symbolizes the continuing relationship between the world of the living and the world of the dead, and this is also part of a woman's responsibility. Women carry offerings of food to the graves of deceased family members and prepare the ritual *koliva* (a confection of boiled wheat) to take to the cemetery on All Souls' Day. Once again they serve as mediators, in this case between life and death.[17]

Food, then, is integrally involved with women's roles. Greek mothers have a reputation for the forceful and insistent feeding of their children, and the admonition to "eat!" (*fae!*) often punctuates children's meals. I once saw a woman at the beach, bowl and spoon in hand, follow her small son into the water, trying to get him to take just one more bite.

It would be a mistake, however, to view the symbolism of food only in terms of gender roles. Food is part of a general idiom in which social relationships are expressed. It symbolizes bonds within the family and between the family and the outside world. Men may preside over ritual meals (for example, they are the hosts at the celebration of their name days), and their hospitable serving of food can occasionally reach aggressive proportions worthy of the most insistent Greek mother. One time, a male villager sitting with me at a village festival cut up pieces of meat, skewered them on a fork, and quite literally fed them to me, just as a mother might feed a child. Thus, while women may symbolize nurturance and food, such symbolism does not necessarily coincide neatly with gender roles, and men may also take on patterns of "feminine" behavior as occasion warrants.[18]

Gender roles, then, cannot be analyzed simply in terms of symbolic

oppositions such as nature/culture, pollution/purity (or even private/
public, profane/sacred). Rather than being equated in a simple fashion
with one side of such oppositions, women are concerned with maintaining boundaries, mediating between realms, and transforming substances suitable for one realm into those proper for another.[19] In addition, in their preparation and serving of food, they symbolize, create,
and sustain those bonds necessary for social order. Instead of seeing
women only as potential disrupters of social order (see, for example,
Hoffman 1976), we might gain more insight if we analyze the ways in
which, on both a practical and symbolic level, they provide the "glue"
that helps bind social units.

SOCIAL ORDER AND THE LANGUAGE OF POLLUTION

But even if we end our analysis here, with women's role as mediators
and transformers, we are still taking too narrow a view. We need to
look beyond these roles and ask what the system as a whole is about.
What are Greek beliefs about pollution and sexuality "saying" in some
larger sense? Mary Douglas suggests that ideas about sexual dangers,
rather than expressing something about the actual relations of the
sexes, "are better interpreted as symbols of the relation between parts
of society" (Douglas 1966:14). Following Douglas, I suggest that in the
Greek village in which I worked, and in other villages as well, house
and body represent both each other and the social order, and that the
concerns pertaining to each and the controls that are placed over them
reflect certain important concerns of the social system as a whole.[20]

To determine what these concerns are, it is necessary to discuss
briefly some of the important features of village life. This life has often
been described as "agonistic" (Campbell 1964; Friedl 1962); that is,
relationships among families are competitive, a competition that centers not only around economic advancement but also around family
reputation (filotimo).[21] Reputation is lost or maintained in the public
arena of Greek village life, for it is its attribution, or the withholding of
attribution, by others in the community that determines whether individual families possess it. A family's reputation depends upon a man's
success as provider and his willingness to defend the family from insult,
upon the proper display of hospitality, and upon a woman's appropriate and modest conduct. The conduct of any one family member reflects on the family as a whole. Reputation, once lost, is difficult to re-
gain. Since reputation is something conferred by the judgment of
others, what counts is not so much what one does as whether anyone

6. A young couple with child. (Photograph by Harold Shapiro)

finds out about it.[22] Therefore, any information detrimental to the family should be kept inside the house and not let out "into the street."

Related to this feature of village life is the distinction Greeks make between inside and outside, between "us" (*dhiki mas*, "our own") and "them" (*kseni*, "strangers"). One's own can be trusted, and relationships are diffuse and supportive. Strangers, on the other hand, are not to be trusted; with them, one is under no obligation to behave honorably.[23] The house, as the focus of family life, reflects this dichotomy. Greek houses are built to maximize privacy, and while they may be clustered close together, they are raised above the street and angled away from each other (cf. Friedl 1962), their windows often shuttered and curtained. Thus, despite their proximity, it is almost impossible to see into one house from another.[24]

Within the house is order (mutual obligation and support); without is the "wild" (competition and "strangers"). The house guards the family's reputation and privacy, which is symbolized in the control of things passing over its boundaries. Whether these things are women, information, food,[25] or dirt, their movement must be guarded and controlled. The boundaries between inside and outside are upheld either by preventing passage of certain substances or by transforming these substances into matter acceptable for such passage. Thus, dirt is kept out of the house; food is transformed, through cooking, from a raw natural substance into a culturally created product; and family matters are not discussed outside the house, where they can become "dirt" (gossip), "matter out of place" (Douglas 1966).

Likewise, the body also symbolizes this inside/outside division and the importance of control. Douglas observes that "[i]nterest in the body's apertures depends upon the preoccupations with social exits and entrances, escape routes and invasions" (Douglas 1970:98). "We should expect the orifices of the body to symbolize its especially vulnerable points" (Douglas 1966:145). Concern with what comes and goes in the body, with things that move from inside to out and those that go from outside to in, parallels the concern with what goes inside and outside the house and reflects the larger preoccupation with the boundaries of the family and their protection. Through bodily orifices pollution can occur. The natural impulses of sexuality must be transformed through marriage and controlled through a woman's dropi, or sense of "shame," so that they are channeled into a culturally circumscribed and acceptable act that ensures family continuity. Illicit sexual penetration is a violation of the family; it is, like gossip, "matter out of place," dirt, and, like all dirt, polluting. Through a woman's sexual orifice, dishonor can occur. Through her mouth, gossip and the revelation of family secrets can run uncontrolled. A woman's body thus becomes the symbol of family integrity and purity and, more generally, of society as a whole (cf. Giovannini 1981).

Based on this analysis, we might draw a parallel between the kitchen and the vagina,[26] each an important entryway for the maintenance of the family—through sustenance and procreation, respectively—but each also a potential arena for pollution. The kitchen, the point of entry into the house, is protected by the porch, an area for collecting or deflecting dirt, just as entry into the woman is protected both by modest clothing and the propriety of her own deportment, which deflects improper sexual advances or gossip. Both kitchen and sexual entryway are subject to cultural rules regarding the passage of substances, rules that serve to turn a natural product or impulse into a culturally approved one. And each, because it is a point of entry between inside and out, carries a certain element of ambivalence or liminality.

Thus, a woman can be responsible for the loss of her family's reputation through her failure to maintain the boundaries of house and body. A woman guilty of such a failure earns the designation of dirty (*vromiara*), for she has let matter out of place and threatened social order, but a woman who performs her proper role in boundary maintenance is clean (*kathari*), in body, in house, in her family's reputation. She is a supporter and preserver, rather than a destroyer, of social order.

CONCLUSION

This analysis has not sought to deny that beliefs regarding pollution are associated with gender roles. Obviously, there is a close relationship between the two, and concepts of pollution, although not limited to women, nonetheless have important consequences for women's behavior.[27] What is being suggested, however, is that we must neither confuse gender roles with gender symbolism, nor see them as simple reflections of each other. While the nature/culture dichotomy seems to have some relevance for our understanding of important symbolic realms within the village, equating these realms with female and male respectively is misleading, and focusing on pollution as a female "problem" and a reflection or cause of women's subordinate status leads us to overlook the wider social significance of these beliefs. When we question the female:male :: nature:culture analogy and view pollution beliefs instead as statements regarding social boundaries, we also have to question assumptions about the relationship of such beliefs to women's subordinate status. Ortner views the attribution of defilement "as *implicitly* making a statement of inferior valuation" and as one of the factors that constitutes "evidence that a particular culture considers women inferior" (Ortner 1974:69). But if pollution beliefs are not really "about" women, then we cannot necessarily take them as indicators of women's lower valuation (cf. Faithorn 1975). And if women are to be seen as controllers of nature and maintainers of cultural boundaries rather than simply as more "in" nature than men, then the female:nature equation cannot be associated in any simple way with their presumed lower status. Moreover, "feminine" qualities can be considered valuable and appropriate in certain contexts, for both men and women.[28] This is not to say that ideology plays no role in sexual subordination; rather, it suggests that such ideology cannot be reduced to the nature/culture dichotomy or deduced absolutely from beliefs regarding pollution, since these reflect structural and ideological features that transcend gender roles.

NOTES TO CHAPTER NINE

1. This essay is a revised version of a paper entitled "Culture Enters Through the Kitchen: Women, House and Food in Greece," presented at the annual meeting of the American Anthropological Association in Los Angeles in 1981. I am indebted to Loring Danforth and Renée Hirschon for suggesting to me some of the ideas upon which this paper is based.
2. I have developed this argument more fully elsewhere (Dubisch 1983).
3. Men, on the other hand, are more associated with public space and carry out both business and leisure activities there (see Friedl, this volume).
4. See Danforth (1983) for a discussion of the public aspects of the house.
5. This does not mean that men have no role in the house. They support it by bringing in resources from the outside and laboring on its behalf (see Hirschon 1978). But while a woman is praised for being *tou spitiou*, a man may be criticized for having such a trait (cf. Loizos 1981:28-29).
6. Hirschon (1978) notes the importance of women "keeping busy" with tasks such as embroidery in the urban community she studied.
7. See Hirschon (1978) for similar observations regarding the urban street; cf. Paul (1974:283, 290).
8. See Hirschon (1983) regarding the role of religious excursions in allowing women a legitimate reason for leaving the house. She suggests, however, that because urban women are not engaged in agricultural tasks, the boundary between inside and outside, house and street, is more marked in cities than in rural villages.
9. Hoffman makes a distinction between women's domestic cooking and pub-

lic cooking for ritual occasions which, she states, is carried out by men (Hoffman 1974). However, I found no such differentiation on the island of Tinos.

10. Hirschon (1981) notes the importance of the straight-backed chair in the urban setting. It is an item that can be carried into the street for sitting and socializing, thus serving as a bridge between inside and outside.

11. Okely (1975) notes a similar distinction among gypsies.

12. Hoffman (1976) likewise suggests that women's bodies are a symbol of society, but she stresses the negative aspects of women.

13. Okely (1975) has observed among gypsies a similar separation in the use of utensils.

14. It was Hirschon who first called my attention to the concept of *magarisma*, prior to my beginning fieldwork. She told me of a conversation with a Greek from Mykonos who had recently returned from England complaining about how "dirty" people were there because they did not practice the sort of separation discussed here.

15. We might contrast this concept with the "natural food" movement in American society, in which things that are raw or minimally transformed are given high value.

16. It is interesting to note that women in the village where I lived assumed that foreign women could not cook, and several women remarked to me that I must have had to learn to cook after I arrived in Greece. I do not know to what extent this idea is connected to either the generally assumed immorality of foreigners or the fact that villagers' notion of American cuisine is based on the American canned goods on the shelves of village stores.

On the association of symbolic aspects of woman and their relationship to food in an Italian village, see Giovannini (1981).

17. See Danforth (1982) for an extensive discussion of the relationship between food, women, and mortuary ritual.

18. Cf. du Boulay, Caraveli, and Herzfeld, this volume.

19. Ortner (1974) notes woman's intermediate position and her role as mediator, and also the fact that in some situations she may be aligned with culture. However, this aspect of her argument has received less attention than the nature/culture, female/male dichotomy.

20. Hirschon's work in Piraeus suggests that many of these characteristics may also apply to at least some segments of urban populations (see Hirschon 1978, 1983, 1980).

21. On the concept of *filotimo*, see Campbell (1964), Friedl (1962), and Herzfeld (1980a).

22. As a villager in the mountain community studied by du Boulay expressed it, O *Theos thelei skepasma*, "God wants things covered up" (du Boulay 1976:406).

23. The concepts of dhiki mas and kseni are contextual, and dhiki may include all villagers or, in some cases, even all Greeks, as contrasted to non-Greeks.

24. I do not wish to overemphasize this privacy, however, which is not as great as that found, for example, in some Middle Eastern societies.

25. Things passing between houses may be concealed as they are carried through the street. Whenever anyone gave us food to take home, they always covered or wrapped it so no one would know what they had given us.

26. Cf. Okely's (1975) discussion of the sexual orifice as mouth.

27. Cf. du Boulay, this volume, on the notions of sexuality, sin, and the potential threat to the household posed by women.

28. Cf. Herzfeld, this volume.

TEN

Within and Without:
The Category of "Female"
in the Ethnography of
Modern Greece

MICHAEL HERZFELD

THE ANALYSIS of rural Greek gender ideology has suffered from an excess of generalization. The meticulous particularism of the earlier ethnographic accounts (notably Friedl 1962; Campbell 1964) generated some complementary oppositions (especially honor:shame:: men:women :: public:domestic) that both enabled and bedeviled cross-cultural comparison. While these equations worked reasonably well in particular ethnographic situations, where they functioned as convenient descriptions rather than as substantial theoretical elaborations (see, for example, du Boulay 1974:104), they soon acquired much more disturbing characteristics. They sacrificed *complementarity* to *opposition* and so lost their significance as essentially manipulable and rhetorically subtle symbols. By separating men and women from each other with a rigidity that far surpassed that of the actors they sought to describe, ethnographers for a while ignored the lability of male and female stereotypes and their capacity for variation and change (see, for example, Hoffman 1976; cf. Dimen 1977; see also Danforth 1983). At the same time, the formal structural equations fed a growing tendency to homogenize "Mediterranean society" in terms of a circular argument about "honor and shame" (see, for example, Blok 1981; cf. Herzfeld 1984). Cross-cultural generalization began to undermine ethnographic description, forcing the latter into the larger mold.

The besetting problem was that of finding the appropriate level of generalization. Anthropologists working in Greece have never claimed that their communities were in any sense "typical" of the country.[1] On the other hand, the closely related charge that anthropologists have tended to work in isolation from the national framework is well taken (see, for example, Mouzelis 1978:68). Their particularistic focus has often led them, if not to ignore, then certainly to downplay the role of

nationalistic ideology in the development of local values and identities.[2] As a result, the problems of gender ideology have been treated
within a strictly local frame of reference—one that permits cross-community comparison, certainly, but one that also obscures the possible
effects of nationalistic concepts of Greek identity on how both anthropologists and local people conceive the roles appropriate to men and
women.

In this essay, therefore, I indicate some of the possibly relevant connections. My focus is necessarily programmatic, and the questions I
raise will have to be answered by subsequent fieldwork and archival research. I hope, nevertheless, that the central point will emerge clearly:
that "female" and "male" are symbolic categories, as manipulable and
labile as those of *dropi* and *filotimo* or of "private" and "public," and
that villagers and nationalist writers alike use them to articulate ideas
about what it means, in particular contexts, to be a Greek woman or
man. In this way, I suggest, we can counter the charges of both excessive generalization and excessive particularism by situating the *uses* of
gender symbolism and ideology in an appropriate historical setting—
the experience of national identity at both the national and local levels.

Ever since the early days of Greek statehood, the rural people furnished materials for the symbolic construction of Greekness (Herzfeld
1982a). Foreign anthropologists, perhaps too eager to distinguish
themselves from both "folklorists" and "political polemicists," have
largely ignored these early findings and consequently have lost sight of
the fact that even the most interventionist of official definitions of
Greekness are largely derived from precisely the kinds of small-scale rural societies that anthropologists themselves traditionally study. It
would not be very surprising, therefore, if we were to discover *some*
sort of relationship between the idealized rural Greek society of the nationalistic discourse and what we ourselves find "in the field." We
would also be guilty of extraordinary arrogance and ethnocentrism if
we were to insist on the objectivity of our own observations, while denying that those of indigenous and contemporary observers have any
relevance to our work.

Indeed, I will suggest here that our own focus on gender roles is
something of a distortion, though a useful one if we can learn from it.
Specifically, we have elevated the female/male dichotomy to the level of
a key symbol in our own discourse. In other words, we have persist-
ently viewed the gender dichotomy as though it were unquestionably
the foundation on which other symbolic oppositions rested. In particular, the tendency to treat the private/public opposition as an epiphenomenon of the female/male polarity says something about the con-

cerns of anthropologists but not necessarily about those of the people they study.

I suggest that the reverse would be equally applicable, that the categories of "male" and "female," far from being yoked indissolubly to specific individuals, can be manipulated as symbols of exterior and interior identities of other kinds. They are epiphenomena of a fundamental concern with display and concealment, extroversion and introspection, pride and self-criticism. This does not mean that gender categories are unimportant or insignificant in rural Greece. On the contrary, their immense evocative power is what makes them an ideal device for negotiating the complex relationships between different levels of identity—kin-group, local, regional, and national. Because women are stereotyped as "interior" beings, for example, female images evoke a strong sense of familiarity and comfort, a sense that necessarily allows for the known flaws of one's intimate world. It is thus not so much that women *are* flawed in Greek gender ideology, as that they *can stand for* the flaws, as well as the benefits, that Greeks recognize as characteristic of their own families, villages, regions, and even nation. Herein lies the significance of women as simultaneously virginal mothers and diabolical strumpets (see, for example, Campbell 1964:31, 277, 354; du Boulay 1974:102, 173; cf. also Giovannini 1981 for a comparable Italian example). Because women are formally associated with what is interior and intimate, they symbolize self-knowledge. Their very existence is an appropriate metaphor for that condition. Just as self-knowledge is discomfiting in a public context yet comfortingly familiar in a private one, so women both diabolically threaten the men with public exposure yet also provide them with the maternal and uxorious comforts of domesticity.

BEING GREEK: CONFLICTING IMAGES

Modern Greeks entertain two quite disparate images of their national culture. One of these stereotypes, the so-called Hellenic model, represents the self-conscious classicizing and archaizing ideology of the establishment and political right wing, subsumes the purist language movement, and is extensively involved with the development of a national ethnological (or laographic) tradition in Greek scholarship (see Herzfeld 1982a). Opposed to this model is a second stereotype, which I call the "Romeic," and which, most characteristically exemplified by linguistic demoticism, represents the familiar self-image which Greeks entertain about themselves when conversing *among* themselves. These are the two faces of Greek *national* identity that conform to the models of public pride and private intimacy just described.

The two models represent allusions to two different periods of Greek history, one recalling the glories of the classical era and the other recalling the more recent Byzantine and Turkish periods. Greeks do not adopt one or the other model consistently but rather negotiate social relationships and identities by means of the tension that subsists between the two poles. When talking to a foreigner, for example, a Greek may well adopt a Hellenic pose, at least until the foreigner has demonstrated a good feeling for the Romeic alternative. In political discourse, too, a speaker may alternate the two poses strategically, appealing both to a sense of pride in the Periclean past and to exasperation with the familiar absurdities of patronage or the bureaucracy. Since the Hellenic model was developed largely in response to the classicizing tastes of those who supported the Greek national cause from abroad, it should not surprise us that this model should be associated with a form of collective extroversion. By the same token, the willingness of exponents of the Romeic model to acknowledge the importance of Turkish and other non-Western influences on Greek culture corresponds to an ideology that is at once more internationalist and more amenable to domestic *social* (that is, rather than *cultural*) criticism.

This fundamental dichotomy in Greek culture has generated a series of divergences in virtually all the cultural codes that integrate village life with national identity. The most celebrated of these problem areas is the so-called "language question" (*ghlossiko zitima*). The language question in Greece pits a formally archaizing or neoclassical form of Greek (*katharevousa*) against the demotic tongue of everyday discourse. I have argued elsewhere, however, that to describe this problem as diglossia and isolate it as a unique phenomenon in Greek society is to overlook a wide range of similar divergences in other areas of Greek self-expression. I thus prefer to use the term *disemia* to address the whole gamut of these patterns (Herzfeld 1982b). In architecture, for example, we often find that a neoclassical house façade masks an extremely simple, village-style interior. The outside announces to the uninitiated that here lives a true Hellene. The inside, with its familiar intimacy, is an environment that every Greek recognizes as characteristic of the culture as a whole, though not necessarily one that should be displayed to outsiders. Thus, the style of domestic architecture, like the extensive code-switching that takes place in language between katharevousa and demotic Greek, reproduces the fundamental historical and ideological experience of the Greek nation as an entity. The symbols of national culture become negotiable elements in a social discourse. It is not that Greeks consciously think all the time about the reproduction of national history in everyday interaction; on the contrary, these associations have become part of the daily cultural style that every Greek takes for granted.

In this context, it becomes easier to see how the movement of men and women alike across the boundaries of inclusion and exclusion may suggest that what we have been accustomed to perceiving as specifically *gender* roles are actually facets of a more general rhetoric of concealment and display. Such rhetoric is paralleled in other societies. In Kabylia, for example, Bourdieu notes the extraordinary significance of covering and interiority as a component both of female identity and of its complement, male self-regard (Bourdieu 1965:221-225). The association of women with the value of dropi, commonly if inadequately glossed as "shame," frequently has been associated in the ethnographic literature with such characteristic behavior patterns as the disguising of sexuality through drab clothing and the concealment of female interaction behind closed doors (see, for example, Campbell 1964:287). Ethnographically well argued, these observations take on added meaning in the context of discourse about *national* identity. The male/female dichotomy then appears less as a mere epiphenomenon of the distinction between public and private than as a model that serves for the exploration of other social boundaries as well.

A few ethnographic illustrations from my own fieldwork in the villages of Pefko, on the island of Rhodes, and Glendi, on the island of Crete, will serve to make the point more effectively.[3] When a Pefkiot woman slapped her drunkard husband during one of my visits to their home, she was effectively signaling my inclusion into their domestic circle. She was not behaving like the submissive woman of the ethnographic stereotype; rather, she was adopting a different female role, one that was more appropriate to the intimacy of "inside." A young married couple who did ethnographic research in Methana similarly discovered not only that household economy often was controlled by "physically and socially strong women," but also that sexual joking was acceptable in mixed company "so long as everyone present was married" (Clark 1983:122-123). Clearly, what is important here is the audience; the actors' social competence encompasses the ability to shift between intimacy and formality as the occasion demands.

The converse of this principle also applies: a person's disregard for context will induce sharp criticism. A Glendiot woman who entered a coffeehouse—a definitively "public" and "male" space—aroused considerable contempt by screaming at the proprietor about his son's violence against her own boy. One of the patrons commented that she was a "male-female"—she had violated the spatial conventions not by entering the coffeehouse, but by doing so as an *unrelated* female and by behaving in an aggressive way more appropriate to a man. Had she merely entered to make a purchase, she would have been treated politely and would probably have aroused no comment. Her behavior, however, confused the lines of demarcation; it would have been appropriate at home, even if directed at her own husband, and it would have been appropriate in public had she been a man. Other women, especially the close kin of coffeehouse proprietors, not only enter these places but help with the serving and sometimes take charge on their own. But they act meekly and as though offering hospitality to strangers in their own homes. What they do *not* do is behave as though they were at home with immediate family or other intimates.[4]

It is generally understood that women do exercise far more authority in intimate settings than in public. Du Boulay (1974:129) reports that an Ambeliot husband is considered "a guest in the house" (a stock phrase also heard in Serbia [Halpern 1956:142]). Because discussion so far has centered primarily on the research categories of "sex roles" and "public and private domains," and thus on the actual practice of male-female relations, little attention has been paid to the possibility that the domestic inversion of public authority patterns might be a metaphor for and icon of the Romeic ideology. Just as anthropologists have tended to adopt the Hellenist rather than the Romeic stereotype of Greek culture, they have tended to emphasize male authority in general and to overlook the extent to which it is transformed into a measure of subordination within the family home. Since the very idea of a man being slapped by his wife is perhaps more familiar—and certainly more embarrassing—than most writers acknowledge, it belongs properly with the Romeic rather than with the Hellenist model. It is an aspect of the everyday reality of Greek life, not of the generalized ideal.

The omission of any such considerations from the published ethnographies has probably been reinforced by the fact that until recently most anthropological work was done by foreigners, who may have been actively discouraged from gaining access to the Romeic side of Greek identity. Certainly, at least one Greek ethnographer has stressed the significance and the great complexity of the interrelationships between gender roles and categories of inclusion and exclusion in modern Greek rural culture (see Skouteri-Didaskalou 1980).

This is an important and comparatively rare insight. Both Greek and foreign ethnographers have had to contend with the strongly elitist implications of their role as "scholars" for their informants, and with the ideological effects of that perception on the resulting discourse. It is certainly significant that Ernestine Friedl, who with great honesty reports that she and her husband were not allowed to perform menial tasks, acquired a good knowledge of the Vasilikans' *classical* pretensions but says relatively little about any negative or jocular stereotyping of Greek identity; her informants even presented the divisiveness of Greek social and political life (which their counterparts in Pefko certainly bewailed as one of the nation's greatest problems) as flowing from an ancestral "love of freedom" (Friedl 1962:105-106). The Vasilikans evidently emphasized the "Hellenist" and androcentric interpretations of Greek culture in their discussions with the visiting ethnographers, and it is a tribute to the ethnographers' sensitivity that, despite the villagers' essentially nationalistic stance, so many hints that they *simultaneously* but *internally* espoused a more Romeic perspective do in fact surface throughout the book. While Friedl succeeded in developing close ties with the women (cf. Clark 1983:127; Friedl 1970:217), the latter were probably not very interested in exploring the problems of "national character." Men, on the other hand, interacted more with her husband, whom they knew to be a distinguished scholar and to whom it was consequently more appropriate to present the Hellenist model of Greek identity. The Romeic model might have slipped through the crack had the ethnographers not been receptive to the often all-too-vague suggestions of its importance in the villagers' own scheme of things.

There are many insights into this "low" model in the various published ethnographies, including allusions to the Greeks' supposed lack of disinterested political detachment (for example, Sanders 1962:238-240), despairing appraisals of the inevitability of graft and influence-peddling in civil and political life (Campbell 1964:256-262), and acknowledgments of the role of guile (*poniria*) in social relations (Friedl 1962:76, 80; Campbell 1964:282-283; du Boulay 1974:167-168, 201-229). The stereotype of "illiteracy" is often predicated on an explicit substitution of the Romeic for the Hellenist model: a common complaint is that the Europeans "received the light [that is, of the intellect] from Greece and have not returned it."

This "warts and all" Greek self-image reproduces the main characteristics of what is usually thought of as the Greeks' model of female identity—cunning, illiteracy (*aghrammatosini*), deprivation, and lack of self-control.[5] Like female identity, it is something to shield from outsiders and a cause for embarrassment or even anger when it is inadvertently exposed to prying eyes. Female modesty, far from being a total separation of female from male interests, is a public reversal of domestic power relations. In the same way, a general reluctance to discuss the less "civilized" aspects of Greek life with foreigners, presented as a desire to become more "European," often actually hides a strong element of condescension toward the effeteness of the West. The male-female complementarity thus provides an apt analogy for the Greeks' view of their general cultural and political subordination to "Europe" (*Evropi*). The relative and symbolic seclusion of women, with its intimations of a stereotypical inferiority that can be leavened but never entirely redeemed by personal guile, is thus analogous to the intimacy and privacy of the Romeic model—a model that is extensively discussed in *Greek* writings (in newspapers, for example) but that often shies away behind the modesty enjoined by "national filotimo"[6] whenever foreigners are present.

WOMEN IN ETHNOGRAPHIC DISCOURSE

These brief observations should make it clear that the villagers' ability to situate any ethnographer in a particular ideological framework must affect the recording of data. The history of ethnographic fieldwork in Greece reflects this. Much excellent work was done by the Greek folklorists, but an internal political and symbolic split between folklore and anthropology, as well as between indigenous and foreign scholarship, has had the unfortunate effect of polarizing the results of research.

Many Greek folklorists in the past have been committed to the presentation of an idealized view of national culture. Some of them, indeed, so presented themselves as high-status individuals to the villagers with whom they talked that they had little or no chance of reflecting an "inside" view of Greek society in their writings. Foreign anthropologists, by contrast, have been committed to the notion of penetration, albeit at a seemingly paradoxical distance; the paradox, of course, is the celebrated precept of participant observation. In practice, there have always been contradictions inherent in both approaches. The Greek folklorist, *as* a Greek, has been in a generally better position than the foreign observer to appreciate subtle differences of nuance and regional style, but he or she may be "marked" by urban and high-status speech styles and other traits, causing reluctance among rural informants to disclose their local traditions. The foreign anthropologist, on the other hand, usually claims a degree of objectivity that goes with being an outsider. This, too, may be a questionable contention: the foreign observer may be tempted to treat nationalistic poses as mere rhetoric, rather than as crucial elements in the mutual articulation of village and national levels of identity. As a result, whether we read the relatively scarce accounts of womanhood in the writings of nationalist folklorists or the much more frequent mentions of gender roles in the writings of foreign anthropologists, we soon get a sense that they are talking about two entirely different societies. In fact, the relative paucity of references to gender roles in the indigenous folklore literature and the relative frequency of such citations in the foreign anthropological literature together represent a fundamental result of the very phenomenon that we are examining here. Folklorists of the nineteenth century, for example, evinced a certain reluctance to discuss female roles, since what was largely domestic could not effectively be connected with the glories of high antiquity.

Thus, in the nineteenth century, Greek scholarly writing on female roles was limited in both quantity and topical range. Admittedly, Dora d'Istria, a renowned early feminist and advocate of several Balkan *risorgimenti*, devoted a significant amount of energy to both the ethnographic study and the practical emancipation of Balkan womanhood. She was not a native-born Greek, however, but received her Hellenic nationality by a special act of Parliament. Other references to the position of women in the nineteenth-century laographic literature are few and far between and usually extremely uninformative. This paucity, as I have suggested above, is the product of an existing bias in the perspective of most of the writers at the time. The assumption seems to have prevailed throughout that woman's place was very much in the home. In the works of those folklorists who were concerned to describe the domestic life of the modern Greeks, we do encounter somewhat dismissive references to the position of women. However, most of the nineteenth-century folklorists were more interested in recording texts of songs and tales, and even though many of them received examples of this folk literature from female informants, they were not sufficiently interested in the context of recording to elicit much information about the status of the performers themselves.

We do encounter references to the women of *ancient* Greece, however, since the study of women provided scholars with evidence of continuity between the ancient and modern cultures. What we see in such writings is to a large extent a replication of attitudes toward female abilities and weaknesses that are also recorded among the rural populations by foreign ethnographers. Thus, women emerge as either domestic or diabolically clever. Just as, for example, one might be told in a Greek village that when women decide to take up letters they adopt the abilities of the devil, so too one discovers a grudging admiration on the part of male writers for the intellectual skills of their female predecessors. Here is Dragoumis, writing about the women of ancient times.

> [B]ut however these works are written, they are not without value, since they relate customs and practices at the same time as demonstrating the temper of the times during which they were written. Of course it would have been preferable had the literate women of antiquity written, as they do in our own day, memoirs, travel accounts, descriptive passages, and notes and observations; how many details of what to us is the unknown life of the ancients would we have today—details which only women, much more observant than men, perceive! (Dragoumis 1866:347)

There is admiration here, certainly, but it is admiration of a curiously qualified kind. It occurs in an article that also, somewhat surprisingly, attributes to the advent of Christianity a liberation of Greek womanhood from its former travails. The implication in this passage, that it is appropriate for women to concern themselves with the observation of domestic detail, reproduces the predominant emphasis of travel writing by Western European observers, as well as the establishment ideology of Greece at that time. Men should concern themselves with public affairs, it is hinted; women more appropriately should busy themselves with describing the domestic niceties that escape men's more coarsely grained intellects.

At any rate, Greeks of the mid-nineteenth century did not consider the education of women to be more important than that of men. The effects of this indifference are of course still felt in the countryside, where it is common to hear complaints that "we women are illiterate." Among urban sophisticates, on the other hand, it was a sign of real achievement if the women of one's family were formally educated. The reasons behind this attitude were hardly emancipatory. What they do show is a concern with setting a "European" example for the benighted East, thereby reproducing the paternalistic ideology of the tutelary Western European nations and at the same time revealing how simplistic it would be simply to dismiss the role of women in early modern Greece as a purely domestic one.

> Among the domestic topics suitable for your hearing, I wish today to turn to the study of woman, and particularly Greek woman, inasmuch as concerns her national education, thinking that the discussion about her is important for the present time in which we are undergoing social and political change, and during which there is a great danger of corruption. . . . I am convinced that a substantial

part of the Greek resurgence is due to Greek woman, who with God's will is fated to shine forth for the good of the East and of all lands whither extend the margins of Hellenism. [This is] because when the son is educated, the man is illuminated, but when the daughter is educated, the entire family is illuminated. (Pappadopoulos 1866:81)

This passage illustrates a very important point. Even though women's place is considered to be in the home, they play a major role in the education and moral fashioning of their offspring, and in a world in which Greece claims "European" status, the nation's women must be correspondingly well educated. The example they set to the nations of the East is predicated upon their innate ability to act as the representatives of a fundamentally European culture. This is, in fact, a clear expression of the extroverted Hellenist ideology at work. The very concept of education as "national" (a characterization that is still preserved in the name of the appropriate government ministry in Athens) illustrates the degree to which the ideology of female gender is refracted through the prism of an extroverted nationalist concern.

"Illiteracy" is a stereotypical attribute that is applied not only by Greeks to the people of Turkey, but also by Greek men and women to the female part of their own population. "Having letters" is a sign of cultural superiority, and the variable use of illiteracy as a characteristic of Turks in some contexts and of women generally in other contexts illustrates the idea that internally Greek women may be inferior to Greek men, but externally they must be presented as superior to all Turks (see Herzfeld 1980b). An educated female population is a necessary part of the claim to European status and justifies a discrimination between Greek and Turkish identities. As further confirmation of this position, the same author continues:

I would like to mention a few brief details of her education, avoiding any exposition of the upbringing of the Greek woman in ancient times . . . because the ancient Greek woman unfortunately cannot know her modern counterpart. . . . The majority of such discussions are alien to the situation in the East, and the introduction of untried and foreign systems of education is extremely dangerous and disruptive. (Pappadopoulos 1866:81)

In other words, at the same time as the Greek woman is upheld as a model of intelligence by comparison with her Turkish counterpart, she is to be kept in a relatively submissive role, far more so than her counterpart in the countries of Western Europe.

But my intention is not to expound in detail upon the fortunes of women, nor to depict the benighted communities of the East, where the multiple organization of the family which derives from polygamy and indeed from the subjugation of woman is the principal cause of the animal degradation in which those peoples live, dragging a heavy chain of familial, theocratic, and political tyranny. It is sufficient for us to observe that in the ancient Greek society man was not the master of woman, but rather her protector. ... But the Greek mistress of the house, despite the fact that she holds a position of honor within the household, is nevertheless shut up in the female quarters; her upbringing is thus only directed to making her a good housewife [*ikonomos*]. (Pappadopoulos 1866:81)

And this same author then proceeds to lead off again in a discussion of classical parallels.

The ultimate objective of all these paternalistic assumptions is to ensure the continuity of the Greek nation through the excellence of its domestic governance.

To women, however, as we have already often said, falls the future of the fatherland, because anything which does not derive from the family hearth has no influence on social order. Woman softens the harshness of our customs. (Pappadopoulos 1866:81)

The special fascination of these passages lies in their expression of attitudes that are remarkably similar to those that emerge from ethnographic description. For example, women may exercise a restraining role on the excessive self-regard of the men. In Glendi, women attempt to use their *domestic* moral authority to entreat their husbands and sons not to go raiding the flocks of nearby villages, and they condemn such actions as pure stupidity. Friedl also reports that the women of Vasilika are contemptuous of the relatively mild forms of male self-regard usually found in their community (Friedl 1962:90). If the "harshness" of the stereotypical male is somehow necessary for the extroverted display of national as well as familial *eghoismos*, it is woman who, through her supposedly innate gentleness and cowardice, softens this behavior.

What we discover in Pappadopoulos' discussion of womanhood, above all, is a view of woman as the mediator not only between male individuals and groups, but also, indeed, between the nations. Thus, the education of Greek woman is seen as simply an expansion to the national scale of the role of woman as a mediator in quarrels and disputes, already well known from the ethnographic literature. Her education is designed not to emancipate her but to make her a suitable domestic ally for the man who will conduct public affairs. This attitude is integrated with the ideology of national extroversion in such a way as to suggest that one of the principal functions of female education is in fact to differentiate the Greek nation as a whole from the supposedly backward and oppressive culture and society of the Turks.

There is in Friedl's ethnography an important suggestion of the actual dynamic linking maleness to *national* identity (in the Hellenist sense) and femaleness to those aspects of the national self-image that have more to do with supposedly foreign but in fact much more familiar realities.

> Most of the villagers of Vasilika, in 1961, still called the village "Kravasaras." Indeed, the new sign pointing to the dirt road which leads into the settlement reads Kravasaras, in spite of the designation of the village in the provincial records as *Vasilika*. This type of double nomenclature is common in the entire region. The wives of Vasilika, most of whom come from the surrounding ocean villages, frequently refer to their former houses by their older Turkish names. These are the names which evoke for them the emotions associated with "my village." Their husbands on the other hand, often refer to their wives' home villages by the newly given names. (Friedl 1962:7)

This paragraph is extremely revealing. Vasilika is a virilocal community, so that it is the women, normatively, who move from one village to another. Such motion contrasts markedly with their status as people of the symbolic interior. Their use of Turkish names for their home villages implies and alludes to the intimate nature of their relationship with their natal families and communities. It also suggests a measure of their exclusion from the modern political realities, with all the associated emphasis on extroversion and public display. Thus, in this illuminating passage from Friedl's ethnography, we see how social interaction replicates the discourse of historical experience. This connection is closely akin to what has already been observed in language: that "Turkish" forms are associated with some sort of conceptual inferiority, as well as with things that should not be disclosed to outsiders (see Joseph 1983).

Greeks tend to regard the Turkish elements in their culture as the results of a kind of original sin attributable to the Fall of Constantinople, which in turn is analogous to that original Fall from grace to which are attributed all common social ills (Campbell 1964:326-340; cf. Herzfeld 1980b:299). Women, as the descendants of Eve, are closer to the origin of that primal Fall than are men; therefore, it is appropriate that they be associated with "Turkishness." At this point, one may recall the "illiteracy" (aghrammatosini) thought to be characteristic of Turks and women alike (Herzfeld 1980b:296-297). Yet the association with Eve is not entirely negative, since Eve was the source of all subsequent human creation. As a Rhodian wedding couplet that I heard in Pefko expresses it:

> I wish that you may branch forth as the mint-bush branches,
> as Eve branched forth so that the world was filled.

It is a condition of human existence that one's life is vitiated by social flaws, and it is a condition of being Greek—of being that *Romios* whom every Greek recognizes as the archetype of himself or herself— that elements of Turkish culture spoil the purity of every man's Hellenism.

The disemic structuring of the analogy between non-Greekness and female identity is also evident in another, seemingly trivial, but actually extremely observant passage from Friedl's ethnography. She notes that adults' use of footwear in the village displays a pattern quite unlike that of adults in North America, even though the Vasilikans use Western material models. In fact, as we shall see, it is precisely this use of "European" material models that enables footwear to serve as a device for the expression of disemic contrast. She writes:

> Shoes and slippers are purchased, not manufactured by each family; men and women do not wear the same types; the man's shoe is a standard low small oxford tie, and the women wear leather pumps with medium high heels, or cloth slippers. . . . Men in Vasilika wear ordinary oxfords for work in the fields, for walking in mud, rain, and even snow during the winter—with no other foot protection. When the fields are flooded for irrigation, men remove their shoes and work barefoot. Within their houses, men do not change into slippers; they do not own any. Women, on the other hand, wear cloth slippers both indoors and outdoors, around the house and in the fields, in all weathers and in all seasons. Their leather pumps are saved for church, for holidays, and for journeys. On such occasions women wear pumps regardless of the weather. (Friedl 1962:5)

It is clear from this passage that practical considerations have very little to do with what kind of footwear is worn on which occasion. What seems to be much more significant is a consistent differentiation be-

tween public and private roles—a differentiation that does not correspond precisely to the distinction between men and women. Let it be
noted first of all that shoes and slippers are purchased; this renders
them, relatively speaking, a status item and makes them a particularly
ideal device for emphasizing the Western character of the act of wearing. Slippers are clearly defined as domestic footwear and therefore as
appropriate only for women; this is why men do not wear shoes during
the flooding of the fields but will appear dressed in their oxfords during
extremely bad weather when they are walking around under public
scrutiny. The fact that men do not change into slippers in their homes
is a further affirmation not only of their maleness, but also of the fact
that they are "guests in their own houses."

Women demonstrate in their footwear an equally clear but differently organized distinction between public and private. They only wear
their leather pumps in church or other festive settings, since this kind of
footwear is indicative of the high status of the occasion and of the ability of their husbands to provide for their public display. At a certain
level, it would not be too far-fetched to draw an analogy between this
pattern and the nineteenth-century writer's use of the education of
Greek women as a symbol of differentiation from alleged Turkish
backwardness.

Although the ethnographic data upon which these comments are
based are given a relatively minor place in the book from which they
are taken, they are in fact of extreme importance when one is trying to
gain some sense of the correlation between local-level sex role differ-
entiations and village identities, as well as the integration of both of
these with stereotypical views of the Greek national character. In other
words, we cannot accurately understand the behavior of village
women, and the apparent differences between their public and private
demeanors, without reference to the larger national context of which
the village is both a microcosm and a part. The difference between male
and female footwear, for example, is not simply a matter of cultural
patterning. It is one expressive device that links Greek village actions to
the wider national context in which personal behavior becomes ultimately accountable. Even in those more isolated communities, like
Glendi, where social behavior is self-consciously opposed to the norms
of the state, the very fact of opposition to a nationalist and statist ideology is itself evidence of an awareness that such an ideology exists. In
a village like Vasilika, which demonstrates a far higher degree of conformity with national norms, there can be no question that there is considerable awareness of national standards of behavior.

The Virgin and the Devil:
The Richness of Ambiguity

The foregoing discussion will help us to resolve a puzzle that has bemused ethnographers working in Greece for some time—that of the apparent conflict between the stereotypical views of the Greek woman as both diabolical and angelic. Accounts by J. K. Campbell (1964) and Juliet du Boulay (1974), among others, have made this conflict a matter of considerable theoretical elaboration. I would like to suggest, however, that, once again, we can make much better sense of the apparent contradiction by linking it to the ambiguity of the overarching disemic structure; that is, the apparent ambiguity of female moral status replicates the ambiguity of the Greek in general, as he or she is between the two poles of the disemic contradiction.

I illustrate this section of the essay with some data drawn from my own fieldwork. I encountered in Pefko an elderly priest who clearly considered the advanced education of women to be an evil phenomenon. He was concerned that female emancipation was causing a nationwide and indeed global disruption of moral values, and he pointed out that education in general entailed a loss of innocence. When women acquired learning, he insisted (though with a certain amount of grudging admiration), they were truly possessed by the devil!

The ethnographic accounts of rural Greece are indeed full of references to the low cunning characteristic of women. This cunning, or poniria, is also considered to be a national characteristic of the Greeks as the latter are represented in the more inwardly directed, or Romeic, ideology. Thus, we immediately see a correlation between the position of women as potentially intelligent and even dangerous subverters of the male-controlled social order and that of the Greek *rayadhes* who, especially in the antihero figure of Karaghiozis (Danforth 1976), supplant the authority of the hated Turk with their cheeky subordination. Women are not simply the chattels of men, any more than the Greeks in general were of the Turks. That there was subjugation and subordination is without doubt. However, this should not be taken to mean that these sad conditions could not be alleviated by systematic inversion, and this in fact is precisely what we see, both in the gender role distinction and in the free play given to poniria in the folklore of the Romeic point of view.

What is more, this ambiguity, and the possibility of its being negotiated between levels, sometimes leads to curious switches of role. A tale from Pefko will suffice to illustrate this point (for a more detailed version, see Herzfeld 1984). A woman wagered with the Devil, who claimed that she would not be able to outwit him and that he would therefore be able to take her soul down to Hell. He told her that, in order to escape on this occasion, she would have to run a race with him without getting wet. She readily consented, and they set off. At this point, a downpour began, as the Devil had known it would. Not a whit dismayed, the woman stripped off her clothes and only replaced them on reaching her destination, whereupon the Devil saw that he had indeed been defeated. This story was recounted to me by a *man*, who then went on to explain that he had recalled the story one day, when a sudden rainstorm broke while he was walking between two nearby villages. He immediately stripped off his clothes and dived into a roadside ditch every time a vehicle came by. When he arrived in the village of his destination, people were amazed that he appeared to be totally dry. He was able to gain a great deal of satisfaction from their surprise and astonishment and a good deal of credit also for his display of poniria—a poniria that was truly reflexive, since he showed cunning not only in being able to keep himself dry, but also in being able to relate his behavior to an archetypical example.

The protagonist of the tale from which he drew his model was a woman. Are we to assume, then, that the male narrator was regarded as in some sense effeminate? In fact, nothing could be further from the truth. On the contrary, both his action and his use of the tale simply illustrate the negotiability of role definitions, as well as the fact that a female model is not exclusively *female* but may also serve as a guide to appropriate forms of poniria for situations in which *men* find themselves. The intimacy of the man's uncovering himself nicely captures the significance of the female image: just as there are circumstances under which a woman's interiority is evil and polluting and others under which it is warm and welcoming, so too there are circumstances under which a true Greek man should not emulate women and others under which his very Greekness—as defined by poniria—is enhanced by his doing so.

Thus, to focus on "gender roles" as the appropriate category of analysis would distort the significance of this tale. On its own, it could indeed easily illustrate the negative evaluation of female character in traditional village ideology. But this analysis would disregard the extremely valuable insight afforded by the context of performance in which the tale was recorded. That it was told to me by a man, who was able to relate it to his own behavior in such a creative manner, shows that we should view the gender role as an expressive trope for the more fundamental discrimination that marks as a national characteristic the cunning of self-recognizing Greeks. Perhaps it is not always praiseworthy, but certainly it is a trait that one cannot do without, given the fallen condition not only of women but, analogically, of the human world in general.

THE OTHER SIDE OF "GREEK IDENTITY": AWAY FROM ANDROCENTRISM

The Greeks express the duplicity of history through their mutually conflicting models of national identity. These models oppose an idealized Hellene to a gloriously insubordinate Romios. Greek woman functions, literally and metaphorically, as an apt trope for the condition of the Greeks generally. While Greek male pride and female submission may serve as the exemplars as far as the extroverted ideology is concerned, the poniria of Greek women is a hypotactic model of *Romiossini*, or Romeic identity. In this nationalistic discourse, the tension between Virgin and Devil is replicated between Pericles and Karaghiozis.

There is even some linguistic evidence that feminine grammatical gender is associated with the less-controlled but more familiar aspects of male sexuality; the male organ, which in clinical usage is neuter in grammatical gender, becomes known by a feminine noun in jokes and ribaldry, and there are numerous expressions in which a feminized sexuality expresses a familiar sense of disorder.[7]

The tension between the two extreme models of Greek culture is thus replicated in the tension between the respective stereotypes of male and female in rural Greek society. The roles of male and female may be reversed at both levels. The extreme type of filotimo, once commonly regarded as a male virtue, can be seen in the Glendiots' idealization of the poor old woman whose hospitality consists of all of the little that she owns. Again, if the superhuman quality of the "warrior maiden" (*andriomeni*) in Greek folklore "has as its precondition freedom from woman's ordinary sexual allegiance to a male" (Constantinides 1983:71), then by analogy this heroic figure can be viewed as representing the vindication of the oppressed Romios no less than do the temporary but uproarious triumphs of Karaghiozis.

Like all symbols, the markers male and female, *filotimos* and *dropiasmenos*, and Hellene and Romios are extremely labile. Anthropologists and folklorists necessarily find themselves cast by their informants in terms of these same categories, with important consequences for the picture that emerges thereafter. We should not study "gender roles" in isolation from the symbolism of gender (grammatical as well as personal) or from the political rhetoric of identity. To do so risks reintroducing a reductionist binarism that separates categories from experience and represents men and women in Greek society at large as the slaves of stereotypes that are at times demonstrably inaccurate. If what we seek is an acceptable level of generalization about Greek men and women, then we must locate the analysis within the framework implicitly chosen for it—that of *Greece*, the political and conceptual entity. We must seek to establish more clearly how the existing descriptions and ideologies of gender have been influenced by their entailment in a dialogue between politicians and peasants, anthropologists and folklorists, foreigners and Greeks. The stereotypes that have emerged thus far clearly have been influenced by the conflict between doctrines of national identity, and any study of gender ideology that ignores this encompassing circumstance must also fail to rise above the ethnocentrism and sexism of caricature.

NOTES TO CHAPTER TEN

1. This view runs contrary to the claims of some of their sociological colleagues (notably Vlachos, in Dimen and Friedl 1976:286-288; but cf. the responses of Andromedas, Dimen, and Friedl); as far as I know, the only book with the general title *The Greek Peasant* (McNall 1974) is by a sociologist who also participated in this debate!
2. An important exception, though having to do with Cyprus, is the work of Loizos (1975, 1981).
3. Pefko (pseudonym), where I conducted fieldwork during the first half of 1974, has a population of about 160. Subsequently, I conducted extensive fieldwork, for a total of fifteen months between 1974 and 1981, in Glendi (pseudonym), a West Cretan highland village with a population of over 1,400 (see Herzfeld 1985).
4. This incident is discussed in greater detail in Herzfeld 1985:71-75.
5. On the alleged lack of ability for self-government, note that a common formulaic "justification" for the military junta of 1967-1974 was that the Greeks were supposedly in need of a strong, dictatorial hand.
6. "National filotimo" means the national pride that demands a "covering" of any traits that might seem undesirable to an outsider.
7. Katharevousa neuter noun *peos*; demotic feminine noun *psoli*. See also Herzfeld (1985) for an extended discussion of these idioms in Glendi, where they seem to be more completely elaborated than anywhere else in Greece that I have encountered them.

CONTRIBUTORS

ANNA CARAVELI was born in Athens, Greece. She came to the United States in 1966 to attend college and in 1978 received her Ph.D. in comparative literature from the State University of New York at Binghamton, where she specialized in folk literature and folk culture. She has done fieldwork in Crete and Epiros and, since 1979, has been conducting research on the village of Olymbos on the island of Karpathos and in a settlement of immigrants from this community in Baltimore, Maryland. Her research focuses on identity formation and boundary negotiation and the role of traditional ritual and oral events in these processes. She has taught at SUNY-Binghamton and Cornell and is currently at the Smithsonian Institution in Washington, D.C., where she develops educational programs.

MURIEL DIMEN received her Ph.D. in 1970 from Columbia University and her certificate in 1983 from the New York University program in psychotherapy and psychoanalysis. She is the author of *The Anthropological Imagination* and co-editor with Ernestine Friedl of the New York Academy of Sciences volume *Regional Variation in Modern Greece and Cyprus*. She also has written many articles on the ethnography of Greece, social theory, sexuality, and feminism. She is currently professor of anthropology at Lehman College and is working on a book entitled *Sexual Contradictions*, which will be published by Macmillan in 1986.

JILL DUBISCH received her Ph.D. in anthropology from the University of Chicago in 1972. Her dissertation was on the effects of rural-urban migration on a small island community, and she has written articles on migration, religion, women's roles, gender symbolism, health foods, and medical anthropology. She is an associate professor of anthropology at the University of North Carolina at Charlotte and is currently doing research on healing shrines.

JULIET DU BOULAY read language and literature at Oxford from 1955 to 1958 and then worked until 1961 as a journalist in London. After three years of work and travel in Greece, she returned to take the Diploma of Social Anthropology at Oxford in 1965. Her first period of fieldwork, from 1966 to 1968, resulted in her book *Portrait of a Greek Mountain Village*, published in 1974; a second period of fieldwork, from 1971 to 1973, produced various articles and a book in preparation on cosmology and symbolism. She was Associate Fellow at Antony's College, Oxford from 1970 to 1976 and is currently an Honorary Research Fellow at Aberdeen University.

ERNESTINE FRIEDL is the author of *Vasilika: A Village in Modern Greece* and *Men and Women: An Anthropologist's View*, as well as articles on gender roles, rural-urban migration, fieldwork, and peasant society. She has taught at Queens College of the City University of New York and is currently James P. Duke Professor of Anthropology at Duke University. She is a past president of the American Anthropological Association and has served as Dean of Trinity College of Arts and Sciences at Duke.

MICHAEL HERZFELD received his B.A. from Cambridge in 1966 in archaeology and anthropology, his M.A. from Birmingham in 1972 in the School of Hellenic and Roman Studies, and his D.Phil. from Oxford in 1976 in social anthropology. From 1969 to 1970, he was a student at the University of Athens. His major publications include *Ours Once More: Folklore, Ideology, and the Making of Modern Greece* and *The Poetics of Manhood: Contest and Identity in a Cretan Mountain Village.* He also has to his credit numerous edited volumes and articles in the areas of semiotics, anthropological theory and practice, modern Greek studies, and folkloristics. He is associate professor of anthropology and semiotics at Indiana University, Bloomington, and currently is doing research on the political context of ethnographic research and its consequences for ethnographic theory and practice.

JANA HESSER received her Ph.D. in anthropology from the University of Pennsylvania in 1974. She has done extensive research in biomedical anthropology and taught biomedical and physical anthropology for four and one-half years at Case Western Reserve University. Recently, her interests have turned to applying anthropological research methods to program evaluation and needs assessment in the field of education and to film making. She and her husband, Eleftherios Pavlides, are currently working on a film on vernacular environments. She is employed as a development and evaluation research specialist in the Division of Continuing Education at Kansas State University, where she also holds an adjunct position in the Department of Anthropology.

ROBINETTE KENNEDY received her Ph.D. in psychology in 1981 from Saybrook Institute in San Francisco. She is a psychologist in private practice in Atlanta, Georgia.

ELEFTHERIOS PAVLIDES was born and raised in Athens, Greece. He received his M.Arch. from Yale University, where he studied under Charles Moore and Kent Bloomer. From them he developed an appreciation of the significance of studying vernacular architecture. He received his Ph.D. in architecture from the University of Pennsylvania, where he studied vernacular architecture as an expression of the social life and values of the people who build and inhabit it. He currently teaches design studios, as well as a course on world vernacular architecture in the College of Architecture and Design at Kansas State University.

S. D. SALAMONE received his Ph.D. in history from the State University of New York at Buffalo. His doctoral dissertation, *Diogmos: The Genesis of a*

Rural Greek Community and Its Refugee Heritage, was based on eight years of research in Greece and Turkey. From 1978 to 1979, he did postgraduate research in Turkey at the Netherlands Archaeological and Historical Institute of Istanbul and the Swedish Research Institute of Istanbul. He is presently assistant professor of classics and modern Greek studies at Boston University, where he has been chairman *ad interim* of the Department of Classical Studies since 1982.

J. B. STANTON did her research for this article while working on her master's thesis, "The Institution of Dowry in Amouliani, Greece." She is presently practicing immigration law in San Francisco.

LITERATURE CITED

Alexiou, Margaret
  1974 The Ritual Lament in Greek Tradition. Cambridge: Cambridge University Press.
Allan, G.
  1979 A Sociology of Friendship and Kinship. London: George Allen and Unwin.
Allen, Peter S.
  1976 Aspida: A Depopulated Maniat Community. *In* Regional Variation in Modern Greece and Cyprus: Toward a Perspective on the Ethnography of Greece, M. Dimen and E. Friedl, eds., 268:168-198. New York: Annals of the New York Academy of Sciences.
Ardener, Edwin
  1975 Belief and the Problem of Women. *In* Perceiving Women, S. Ardener, ed., pp. 1-27. London: Malaby Press.
Ardener, Shirley, ed.
  1975 Perceiving Women. London: Malaby Press.
Arensberg, C. M.
  1961 The Community as Object and as Sample. American Anthropologist 63(2):241-264.
Aronowitz, S.
  1974 False Promises. New York: McGraw-Hill.
Aronson, E., and P. Worchel
  1966 Similarity Versus Liking as Determinants of Interpersonal Attraction. Psychonomic Science 5:157-158.
Aschenbrenner, Stanley E.
  1976 Karpofora: Reluctant Farmers on a Fertile Land. *In* Regional Variation in Modern Greece and Cyprus: Toward a Perspective on the Ethnography of Greece, M. Dimen and E. Friedl, eds., 268:207-221. New York: Annals of the New York Academy of Sciences.
Attalides, M.
  1976 Forms of Peasant Incorporation in Cyprus During the Last Century. *In* Regional Variation in Modern Greece and Cyprus: Toward a Perspective on the Ethnography of Greece, M. Dimen and E. Friedl, eds., 268:363-378. New York: Annals of the New York Academy of Sciences.
Babchuck, N.
  1963 The Primary Relations of Middle-Class Couples: A Study of Male Dominance. American Sociological Review 28:377-384.
Banfield, E. C.
  1958 The Moral Basis of a Backward Society. Glencoe, Ill.: Free Press.
Barth, Fredrik
  1965 Political Leadership Among Swat Pathans. London School of Eco-

nomics Monographs in Social Anthropology, no. 19. London: The Athlone Press.

Başgöz, Ilhan
1982 Protest: The Fifth Function of Folklore. Unpublished manuscript.

Beaton, Roderick
1980 Folk Poetry of Modern Greece. Cambridge: Cambridge University Press.

Beidelman, T. P.
1980 The Moral Imagination of the Kaguru: Some Thoughts on Tricksters, Translation and Comparative Analysis. American Ethnologist 7(1):27-42.

Bernard, H. Russell
1976 Kalymnos: The Island of the Sponge Fishermen. *In* Regional Variation in Modern Greece and Cyprus: Toward a Perspective on the Ethnography of Greece, M. Dimen and E. Friedl, eds., 268:291-307. New York: Annals of the New York Academy of Sciences.

Bialor, Perry A.
1976 The Northwestern Corner of the Peloponnesos: Mavrikion and Its Region. *In* Regional Variation in Modern Greece and Cyprus: Toward a Perspective on the Ethnography of Greece, M. Dimen and E. Friedl, eds., 268:222-231. New York: Annals of the New York Academy of Sciences.

Blok, Anton
1981 Rams and Billy-goats: A Key to the Mediterranean Code of Honor. Man (n.s.) 16:427-440.

Blum, Richard, and Eva Blum
1970 The Dangerous Hour: The Lore of Crisis and Mystery in Rural Greece. New York: Charles Scribner's Sons.

Blumberg, Rae Lesser
1981 Rural Women in Development. *In* Women and World Change: Equity Issues in Development, N. Black and A. Cottrell, eds., pp. 32-56. Beverly Hills: Sage Publications.

Boserup, Ester
1970 Women's Role in Economic Development. New York: St. Martin's Press.

Bossen, Laurell
1979 Women in Modernizing Societies. *In* Women and Society. An Anthropological Reader, S. W. Tiffany, ed., pp. 93-119. Montreal: Eden Press Women's Publications.

Bourdieu, Pierre
1965 The Sentiment of Honour in Kabyle Society. *In* Honour and Shame: The Values of Mediterranean Society, J. G. Peristiany, ed., pp. 191-241. Chicago: University of Chicago Press.

Bourguignon, Erika
1976 Possession. San Francisco: Chandler and Sharp Publishers, Inc.

Bourque, Susan C., and Jean Grossholtz
1974 Politics as an Unnatural Practice: Political Science Looks at Female Participation. Politics and Society 4:225-266.

Bourque, Susan C., and Kay Barbara Warren
    1981 Women of the Andes: Patriarchy and Social Change in Two Peruvian
    Towns. Ann Arbor: University of Michigan Press.
Brain, R.
    1976 Friends and Lovers. New York: Basic Books.
Brandes, Stanley
    1980 Metaphors of Masculinity: Sex and Status in Andalusian Folklore.
    Philadelphia: University of Pennsylvania Press.
Callan, Hilary
    1978 Harems and Overlords: Biosocial Models and the Female. *In* Defining
    Females, S. Ardener, ed., pp. 200-219. New York: John Wiley and Sons.
Campbell, J. K.
    1964 Honour, Family and Patronage: A Study of Institutions and Moral
    Values in a Greek Mountain Community. Oxford: Clarendon Press.
    1976 Regionalism and Local Community. *In* Regional Variation in Modern
    Greece and Cyprus: Toward a Perspective on the Ethnography of Greece,
    M. Dimen and E. Friedl, eds., 268:18-27. New York: Annals of the New
    York Academy of Sciences.
Cancian, F.
    1965 Economics and Prestige in a Maya Community: The Religious Cargo
    System in Zinacantan. Stanford: Stanford University Press.
    1972 Change and Uncertainty in a Peasant Economy. Stanford: Stanford
    University Press.
Caraveli, Anna
    1982 The Song Beyond the Song: Aesthetics and Social Interaction in Greek
    Folksong. Journal of American Folklore 95:129-158.
    1985 The Symbolic Village: Community Born in Performance. Journal of
    American Folklore 98:259-286.
Caraveli-Chaves, Anna
    1980 Bridge Between Worlds: The Women's Ritual Lament as Communi-
    cative Event. Journal of American Folklore 93:129-157.
Carlson, R.
    1972 Understanding Women: Implications for Personality Research. Jour-
    nal of Social Issues 28:17-31.
Casselberry, Samuel E., and Nancy Valvanes
    1976 "Matrilocal" Greek Peasants and a Reconsideration of Residence Ter-
    minology. American Ethnologist 3(2):215-226.
Cavounides, Jennifer
    1983 Capitalist Development and Women's Work in Greece. Journal of
    Modern Greek Studies 1(2):321-338.
Chagnon, Napoleon
    1983 Yanomamo: The Fierce People. 3d ed. New York: Holt, Rinehart and
    Winston.
Clark, C. E.
    1976 Domestic Architecture as an Index of Social History: The Romantic

Revival and the Cult of Domesticity in America 1840-70. Journal of Inter-disciplinary History 7:33-56.

Clark, Mari
  1983 Variations on Themes of Male and Female: Reflections on Gender Bias in Fieldwork in Rural Greece. Women's Studies 102:117-133.

Cohen, Y. A.
  1961 Patterns of Friendship. *In* Social Structure and Personality. Y. A. Cohen, ed., pp. 351-386. New York: Holt, Rinehart and Winston.

Collier, Jane Fishburne
  1974 Women in Politics. *In* Woman, Culture, and Society, M. Z. Rosaldo and L. Lamphere, eds. Stanford: Stanford University Press.

Collier, Jane F., and Michelle Z. Rosaldo
  1981 Politics and Gender in Simple Societies. *In* Sexual Meanings: The Cultural Construction of Gender and Sexuality, S. B. Ortner and H. White-head, eds., pp. 275-329. Cambridge: Cambridge University Press.

Constantinides, Elizabeth
  1983 Andreiomeni: The Female Warrior in Greek Folk Songs. Journal of Modern Greek Studies 1(1):63-72.

Crapanzano, Vincent, and Vivian Garrison, eds.
  1977 Case Studies in Spirit Possession. New York: John Wiley and Sons.

Currier, Richard
  1976 Social Interaction and Social Structure in a Greek Island Village. *In* Regional Variation in Modern Greece and Cyprus: Toward a Perspective on the Ethnography of Greece, M. Dimen and E. Friedl, eds., 268:308-313. New York: Annals of the New York Academy of Sciences.

Dahlberg, Frances, ed.
  1981 Woman the Gatherer. New Haven: Yale University Press.

Danforth, Loring M.
  1976 Humour and Status Reversal in Greek Shadow Theatre. Byzantine and Modern Greek Studies 2:99-111.
  1978 The Anastenaria: A Study in Greek Ritual Therapy. Ph.D. diss., Princeton University. Ann Arbor, Mich.: University Microfilms.
  1979a The Role of Dance in the Ritual Therapy of the Anastenaria. Byzantine and Modern Greek Studies 5:141-163.
  1979b Women's Strategies and Powers: A Rural Greek Example. Paper presented at the 1979 meeting of the American Anthropological Association, Cincinnati.
  1983 Power Through Submission in the Anastenaria. Journal of Modern Greek Studies 1(1):203-224.

Danforth, Loring M., and Alexander Tsiaras
  1982 The Death Rituals of Rural Greece. Princeton, N.J.: Princeton University Press.

Davis, Nanciellen
  1981 Women's Work and Worth in an Acadian Maritime Village. *In*

Women and World Change: Equity Issues in Development, N. Black and A. Cottrell, eds., pp. 97-119. Beverly Hills: Sage Publications.

de Beauvoir, Simone
1952 The Second Sex. New York: Alfred A. Knopf, Inc. (Orig. French ed. 1949.)

DeWalt, B. R.
1975 Inequalities in Wealth, Adoption of Technology, and Production in a Mexican Ejido. American Ethnologist 2:149-168.

Diamandouros, N. P.
1985 Political Clientelism and Political Modernization in Nineteenth Century Greece. Bulletin of the Historical and Ethnological Society of Greece. Athens. (In English.)

Dimen, Muriel
1977 Review of Kypseli: Women and Men Apart—A Divided Reality. Film (made by Susannah Hoffman, Richard Cowan, and Paul Aratow). American Anthropologist 79:194-195.
1981 The State, Work, and the Household: Contradictions in a Greek Village. Michigan Discussions in Anthropology Winter:102-125.

Dimen, Muriel, and Ernestine Friedl, eds.
1976 Regional Variation in Modern Greece and Cyprus: Toward A Perspective on the Ethnography of Greece, 268:1-465. New York: Annals of the New York Academy of Sciences.

Dionisopoulos-Mass, Regina
1976 Greece: The Evil Eye and Bewitchment in a Peasant Village. In The Evil Eye, Clarence Maloney, ed., pp. 42-62. New York: Columbia University Press.

Douglas, Mary
1966 Purity and Danger: An Analysis of Concepts of Pollution and Taboo. London: Routledge and Kegan Paul.
1970 Natural Symbols. New York: Random House.

Dragoumis, N.
1866 Peri ton arkheon ellinidhon. Pandhora 17 (1866-1867): 339-347.

Dubisch, Jill
1972 The Open Community: Migration From a Greek Island Village. Ph.D. diss., University of Chicago.
1974 The Domestic Power of Women in a Greek Island Village. Studies in European Society 1(1):23-33.
1976 The Ethnography of the Islands: Tinos. In Regional Variation in Modern Greece and Cyprus: Toward a Perspective on the Ethnography of Greece, M. Dimen and E. Friedl, eds., 268:314-327. New York: Annals of the New York Academy of Sciences.
1983 Greek Women: Sacred or Profane. Journal of Modern Greek Studies 1(1):185-202.

Du Bois, C.
1974 The Gratuitous Act: An Introduction to the Comparative Study of

Kinship. *In* The Compact: Selected Dimensions of Friendship, E. Leyton, ed., pp. 15-32. St. John's, Newfoundland: Memorial University Press.

du Boulay, Juliet
1974 Portrait of a Greek Mountain Village. Oxford: Clarendon Press.
1976 Lies, Mockery and Family Integrity. *In* Mediterranean Family Structures, J. G. Peristiany, ed., pp. 389-406. Cambridge: Cambridge University Press.

Dwyer, Daisy Hilse
1978 Images and Self-Images: Male and Female in Morocco. New York: Columbia University Press.

Evans-Pritchard, E. E.
1940 The Nuer. Oxford: Clarendon Press.
1951 Kinship and Marriage Among the Nuer. Oxford: Clarendon Press.

Ewen, S.
1978 Captains of Consciousness. New York: McGraw-Hill.

Faithorn, Elizabeth
1975 The Concept of Pollution Among the Kafe of the Papuan New Guinea Highlands. *In* Toward an Anthropology of Women, R. R. Reiter, ed., pp. 127-140. New York: Monthly Review Press.

Fallers, Lloyd A., and Margaret C. Fallers
1976 Sex Roles in Edremit. *In* Mediterranean Family Structures, J. G. Peristiany, ed., pp. 243-260. Cambridge: Cambridge University Press.

Finnegan, Ruth
1977 Oral Poetry: Its Nature, Significance and Social Context. Cambridge: Cambridge University Press.

Foster, G.
1965 Peasant Society and the Image of Limited Good. American Anthropologist 67:293-315.
1967 Tzintzuntzan: Mexican Peasants in a Changing World. Boston: Little, Brown.

Fried, M. H.
1953 Fabric of Chinese Society: A Study of the Social Life of a Chinese County Seat. New York: Frederick Praeger.

Friedl, Ernestine
1962 Vasilika: A Village in Modern Greece. New York: Holt, Rinehart and Winston.
1967 The Position of Women: Appearance and Reality. Anthropological Quarterly 40(3):97-108.
1968 Lagging Emulation in Post-Peasant Society: A Greek Case. *In* Contributions to Mediterranean Sociology, J. G. Peristiany, ed. Paris, The Hague: Mouton and Co.
1970 Field Work in a Greek Village. *In* Women in the Field, P. Golde, ed., pp. 195-217. Chicago: Aldine Publishing Company.
1975 Men and Women: An Anthropologist's View. New York: Holt, Rinehart and Winston.

1976 Kinship, Class and Selective Migration. *In* Mediterranean Family Structures, J. G. Peristiany, ed., pp. 363-387. Cambridge: Cambridge University Press.

Gilmore, D.
  1975 Friendship in Fuenmayor: Patterns of Integration in an Atomistic Society. Ethnology 14:311-324.

Giovannini, Maureen J.
  1981 Woman: A Dominant Symbol Within the Cultural System of a Sicilian Town. Man 16(3):408-426.

Goodale, Jane
  1971 Tiwi Wives: A Study of the Women of Melville Island. Seattle: University of Washington Press.

Gough, Kathleen
  1971 Nuer Kinship: A Re-examination. *In* The Translation of Culture: Essays to E. E. Evans-Pritchard, T. P. Beidelman, ed. London: Tavistock.
  1975 The Origin of the Family. *In* Toward an Anthropology of Women, R. R. Reiter, ed., pp. 51-76. New York: Monthly Review Press.

Gramsci, A.
  1971 Selections from the Prison Notebooks. New York: International Publishers.

Gray, J. Patrick, and Linda D. Wolfe
  1982 Sociobiology and Creationism: Two Ethnosociologies of American Culture. American Anthropologist 84(3):580-594.

Halpern, Joel
  1956 A Serbian Village: Social and Cultural Change in a Yugoslav Community. New York: Harper.

Handman, M. E.
  1983 La Violence et la Ruse: Hommes et Femmes dans un Village Grec. Aix-en-Provence: Edisud.

Harris, Marvin
  1975 Culture, People, Nature: An Introduction to General Anthropology. 2d ed. New York: Thomas Y. Crowell.

Harris, Olivia
  1980 The Power of Signs: Gender, Culture and the Wild in the Bolivian Andes. *In* Nature, Culture and Gender, C. P. MacCormack and M. Strathern, ed., pp. 70-94. Cambridge: Cambridge University Press.

Hart, C. W. M., and Arnold R. Pilling
  1960 The Tiwi of North Australia. New York: Holt, Rinehart and Winston.

Hayden, Dolores, and Gwendolyn Wright
  1976 Architecture and Urban Planning. Signs 1 (Summer): 923-933.

Herzfeld, Michael
  1980a Honour and Shame: Problems in the Comparative Analysis of Moral Systems. Man 15:339-351.
  1980b The Ethnography of "Prejudice" in an Exclusive Community. Ethnic Groups 2:283-305.

1981a Performative Categories and Symbols of Passage in Rural Greece. Journal of American Folklore 94:44-57.

1981b An Indigenous Theory of Meaning and its Elicitation in Performative Context. Semiotica 34:113-141.

1981c Meaning and Morality: A Semiotic Approach to Evil Eye Accusations. American Ethnologist 8(3):560-574.

1982a Ours Once More: Folklore, Ideology, and the Making of Modern Greece. Austin: University of Texas Press.

1982b Disemia. *In* Semiotics 1980, M. Herzfeld and M. D. Lenhart, comps., pp. 205-215. New York: Plenum.

1983 Semantic Slippage and Moral Fall: The Rhetoric of Chastity in Rural Greek Society. Journal of Modern Greek Studies 1(1):161-172.

1984 The Horns of the Mediterraneanist Dilemma. American Ethnologist 11(3):439-454.

1985 The Poetics of Manhood: Contest and Identity in a Cretan Mountain Village. Princeton: Princeton University Press.

Hirschon, Renée

1978 Open Body/Closed Space: The Transformation of Female Sexuality. *In* Defining Females, S. Ardener, ed., pp. 66-88. New York: John Wiley and Sons.

1981 Essential Objects and the Sacred: Interior and Exterior Space in an Urban Greek Locality. *In* Women and Space, S. Ardener, ed. London: Croom Helm.

1983 Women, the Aged and Religious Activity: Oppositions and Complementarity in an Urban Locality. Journal of Modern Greek Studies 1(1):113-130.

1984 Women and Property—Women as Property. Ed. New York: St. Martin's Press.

Hirschon, Renée, and John R. Gold

1982 Territoriality and the Home Environment in a Greek Urban Community. Anthropological Quarterly 55(2):63-73.

Hoffman, Susannah

1974 Kypseli: Women and Men Apart—A Divided Reality. Film (made with Richard Cowan and Paul Aratow).

1976 The Ethnography of the Islands: Thera. *In* Regional Variation in Modern Greece and Cyprus: Toward a Perspective on the Ethnography of Greece, M. Dimen and E. Friedl, eds., 268:328-340. New York: Annals of the New York Academy of Sciences.

Honko, Lauri

1974 Balto-Finnic Lament Poetry. Studio Fennica 17:9-61.

Horkheimer, M.

1972 Critical Theory: Selected Essays. M. J. O'Connell et al., trans. New York: The Seabury Press.

Illich, Ivan

1982 Gender. New York: Pantheon Books.

Janeway, Elizabeth
1981 The Powers of the Weak. New York: Morrow Quill Paperbacks.
Jordanova, L. L.
1980 Natural Facts: A Historical Perspective on Science and Sexuality. *In* Nature, Culture and Gender, C. P. MacCormack and M. Strathern, eds., pp. 42-69. Cambridge: Cambridge University Press.
Joseph, Brian D.
1983 Language Use in the Balkans: The Contributions of Historical Linguistics. Anthropological Linguistics 25(4):275-287.
Kaberry, Phyllis
1970 Aboriginal Woman: Sacred and Profane. London: Routledge and Kegan Paul. (Orig. ed. 1939.)
Karp, Ivan
1980 Beer Drinking and Social Experience in an African Society. *In* Explorations in African Systems of Thought, I. Karp and C. S. Bird, eds., pp. 83-119. Bloomington, Ind.: Indiana University Press.
Karp, Ivan, and Patricia Karp
1979 Living with Spirits of the Dead. *In* African Therapeutic Systems, Z. A. Ademuwagun et al., eds., pp. 22-25. Boston: Crossroads Press.
Karp, Ivan, and Martha B. Kendall
1982 Reflexivity in Field Work. *In* Explaining Human Behavior: Consciousness, Human Action and Social Structure, Paul F. Secord, ed., pp. 249-273. Beverly Hills: Sage Publications.
Kelly, E. A.
1967 Peer Group Friendship in One Class of High School Girls: Change and Stability. Ph.D. diss., Michigan State University.
Kenna, Margaret
1976 Houses, Fields and Graves: Property and Ritual Obligation on a Greek Island. Ethnology 15:21-34.
Kessler, Clive S.
1977 Conflict and Sovereignty in Kelantanese Malay Spirit Seances. *In* Case Studies in Spirit Possession, V. Crapanzano and V. Garrison, eds., pp. 295-331. New York: John Wiley and Sons.
Kuenstler, G.
1978 Personal communication.
Kuhn, A.
1978 Structures of Patriarchy and Capitalism in the Family. *In* Feminism and Materialism, A. Kuhn and A. Wolpe, eds., pp. 42-67. London: Routledge and Kegan Paul.
Kuhn, A., and A. Wolpe, eds.
1978 Feminism and Materialism. London: Routledge and Kegan Paul.
Lambiri, Ioanna
1968 The Impact of Industrial Employment on the Position of Women in a Greek Country Town. *In* Contributions to Mediterranean Sociology, J. G. Peristiany, ed., pp. 261-268. The Hague: Mouton.

Lamphere, Louise
    1974 Strategies, Cooperation and Conflict Among Women in Domestic
    Groups. In Woman, Culture and Society, M. Z. Rosaldo and L. Lamphere,
    eds., pp. 97-112. Stanford: Stanford University Press.
Leibowitz, Lila
    1975 Perspectives on the Evolution of Sex Differences. In Toward an An-
    thropology of Women, R. R. Reiter, ed., pp. 20-35. New York: Monthly
    Review Press.
Levenson, E.
    1978 Psychoanalysis: Cure or Persuasion? Contemporary Psychoanalysis
    14:1-17.
Lévi-Strauss, Claude
    1969 The Raw and the Cooked. New York: Harper and Row.
Lewis, I. M.
    1975 Ecstatic Religion: An Anthropological Study of Spirit Possession and
    Shamanism. Harmondsworth, England: Penguin. (1st ed. 1971.)
Lewis, Oscar
    1960 Tepotazlan: Village in Mexico. New York: Holt, Rinehart and Win-
    ston.
Loether, H. J.
    1960 Propinquity and Homogeneity as Factors in the Choice of Best Bud-
    dies in the Air Force. Pacific Social Review 3:8-22.
Loizos, Peter
    1975 The Greek Gift: Politics in a Cypriot Village. Oxford: Blackwell.
    1976 Notes on Future Anthropological Research in Cyprus. In Regional
    Variation in Modern Greece and Cyprus: Toward a Perspective on the
    Ethnography of Greece, M. Dimen and E. Friedl, eds., 268:355-362. New
    York: Annals of the New York Academy of Sciences.
    1981 The Heart Grown Bitter: A Chronicle of Cypriot War Refugees. Cam-
    bridge: Cambridge University Press.
Lomax, Alan
    1968 Folksong Style and Culture. Washington, D.C.: American Association
    for the Advancement of Science.
Lord, Albert Bates
    1965 The Singer of Tales. New York: Atheneum. (1st ed. Harvard Univer-
    sity Press, 1960.)
Loukatos, Dimetrios
    1978 Eisagogi Stin Elleniki Laografia. Athens: Morfotiko Idrima Ellinikis
    Trapezis.
MacCormack, Carol P., and Marilyn Strathern, eds.
    1980 Nature, Culture and Gender. Cambridge: Cambridge University
    Press.
McGrew, W. C.
    1981 The Female Chimpanzee as a Human Evolutionary Prototype. In
    Woman the Gatherer, F. Dahlberg, ed., pp. 35-74. New Haven: Yale Uni-
    versity Press.

McNall, Scott
1974 The Greek Peasant. ASA Rose Monograph Series. Washington, D.C.: American Sociological Association.

Marsden, E. N.
1966 Values as Determinants of Friendship Choice. Connecticut College Psychology Journal 3:3-13.

Martin, M. Kay, and Barbara Voorhies
1975 Female of the Species. New York: Columbia University Press.

Mead, Margaret
1935 Sex and Temperament in Three Primitive Societies. New York: William Morrow and Co.

Meigs, Anna S.
1984 Food, Sex and Pollution: A New Guinea Religion. New Brunswick, N.J.: Rutgers University Press.

Mitchell, J.
1971 Women's Estate. London: Penguin.

Morgen, Sandra
1983 Towards a Politics of "Feelings": Beyond the Dialectic of Thought and Action. Women's Studies 10(2):203-223.

Morsy, Soheir
1978 Sex Roles, Power and Illness in an Egyptian Community. American Ethnologist 5(1):137-150.

Mouzelis, Nicos
1978 Modern Greece: Facets of Underdevelopment. London: Macmillan.

Okely, Judith
1975 Gypsy Women: Models in Conflict. In Perceiving Women, S. Ardener, ed., pp. 55-86. London: Malaby Press.

Ortner, Sherry B.
1974 Is Female to Male as Nature Is to Culture? In Woman, Culture and Society, M. Z. Rosaldo and L. Lamphere, eds., pp. 67-87. Stanford: Stanford University Press.

Ortner, S., and H. Whitehead, eds.
1981 Sexual Meanings. New York: Cambridge University Press.

Paine, R.
1969 In Search of Friendship: An Exploratory Analysis of "Middle Class" Culture. Man 5:505-524.

Papaharalambos, T. X.
1968 I Kypriaki Oikia. Leukossia.

Pappadopoulos, G. G.
1866 Peri Yinekos ke Ellinidhos. Pandhora 17 (1866-1867):81-88, 405-412.

Parsons, E. C.
1915 Friendship, a Social Category. American Journal of Sociology 21:230-233.

Pasadaiou, Aristides
1973 I Laiki Architectoniki tis Imbrou. Athens.

Paul, Lois
    1974 The Mastery of Work and the Mystery of Sex in a Guatemalan Village.
        In Woman, Culture and Society, M. Z. Rosaldo and L. Lamphere, eds., pp.
        281-300. Stanford: Stanford University Press.
Pelto, P. J., and G. H. Pelto
    1975 Intra-cultural Diversity: Some Theoretical Issues. American Ethnolo-
        gist 2:1-18.
Peristiany, J. G., ed.
    1965 Honour and Shame: The Values of Mediterranean Society. London:
        Weidenfeld and Nicolson.
    1976 Mediterranean Family Structures. Cambridge: Cambridge University
        Press.
Psacharopoulos, George
    1983 Sex Discrimination in the Greek Labor Market. Journal of Modern
        Greek Studies 1(2):339-358.
Radford, A., and G. Clark
    1974 Cyclades: Studies of a Vernacular Environment. *In* Shelter in Greece,
        O. B. Doumanis and P. Oliver, eds. Greece: Architecture in Greece Press.
Rapp, R., E. Ross, and R. Bridenthal
    1979 Examining Family History. Feminist Studies 5:174-200.
Redfield, Robert
    1960 The Little Community/Peasant Society and Culture. Chicago: Chi-
        cago University Press.
Reiter, Rayna R.
    1975a Men and Women in the South of France: Public and Private Do-
        mains. *In* Toward an Anthropology of Women, R. R. Reiter, ed., pp. 252-
        282. New York: Monthly Review Press.
    1975b Toward an Anthropology of Women. Ed. New York: Monthly Re-
        view Press.
Rosaldo, Michelle Zimbalist
    1974 Woman, Culture and Society: A Theoretical Overview. *In* Woman,
        Culture and Society, M. Z. Rosaldo and L. Lamphere, eds., pp. 17-42.
        Stanford: Stanford University Press.
Rosaldo, Michelle Zimbalist, and Louise Lamphere, eds.
    1974 Woman, Culture and Society. Stanford: Stanford University Press.
Rubbo, Anna
    1975 The Spread of Capitalism in Rural Columbia: Effects on Poor
        Women. *In* Toward an Anthropology of Women, R. R. Reiter, ed., pp.
        333-337. New York: Monthly Review Press.
Sacks, K.
    1976 State Bias and Women's Status. American Anthropologist 78(3):365-
        369.
Safilios-Rothschild, C.
    1976 The Family in Athens: Regional Variations. *In* Regional Variation in

Modern Greece and Cyprus: Toward a Perspective on the Ethnography of Greece, M. Dimen and E. Friedl, eds., 268:410-418. New York: Annals of the New York Academy of Sciences.

Sahlins, Marshall D.
  1976 The Use and Abuse of Biology. Ann Arbor: University of Michigan Press.

Salamone, Jill Stanton
  1978 The Institution of Dowry in Amouliani, Greece. Master's thesis.

Salamone, Stephen D.
  1986 In the Shadow of the Holy Mountain: The Genesis of a Rural Greek Community and its Refugee Heritage. Athens: Epoteia Press.

Salamone, J. (Stanton), and S. D. Salamone
  1980 The Noikokyris and the Noikokyra: Complementary Sex Roles in a Changing Socio-Economic System. Paper delivered at the 1980 Symposium of the Modern Greek Studies Association. Philadelphia.

Sanday, Peggy Reeves
  1981 Female Power and Male Dominance: On the Origins of Sexual Inequality. Cambridge: Cambridge University Press.

Sanders, Irwin T.
  1962 Rainbow in the Rock: The People of Rural Greece. Cambridge: Harvard University Press.

Schein, M. (Dimen)
  1970 Change and Continuity in a Greek Mountain Village. Ph.D. diss., Columbia University.
  1972 Only on Sundays. Natural History 80:52-61.
  1974 Social Stratification in a Greek Village. In City and Peasant: A Study in Sociocultural Dynamics, A. L. LaRuffia et al., eds., 220:488-495. New York: Annals of the New York Academy of Sciences.
  1975 When is an Ethnic Group: Ecology and Class Structure in Northwestern Greece. Ethnology 14:83-97.

Scheper-Hughes, Nancy
  1983a Introduction: The Problems of Bias in Androcentric and Feminist Anthropology. Women's Studies 10(2):109-116.
  1983b From Anxiety to Analysis: Rethinking Irish Sexuality and Sex Roles. Women's Studies 10(20):147-160.

Schneider, David
  1968 American Kinship: A Cultural Account. Englewood Cliffs, N.J.: Prentice-Hall.

Schneider, H. K.
  1977 Prehistoric Transpacific Contact and the Theory of Culture Change. American Anthropologist 79:9-25.

Schneider, P., J. Schneider, and E. Hansen
  1972 Modernization and Development: The Role of Regional Elites and Non-corporate Groups in the European Mediterranean. Comparative Studies in Society and History 14:328-350.

Sciama, L.
    1981 The Problem of Privacy in Mediterranean Anthropology. *In* Women and Space, S. Ardener, ed. London: Croom Helm.
Sherman, Julia A., and Evelyn Torton Beck, eds.
    1979 The Prism of Sex: Essays in the Sociology of Knowledge. Madison: University of Wisconsin Press.
Silverman, S.
    1968 Agricultural Organization, Social Structure, and Values in Italy: Amoral Familism Reconsidered. American Anthropologist 70:1-20.
Sinos, Stefanos
    1976 Anadromi Sti Laiki Arhitektoniki tis Kyprou. Athens.
Sivignon, M.
    1968 Personal communication.
Skouteri-Didaskalou, N.
    1980 Ya Tin Idheoloyiki Anaparaghoyi Ton Kata Fila Dhiakriseon: I Simiodhotiki Litouryia tis "Teletouryias tou Ghamou." *In* Simiotiki ke Kinonia, Karin Boklund-Lagopoulou, ed., pp. 207-223. Athens: Odhisseas.
Slocum, Sally
    1975 Woman the Gatherer: Male Bias in Anthropology. *In* Toward an Anthropology of Women, R. R. Reiter, ed., pp. 36-50. New York: Monthly Review Press.
Stevens, Evelyn P.
    1973 Marianismo: The Other Face of Machismo in Latin America. *In* Female and Male in Latin America, Ann Pescatello, ed., pp. 89-101. Pittsburgh: The University of Pittsburgh Press.
Stott, Margaret
    1973 Economic Transition and the Family in Mykonos. Greek Review of Social Research 12:122-133.
Strathern, Marilyn
    1980 No Nature, No Culture: The Hagen Case. *In* Nature, Culture and Gender. C. P. MacCormack and M. Strathern, eds., pp. 174-222. Cambridge: Cambridge University Press.
    1981 Culture in a Netbag: The Manufacture of a Subdiscipline in Anthropology. Man 16(4)665-668.
Tanner, Nancy Makepeace
    1974 Matrifocality in Indonesia and Africa and Among Black Americans. *In* Woman, Culture and Society, M. Z. Rosaldo and L. Lamphere, eds., pp. 129-156. Stanford: Stanford University Press.
    1981 On Becoming Human. Cambridge: Cambridge University Press.
Tiger, Lionel
    1969 Men in Groups. London: Nelson.
    1974 Sex Specific Friendship. *In* The Compact: Selected Dimensions of Friendship, E. Leyton, ed., pp. 42-48. St. John's, Newfoundland: Memorial University Press.

Tiger, Lionel, and Robin Fox
1971 The Imperial Animal. New York: Holt, Rinehart and Winston.
Tzakou, Anastasia
1975 Central Settlements on the Island of Siphnos: Form and Evolution in a Traditional System. Athens.
van den Berghe, Pierre L., and David P. Barash
1977 Inclusive Fitness and Human Family Structure. American Anthropologist 79:809-823.
Weiner, Annette B.
1976 Women of Value, Men of Renown: New Perspectives in Trobriand Exchange. Austin: University of Texas Press.
Wekerle, Gerda R., Rebecca Peterson, and David Morley, eds.
1980 New Space for Women. Boulder, Colo.: Westview Press.
West, J.
1945 Plainville, New York: Columbia University Press.
Whitehead, Ann
1984 Men and Women, Kinship and Property: Some General Issues. *In* Woman and Property—Woman as Property, R. Hirschon, ed., pp. 176-192. New York: St. Martin's Press.
Zaretsky, E.
1976 Capitalism, The Family and Personal Life. New York: Harper and Row.
Zihlman, Adrienne
1981 Women as Shapers of the Human Adaptation. *In* Woman the Gatherer, F. Dahlberg, ed., pp. 75-120. New Haven: Yale University Press.
Zourou, Frosso M.
1974 O Gamos sti Voria Lesbo. Mytiline.

INDEX

Anastenaria, 19, 27-28
actor-oriented analysis, 27-30
anthropologist: in the field, 5, 32-33, 35-
  36, 41n, 95n, 156, 169, 216, 220-23;
  influence of gender on fieldwork, 26,
  33, 39n, 169, 220; as outsider, 33, 35,
  220-23. *See also* ethnography, in
  Greece; reflexivity
agora, 43-44. See also *platia*
Ardener, Edwin, xii-xiii, 5, 32
Asia Minor, 71-72, 97, 99-102, 109, 111,
  119n
Athens, influence on architecture, 83-84.
  See also marriage, to urban grooms;
  migration: rural/urban

Balkan Exchange. *See* refugees
biological determinism, in gender roles.
  See gender roles: and biology
biology, as cultural construct, 7
body, symbolism of, 37, 195-96, 202,
  208-211

café. See *kafenio*
Campbell, John, viii, 168n, 215, 221
coffeehouse. See *kafenio*
cooking, 26, 201; as mediation between
  nature and culture, 203-205; and role
  of women, 205-207, 212n-13n. *See
  also* kitchen

daughters, as burden, 46, 95n, 111. *See
  also* mother-daughter relationship
death. *See* laments; mourning
"destiny," and gender roles, 157-58, 161-
  67
dhiki (dhiki mas), 35-36, 210, 213n. *See
  also* inside/outside
disemia, 218-19, 228-30
domestic life: general features of, 9-10;
  and modernization, 30; and spatial arrangements, 10, 72-73, 197-201; and
  the state, 56-59, 66-67
domestic/public division, 9-12, 36, 42-48,
  53-54, 57-60, 68-69, 122-23, 197-201,
  215-17; association with power, 12-13,

16, 18-20, 24, 30, 42-43, 53; and the
  state, 14, 53-54, 56-58
Douglas, Mary, 37, 208-210
dowry, 26, 72, 95n, 100, 102, 107-112,
  197; changes in, 80, 89-92; "groom's
  dowry," 112-13; house as, 11, 72-73,
  77, 89-91, 95n, 197; and hypergamy,
  50-51; items included in, 73-77, 107-
  111; value of, 77, 107-108, 109, 119n;
  woman's labor and, 73, 82-83, 89-91,
  107; and women's power, 16, 22, 29,
  49-51, 159-60. See also *rouha*
dropi, 162, 196, 210, 216, 219, 232

ethnography, in Greece, xi, 5-6. *See also*
  anthropologist
Eve, women's identification with, 23, 34,
  140, 144, 148, 156-59, 161-67, 228
evil eye, 18, 40
extramarital affairs: of men, 151-53; of
  women, 124-26, 200

family: in Amouliani, 102-103, 118,
  119n; as image of divine order, 143,
  158, 166, 168n, 197, 207; in Kriovrisi,
  53, 59-60, 64-65; role in Greek village
  life, 42, 51, 97-98, 141-43, 145-47
feminist anthropology, 53, 57-58
filotimo (philotimo), 103-104, 122, 125,
  129, 138n, 208-211, 216, 232; "national filotimo," 222, 233n
folklorists, Greek, 216, 222-23
food, symbolism of, 205-207. *See also*
  cooking
Friedl, Ernestine, ix, 5, 16-18, 20-22, 29,
  97, 99, 158-59, 215, 221, 226-28
friendships, of women. *See* women's
  friendships

gender: cultural construction of, 6-7, 27-
  28; and nationalist ideology, 36, 216-
  17, 219, 220-22, 226-29, 232-33; vs.
  sex, 6-7; symbolism of, 35-38, 195,
  207-208, 216-17, 232-33
gender roles: and biology, 6-8; changes

Library of Congress Cataloging-in-Publication Data

Gender & power in rural Greece.

Bibliography: p.   Includes index.
1. Sex role—Greece—Addresses, essays, lectures. 2. Women—Greece—Social condi-
tions—Addresses, essays, lectures. 3. Greece—Social life and customs—Addresses, es-
says, lectures. 4. Greece—Rural conditions—Addresses, essays, lectures. I. Dubisch,
Jill, 1943-   . II. Title: Gender and power in rural Greece.
HQ1075.5.G8G46 1986   305.3′09495   86-3183
ISBN 0-691-09423-3 (alk. paper)
ISBN 0-691-02833-8 (pbk. : alk. paper)

DATE DUE